NORFOLK TABLE
ONE COUNTY, TWENTY CHEFS

cookbook & food lovers' guide

Tessa Allingham and Glyn Williams

Foreword by David Adlard

In memory of my dear father-in-law and Norfolk farmer,
Edwin Allingham, who would have loved this book. T.A.

Contents

5

Foreword
David Adlard

Scroll back to the mid-eighties when I first put up the sign 'Adlard's' and opened my fine-dining restaurant in Wymondham... Norfolk was a restaurant wasteland in those days and a home-cooking culture meant that customers were few and far between.

But enough of me – my cuisine of the eighties can't hold a candle to what is being produced now! Scroll forward to 2016, and a culinary revolution has happened. Over the last ten years or so, interest in food has sky-rocketed, people eat out more and we find ourselves living in a glorious food paradise.

How has that happened? It's difficult to pin down the reasons: perhaps it's thanks to the media and communication in all its forms, the fact that we travel more, expect more and that unusual ingredients are more readily available.

Norfolk is right at the heart of this surge in foodie interest – just look at the number of wonderful, thriving restaurants throughout the county, many of them featured in this book.

As a county, it stands unique, blessed by a special 'terroir' making it a gem of a region for curious chefs and interested customers to discover. It is generally drier, warmer and sunnier than other parts of Britain, but the conditions vary dramatically even within the county because the border is a giant half-circle opening up onto the North Sea. Along the coast, famous Cromer crabs, Morston mussels, King's Lynn brown shrimps, and samphire are common currency for us Norfolk chefs. And inside that remote coastline of creeks and marshes, the land opens up to fields of crops, whiskers of wheat and barley shivering in the breeze, canary-yellow stretches of oilseed rape glowing as far as the eye can see. Even pigs and poultry nudge into our rural landscape making it one of the most densely-populated with livestock of that kind in the country. The kaleidoscope of different soils allows a feast of products to be harvested and leaves space for an interjection of heaths and forests, a must for foraging.

The land is open to the elements. In summer there is nowhere for crops to hide from the sun, making for well-defined seasons and produce with stunning flavours. With no surrounding hills, clouds are blown quickly away, leaving summer fruits to enjoy long, sunny weeks to turn sweet and juicy.

I had a discussion recently with one of our renowned chefs while he was handling some black truffles from 'somewhere near Dereham'. He said 'it's so simple just to use local ingredients'. If we buy on our doorstep and respect our seasons, we will bring back variety and excitement throughout the year. That's exactly what the twenty enterprising and entrepreneurial chefs in this beautiful book are doing, and I am delighted to introduce them and their restaurants to you.

Pictured: Glyn, Da and David Adlard, and Tessa enjoying a feast of Jeremy Thickitt's Norfolk lamb and asparagus on the terrace at The Fritton Arms

Editors' thanks

David Adlard, Norfolk's first Michelin-starred chef, has influenced a generation of chefs across the region and further afield. He and his wife, Da, ran their restaurant, Adlard's, for 25 years (oringinally in Wymondham, latterly in Norwich) throughout that time pioneering an approach to food and cooking predicated on using the best local ingredients.

His protégés include renowned chefs Aiden Byrne and Tom Kerridge, the two Michelin-starred chef-owner of The Hand and Flowers,

Marlow. Writing in *The Guardian* in 2014, Tom described David as 'one of my culinary heroes': "David's cooking was a superlative example of the way many chefs cook in East Anglia: solid, ingredient-led and honest to their surroundings (with a dash of great British eccentricity thrown in for good measure)."

David and Da now run Adlard's In The Country from their home, White House Farm in West Somerton. It's a unique place to stay and dine in simple style between the Broads and the

coast, and somewhere you can be assured of the warmest of welcomes.

Norfolk food and cooking couldn't wish for a better champion, and we are thrilled that he has supported the idea of our book, *Norfolk Table: One County, Twenty Chefs* so enthusiastically.

Happy feasting!
Tessa and Glyn

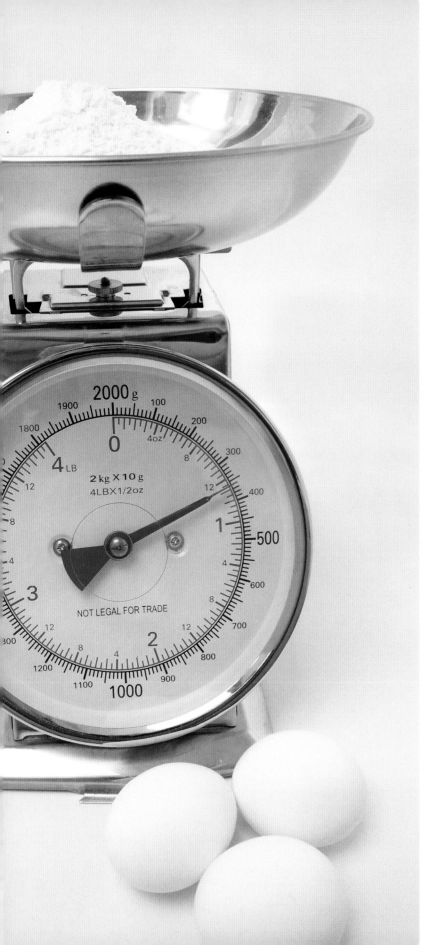

Cooking notes

We want you to enjoy the exciting, original recipes from some of our favourite Norfolk chefs, that are included in this book. To ensure you get the best out of the dishes, please take time to read the following tips and a few words of caution. Much of it will be second nature to many home cooks, but if in doubt, do refer to these notes.

WELFARE IN THE KITCHEN

Sharp tools, high temperatures and close proximity to humans and pets make the kitchen a potentially dangerous place. Accidents can happen when cooking, so please minimise the risk by applying appropriate caution, care and common sense.

COOKING TEMPERATURES AND TIMINGS

Cookers, and especially ovens, can be fickle pieces of equipment. Please treat all temperatures and times as a general guide and adjust to suit your own cooker.

Temperatures and timings are based on the use of a domestic, electric, non-fan oven so please adjust to the appropriate equivalent level, if you have a different cooker type.

MEASUREMENTS

- General cookery rules and common sense apply
- Spoonfuls are measured level
- Handfuls and pinches are based on an 'average' woman's hand and fingers (apologies if that's non-PC!)
- Bunches for herbs are standard retail sizes
- Eggs are large and free range from a local, happy farm flock preferably
- Milk used is full fat unless otherwise stated

SEASONING

Recipe seasoning instructions refer to adding salt and pepper to taste. We choose to use local Maldon sea salt flakes, crushed between clean fingers or milled for fineness, and black peppercorns, freshly-ground to order. Some dishes may taste or look better on the plate with the alternative use of white peppercorns, eg fish dishes and cream sauces.

GENERAL TIPS

- Rapeseed oil should be cold-pressed, good quality and local where possible.

- Keep warm plates to hand both for storing cooked elements of dishes hot while finishing recipes and then to serve up on as required.

- All recipes assume ingredients are ready to be consumed ie washed and dried, cleaned, peeled or prepared as one would generally expect, unless stated otherwise.

- To rest food, leave somewhere hot on a warm plate, loosely covered with foil if your kitchen is cool or draughty, until required.

FOOD SAFETY

It goes without saying that ensuring the health and well-being of the people eating your food is vital! Use your common sense backed up with a bit of research and advice from reputable books and online sources.

Please do pay particular attention to:

- Quality and freshness of ingredients – check expiry and best-before dates

- Storage of produce and ingredients in the kitchen

- Use of raw and partly-cooked eggs

- Allergen risks

- Cooling and refrigeration where dishes are stored mid-preparation before finishing

- Fridge temperature – are they low enough for safe storage?

- Oven temperatures – is it hot enough before you start cooking?

- Core temperature of cooked dishes – has the food reached the right temperature before consumption?

- Finished dishes, not consumed immediately after preparation – are they stored at appropriate temperatures and consumed within safe time limits?

If in doubt, consult the Government's own online health and nutrition website for food safety advice at www.nhs.uk/livewell

THE WHITE HORSE
FRAN HARTSHORNE

TIPI IN THE PADDOCK
MATTHEW
OWSLEY-BROWN

TITCHWELL MANOR
ERIC SNAITH

CONGHAM HALL
NICK CLAXTON-WEBB

Meet the chefs

Here are our twenty talented Norfolk chefs!
From King's Lynn to Norwich and Thornham to
Swaffham, they produce some of the tastiest food
to be had in the county, dishes that are testament
to the creative flair and dedication that it takes to
be a good chef.

Do visit them! Some will surprise you with inventive,
boundary-pushing plates, others will make more
straightforward food, the sort you'd happily eat
every day; some take their inspiration from classic
French cooking, others enjoy the rustic thrill of
cooking over an open fire. All of them celebrate
the produce that grows so abundantly in this
extraordinary, special, county of Norfolk.

So, whether you find yourself eating by a log fire
in a cosy country pub, in an elegant conservatory,
under convivial canvas, or in a welcoming
town-centre neighbourhood spot, enjoy your
meal and maybe raise a glass to the people who
produced the ingredients, and the chefs who
brought them to your table.

THE DABBLING DUCK
JASON 'MITCH' MITCHELL

THE VICTORIA INN
NIK HARE

KINDREDS
MARK DIXON

NORFOLK RIDDLE
NEIL RUTLAND

12

THORNHAM DELI
GEMMA ARNOLD

STRATTONS
VANESSA SCOTT

MARKET BISTRO
RICHARD GOLDING

THE DUCK INN
BEN HANDLEY

THE FRITTON ARMS
STEPHEN DAVID

THE KING'S HEAD
LEIGH TAYLOR

THE GUNTON ARMS
STUART TATTERSALL

THE GLOBE INN
WILL JACKSON

THE WIVETON BELL
SIMON HAYNES

THE SARACEN'S HEAD
MARK SAYERS

SHUCK'S AT THE YURT
PHIL MILNER

ROOTS
GARETH CRIMMINS

The might of mussels

Glossy bivalves are at the heart of Fran Hartshorne's powerfully-local menu

On the saltmarsh at the back of The White Horse in Brancaster Staithe is a small white-painted wooden boat called *Faith*. A bit further out, also skewered on her hull in the low tide, is *Eve*. The boats are named after Cyril Southerland's granddaughters and are his workhorses, capable of ferrying a two-tonne load of mussels from the shallow creek beds where the shellfish grow to the foreshore where they are sorted and bagged for sale.

As offices go, Cyril and his son Ben's is surely unrivalled. At low tide, small boats like *Faith* and *Eve* – and *Isaac*, a third vessel, named after the girls' cousin – wait, marooned, for the tide to bring them back to bobbing life. An occasional small sailing boat drifts past in deeper water, gulls play on the breeze, ramblers and their dogs walk the Norfolk Coast Path. In the distance, the sandy expanses of Scolt Head Island beckon; look east and the lazily-turning blades of Sheringham's offshore wind farm are visible. Here, the sky, whether heavy with winter rain, faultlessly summertime blue or glowing with a flamboyant sunset, is magnificently big. This is a mesmerisingly beautiful spot.

It's not surprising that The White Horse's head chef, Fran Hartshorne, has chosen to stay a loyal ten years in the kitchen a stone's throw from the marshes. "It's a very special place," she agrees. "When people ask where the mussels come from, I point to Cyril's boat and they are amazed. I am so lucky to have a product like this grow literally yards from my kitchen – we don't really talk food miles!"

Fran, who leads an organised seven-strong core brigade (the team swells to thirteen in the peak season), shucks swiftly as we speak,

THE WHITE HORSE FRAN HARTSHORNE

The end of the mussel season is imminent when we meet, but for now they are at the heart of Fran's cooking. There is always a classic moules marinières on the menu, but on Monday Mussel Nights she will play with other flavours, steaming the shellfish in The White Horse's own Brancaster Brewery ale and serving them with local Smoked Dapple cheese; preparing them with Moroccan ras-el-hanout, raisins, carrots and almonds; or using a fragrantly-spicy Thai tom yum broth. Needless to say, the assiette of all four flavours is a popular choice.

Back on the foreshore, the Southerlands – Ben is the fifth generation of his family to fish – sort the haul, a job they do daily during the winter months, whatever the weather. They pump seawater from an adjacent reservoir into a handmade riddle that turns, allowing debris and small mussels to fall through the gaps. Bigger ones make it onto a conveyor belt where Cyril and Ben, protected in heavy yellow oilskins and thick blue gloves, run their hands expertly, swiftly, over the shells allowing the best to tip into a basket, discarding the rest. Purified and bagged, the shellfish are later barrowed to the back door of The White Horse.

Fran plunders the rich area around Brancaster Staithe for other ingredients too, happy to take a 'when it's gone, it's gone' approach to planning dishes. Local grower Ian Sutherland brings in asparagus from his beds in the village, while sea vegetables – beets, purslane, samphire – are foraged in the saltmarsh, and wild garlic is picked from hedgerows. "I work the menu round what's in season of course, and if the local ingredient is the best then I buy locally – but I'm not a slave to that. I'll always go to Simon Letzer for smoked fish, and Richard Loose is fantastic for oysters, but generally I like to hear from my suppliers what's good and then think on the hoof to create the menu."

preparing in moments a simple dish of the glossiest oysters, served with a classic Hendrick's gin and cucumber mignonette. Plate done to her liking, she turns her attention to the mussels, using them to create classic creamy chowder, setting aside the most attractive as a garnish. A firm-fleshed piece of smoked cod is topped with creamy pipings of mashed potato (she uses Hillfarm Oils cold-pressed rapeseed oil and Smoked Dapple cheese to finish the mash) and placed on top of the chowder. The showpiece mussels, open to reveal luscious dark orange flesh, are arranged alongside. "I love this dish," says Fran. "It's simple, fresh, the flavours are uncomplicated and they showcase the ingredients brilliantly. When the mussels are over, I use cockles or King's Lynn brown shrimps."

Moments later, Fran is onto another dish, forming quenelles of goats' curd, tangy and fresh, placing them carefully on a slate and adding lightly-charred asparagus spears and panéed quails' eggs ("cooked for two and a quarter minutes precisely!"). Halved, they spill their yolks, orange and tempting. A scattering of micro leaves from Nurtured in Norfolk finishes the dish. "I like quick dishes," she says. "We can easily do 700 covers a day in summer so it makes sense, especially as I want to prepare everything to order."

I wonder if Cyril, fifty years a mussel-man, would order a pan of Fran's mussels? "I do enjoy mussels, yes," he says. "At home we have them simply with vinegar and bread and butter, but I like coming up to The White Horse every so often to have them cooked by an expert."

17

Cyril's mussel chowder, smoked cod, rapeseed mash, pancetta and Norfolk Dapple

Simon Letzer's home-smoked cod from Brancaster village, is a perfect match for Cyril's plump mussels and served with mash from lovely floury Norfolk-grown potatoes, local cheese and rapeseed oil. (Serves 6)

If you like, save the smoked cod skin to flavour the chowder stock or alternatively use the skin from a piece of good cured gammon. Cook the vegetables for the chowder while the mussels are steaming. And to serve, you need to coincide grilling the cod and glazed mash top while cooking the pancetta, shallots and peas.

Mussel chowder
100ml dry white wine
1kg live mussels, cleaned and de-bearded
500ml fish stock
Rapeseed oil
3 carrots, finely diced
6 sticks celery, finely diced
300ml double cream

Discard any open mussels, which won't shut when tapped. Pour the wine into a large lidded saucepan over a high heat, bring to a boil and carefully tip in the mussels. Cover, cooking while stirring the shells up occasionally, until all or nearly all have opened fully. Tip through a colander over a saucepan to save the liquor. Sort through the mussels, removing and setting aside the meats from any open ones and discarding any closed shells. Reserve some still in their shells for garnish later. Strain the liquor through a sieve and set aside. Keep mussel meats, mussels in shells and the stock warm.

Meanwhile, in a lidded sauté pan, heat up a little oil over a medium heat. Add the carrot and celery, cover, and cook until soft but do not allow to colour. Add the mussel liquid, fish stock and the skin of the smoked cod (not the fish), if using. Simmer for 10 -15 minutes uncovered so that it reduces by a third. Remove the fish skin and add cream, bring back to the simmer and reduce again by a third or to a creamy chowder texture. Adjust seasoning to taste,

generally I find just pepper is required. Return the mussel meats and those in shell to the pan. Bring to a gentle simmer and keep warm.

Rapeseed mash
1.5kg good Norfolk mashing potatoes
100g unsalted butter
100ml rapeseed oil

Peel potatoes and cut into chunks. Cover with cold water in a covered saucepan and simmer until soft, perhaps 20 - 25 minutes, drain and put through a potato ricer or thoroughly mash. Melt the butter and add with the oil to the potatoes and stir well. Season to taste before a final mix and then keep warm.

To serve
700g smoked cod fillet, skin removed and kept
Rapeseed oil
Unsalted butter
500g pancetta, de-rinded and cut into thin lardons
6 shallots, thinly sliced
200g petit pois or garden peas
(cooked from fresh or defrosted)
50g Norfolk Dapple cheese, grated

Pre-heat grill to very hot. Cut cod into 6 portions and brush with oil, season to taste and add a knob of butter on top of each. Grill until just flaking but cooked through.

Meanwhile, heat a sauté pan, add a small glug of oil, and fry the pancetta until light-golden and crispy. Remove with a slotted spoon to kitchen paper. Over a lower heat, soften the shallots in a little more oil until translucent, add the peas to heat through and then remove from the heat.

Place mash into a warmed piping bag. When the fish is cooked, pipe the mashed potato on top and sprinkle over the cheese and grill again until golden. Ladle the mussel chowder over a bed of the pancetta mix in deep wide bowls and top with the glazed fish.

18

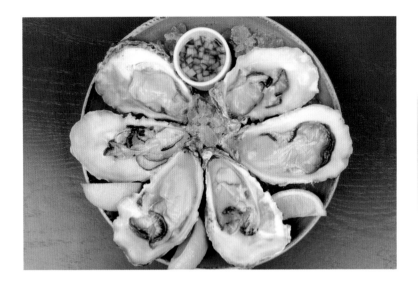

Brancaster oysters, Hendricks gin and cucumber vinaigrette

Like our lovely mussels, our oysters are sourced from a local shellfish farmer in the village, Richard Loose. The gin is heated to remove the alcohol and retain the flavour but if you are sensitive to spirits with shellfish, best to avoid this dish. (Serves 4)

Hendricks gin vinaigrette
200ml Hendricks gin
200ml white wine vinegar
100g caster sugar
1 whole cucumber

Place the gin, vinegar and sugar into a heavy saucepan, bring to a simmer, stir well to dissolve and remove from the heat. Decant and cool. Halve and deseed the cucumber. Dice into half cm cubes. Add to the vinaigrette and mix before chilling again.

To serve
12 oysters, shucked and detached, chilled in the half shell
1 lemon, cut into trimmed wedges

Place a bed of crushed ice or salt onto a wide platter, arrange your oysters in their shells on top with a ramekin of the vinaigrette at the centre and a garnish of the lemon wedges.

Norfolk tapas of fennel salami, wild garlic and granola

We love Jackie's Marsh Pig salami and cured meats, using wonderful Blythburgh free range pork. (Serves 4 as a nibble with drinks)

Granola
2 tbsp honey
125g unsalted butter
300g rolled oats
1 tsp ground cinnamon
½ tsp ground nutmeg
1 tsp ground ginger
1 tsp salt

Pre-heat the oven to 160c. Melt the honey and butter together in a deep pan. Mix the dry ingredients in a bowl and stir in the melted mixture. Transfer to a roasting tray and bake for 40 minutes, stirring every 10 minutes. Allow to cool.

500g Marsh Pig fennel salami
500g wild garlic leaves

Dice the salami into 1cm cubes. Add a splash of oil to a hot frying pan and sauté the salami. When just crisping, add the wild garlic and toss to wilt like spinach. Remove and stir 200g of the granola through the pan, season to taste and serve in a hot earthenware dish or from the pan.

Asparagus, goats' curd and quails' eggs

The charred spears and crisp Scotch egg work well with the cheese and the mustard dressing. Our asparagus comes from local grower Ian Sutherland. Panko crumbs on sale in good delis. (Serves 6)

30 asparagus spears, trimmed (use the woody bits for soup)

Blanch the spears in salted boiling water for a few minutes until al dente and then transfer to iced water to stop them overcooking. Drain and refrigerate.

12 quails' eggs
25g plain flour
2 hens' eggs, beaten
250g panko breadcrumbs

Gently cook the quails' eggs in constantly simmering water for 2½ minutes to keep the yolk runny. Carefully transfer to iced water. Once cooled, peel and lay onto kitchen paper to dry.

Season the flour well, then place into a shallow wide bowl. Put the beaten eggs and the crumbs into separate bowls. Line a tray with baking parchment. Dip the quails' eggs a few at a time into the flour bowl, then the beaten eggs, then the crumbs, back into the eggs and again into the crumbs, not

allowing them to touch. Remove one at a time and, shaping the coating, lay them separately onto the tray. Repeat with all the eggs and chill.

Mustard dressing
1 tbsp white wine vinegar
1 tsp Dijon mustard
1 tsp honey
3 tbsp rapeseed oil
1 tsp wholegrain mustard

Hand blend the first 3 ingredients together in a jug and then add a few drops of oil as you continue to blend, increasing to a light drizzle off the spoon. Once all spoonfuls have been added, stir in the wholegrain mustard by hand and season to taste with more honey, if preferred.

500g goats' curd
Favourite leaves or micro herbs for garnish

Pre-heat the deep fryer with sufficient oil to 170c. Meanwhile, char the asparagus with a chefs' blowtorch or in a very hot chargrill pan. Deep fry the crumbed eggs carefully for about 1 minute until golden brown. Gently remove onto kitchen paper, season to taste and serve with spoonfuls of curd, the mustard dressing and leaves to garnish.

DREAM DINNER?

It would be some crazy mad hatter's tea party where nothing tastes or smells as you expect. I'd get Heston [Blumenthal] to cook it – it would be right up his street! – and I'd enjoy it with my husband, family and best friends.

RECENT FOODIE DISCOVERIES?

It's not new but I like BBQ flavours, charring vegetables, fish and meat. If the ingredient is marinated and cooked properly – not overcooked – it can bring out amazing tastes and textures.

SIGNATURE DISHES

Starters

Norfolk pigeon, quails' eggs, wild mushrooms, edamame beans, seaweed

Baked garlic queen scallops, King's Lynn brown shrimp, gremolata

Smoked Dapple brûlée, tenderstem broccoli, pumpkin seeds

Mains

Smoked pork fillet, pancetta, butterbeans, pickled onions, cavolo nero

Confit sea trout, fennel & apple, potato, sea beets, lobster bisque

Norfolk Red Poll steak, fries, garlic butter

Puddings

The White Horse lemon tart

Dark chocolate ganache, coconut ice cream, chocolate granola

Set custard, poached rhubarb, gingerbread

UNFULFILLED DREAM JOB?

I'd love to run my own little bistro in Australia with my husband with no cares in the world and just being very successful and having people fighting to come through the door to eat the food that I love to cook!

BEST DISHES EVER EATEN?

I can't remember exactly what I ate – it was a while ago – but it was the taster menu at Launceston Place, South Kensington. I was blown away by the flavours, it was my first taste of top class Michelin star food.

FAVOURITE TIME OF YEAR FOR FOOD?

Autumn – there are so many more ingredients coming into season then, and it's such fun to create menus. I love it also when I can pick samphire from the marshland round the pub and get a real taste of the sea on my menu.

FRAN ON HER...

CHEF'S TIPS?

Use a scallop shell in a scraping motion to scale fish – it's really quick.

INSPIRING NORFOLK VIEW?

It's got to be the panoramic view across the tidal marsh looking out from the restaurant at The White Horse towards Scolt Head Island and the sea beyond. It is an ever-changing view, there's different light at different times of the day, always something to look at. The first thing we do every morning is to get a 'fix' of that view – it's a great start to the day!

QUICK SNACK OR MIDNIGHT FEAST?

I love antipasti and with so many fantastic delis around it's a hobby of mine to find quirky 'bits' for a fast snack.

WHERE ARE YOU HAPPIEST?

On a Saturday night in the middle of summer, 100-plus booked in the restaurant, the deck terrace overflowing and sunset over the marsh. There's a real buzz at times like that, and that's what this job is all about.

FAVOURITE LOCAL FOODIE PLACES?

I love The Duck Inn at Stanhoe, Market Bistro in King's Lynn and Byfords in Holt. They all serve well-cooked food with exciting elements.

Nye on irresistible

I t is hard to imagine that twenty years ago, when Cliff Nye bought the place, The White Horse was nothing more than a run-down, unloved roadside pub. Over the past two decades he, with support from his wife, Tina, has spearheaded its transformation into a magnet for holidaymakers (there are fifteen en suite bedrooms) and locals alike. It is rarely out of the press, the sort of place listed in Sunday supplement 'ten best coastal pubs' or 'best places to eat with view' listings with impressive regularity.

Cliff, chairman of Anglian Country Inns (ACI) which owns The White Horse, and his sons James, managing director, and Howard, operations director, have marked the milestone anniversary with a transforming refurbishment. Vast panes of glass now give an unencumbered view of the marshy coastline and ever-changing sky, and muted colours, organic shapes and materials root the space in its coastal environment. It looks and feels fresh, inviting and comfortable. And while the main dining area is modern and bright – lifted also by the stunning paintings

of lobster and crab painted by Gemma Nye, Cliff's daughter – the bar with its scrubbed pine tables, woodburner and traditional games is a more informal place to linger with a drink and bar nibbles or a light meal. Here, old photographs trace the history of the pub and the people that have propped up its bar, owned it, supplied it, worked in it and in the surrounding area over the years, creating a fascinating history of this stretch of coast.

Stylish outdoor spots – a terrace at the back and a covered outdoor dining area at the front – come into their own during the summer. A second purpose-built kitchen looks after the all day bar menu served in these spaces, enabling the pub comfortably to feed the hundreds of people who come through its doors on a busy sunny day.

ACI's Norfolk portfolio includes The King's Head, Letheringsett and The Jolly Sailors pub, also in Brancaster Staithe, where head chef Nick Ramsay is building a following for smoked dishes prepared in the on-site Jolly Smokehouse.

The White Horse
Brancaster Staithe, PE31 8BY
W: www.whitehorsebrancaster.co.uk
T: 01485 210262
E: reception@whitehorsebrancaster.co.uk
🅵 /WhiteHorseBrancaster
🐦 @WhiteHorseBranc
📷 /whitehorsebranc

Accolades: Waitrose *Good Food Guide* 3; AA Two Rosettes; Three Stars – Sustainable Restaurant Association 'Food Made Good Awards'; East of England Best Pub – 'National Pub & Bar Awards'; Top Ten – Seafish/The Caterer 'Restaurant of the Year Awards'; *Michelin*; *Harden's*; *Sawday's*.

Covers: 100 inside, 100 outside

Cost: carte average £29; wine from £17.50; pint from £3.40

Open: all week L 12-2, D 6.30-9; Sun L 12-2.30

Details: all day bar meals; children's menu; wheelchair access; 15 en suite rooms including the Room at the Top with viewing telescope; family rooms; dogs welcome in garden rooms (£10/night); parking

**TIPI IN THE PADDOCK,
WEST BILNEY**
MATTHEW OWSLEY-BROWN

On fire

A tipi, a campervan and al fresco dining
in the middle of a wooded glade, welcome to
a very cool, under canvas food experience

It was the smell of sage and garlic cooking over an open fire that told us we were in the right place as we pulled up outside 'Conkers', the home and idyllic workplace of Matthew and Caroline Owsley-Brown.

The couple are known round these parts from their time running Fishes, the fine dining restaurant in Burnham Market, but they have cut ties with that scene to focus on a totally different style of cooking and eating, to create their own intriguing take on al fresco dining.

"It is a bit of a cliché to say we are living the good life," says Matthew, "though our friends have been known to call us Tom and Barbara [after the characters in the 1980s television show, *The Good Life*]! What we are trying to do is bring fine food back to its roots, lose the pretensions, eat food made from local ingredients. It just makes sense: for us, the art of good cooking is to get the fullest flavours from the simplest produce – that is what we are trying to achieve.

"I was classically-trained, but I've learnt that I don't like poncing around with food, I like the ingredients to give up their flavours naturally."

Matthew bubbles with ideas, his enthusiasm infectious as he explains his vision. "Whole joints roasting on an open fire; the spices and smells of a clay tandoor oven; cooking outside as the sun sets across the fields..." Where most people see food as a set of ingredients on a plate, Matthew sees it as the focal point in an entire panorama.

Keen foodie travellers, the couple have just returned from a three-week campervan trip to northern Italy. A battered notebook is rammed with recipe ideas and notes about the producers they met. "I just love the simplicity of Italian cooking. It still seems to be the case that the women or mums make the pasta in the osteria we went to..." His voice trails off as he realises he's meandering off track again.

"Look, this is the idea." Matthew grabs a book – *Mallmann on Fire* by the Argentine chef, Francis Mallmann – lying open on the kitchen table. He points at a picture of a group of friends sitting around an old table on a grassy plain overlooking the vine-covered hills of Argentina. To one side a chef is cooking chunks of Argentinian steak on an open fire. "Cooking outside, eating with friends, bringing your own wine – that is the joy of the whole experience, that's what we strive to create here."

And so they are. Living happily in a large sty and pen are the latest additions to the household, three Berkshire pigs that go by the names of Olive, Tulip and Poppy. The three little pigs' predecessors are still making appearances as the edible stars of various culinary affairs and Matthew's signature dish is one of those. "I'm using bacon because it is such a versatile ingredient. I can smoke it, fry it, roast it. It is absolutely delicious whatever you do, and it has travelled absolutely no miles. Surely this is the ultimate respect that you can pay an animal that you have reared?"

Matthew and Caroline might laugh off the Tom and Barbara references but there is an element of the quirky and slightly chaotic around the place. The house – a beautiful Arts and Crafts style building – sits in an acre of land, the couple's smallholding.

Exploring it is like wandering behind the scenes of a cookery programme: an industrial kitchen – the beating heart of the business – sits to one side of the house; the pigs snuffle around contentedly; a greenhouse is just beginning to burst into life with tomatoes, chillies and peppers; random beds house squashes, courgettes,

purple sprouting broccoli, sweetcorn; and pieces of serious cooking equipment – including the fabulous tandoor – are scattered around the place. There is also the restored VW campervan, back from its recent trip to Italy, in which Matthew and Caroline intend to undertake further reconnaissance in search of new culinary ideas.

"Shamefully, when we moved here this had a well-tended garden," says Caroline looking around with a rueful smile. "We are really only just getting it back into shape. It is a work in progress."

'A work in progress' demeans what is happening here in the woods just outside King's Lynn. Matthew is a man with a head full of ideas but with a very strong, core vision. When he talks about food, his whole demeanour becomes electrified, but what he says couldn't be simpler. "I really admire the way they approach food in Italy. On our trip there, we ate very uncomplicated dishes but the flavours were invariably astonishing. That's what I want to do here: make food that is delicious and simple, which people can eat in our unique setting."

Agnolotti piemontese of smoked bacon, spinach and parmesan with capers and sage

We rear our own Berkshire weaners in our paddocks, fattened on the lush produce from our kitchen garden. The resultant slow-matured tasty cuts are cured with maple syrup & fennel seed, and then cold-smoked in our converted oak barrel smoker, becoming melting delicious bacon. (Serves 6)

Pasta dough
300g 00 grade strong pasta flour
200g fine semolina
4 large eggs
6 large egg yolks

Mix the dry ingredients and pulse together with the eggs in the food processor just enough until it becomes a rough dough (trying not to overwork). Empty out and firm up by hand into a tacky ball. Place in a floured bowl, clingfilm the top and refrigerate for 30 minutes.

Filling
250g spinach leaves
550g smoked bacon, shredded and fried
2 egg yolks, lightly beaten
1 egg, lightly beaten
50g Parmesan, grated

Blanch the spinach in boiling salted water for one minute then refresh in lots of iced water. Drain well and squeeze out the spinach twisted into a clean tea towel. Chop well and put into a large mixing bowl with the bacon. Once mixed, stir in the egg yolks, whole egg and Parmesan before seasoning to taste. Place in a food processor and pulse mixture to a semi-smooth paste. Chill for 30 minutes and then form into 3cm balls.

Agnolotti
Semolina for dusting
Beaten egg yolks for brushing pasta

Take the chilled dough, press it flat with your hands and dust generously with semolina. Pass it through the rollers in one continuous movement. Dust it again, fold it to fit, dust again, reset the roller one notch narrower and roll again. Repeat the process until you get through the narrowest setting. The dough should be dry but holding together.

Place the rolled out pasta sheet on a clean flat worktop, lightly dusted with semolina. Brush with egg yolk and place the balls of filling in the centre of the sheet with a 5cm gap between each ball. Fold the pasta sheet in half over the balls and carefully press down between each mound expelling as much air as possible. Now using a crimpled pastry wheel, cut firmly but carefully around each filling, leaving a 2cm frill to form the agnolotti. Pick each up in turn and press round the edges with your fingers to seal the filling in and to expel the air. Drop into a deep tray of semolina as you go, dredging well and avoiding them touching.

To serve
Handful sage leaves, roughly shredded
1 tbsp capers
250g cold butter, diced
1 lemon, juice only
Parmesan, grated

Boil a very wide pan of salted water. Carefully lower in the agnolotti and cook on a rolling boil for 7-10 minutes until the pasta is al dente while preparing the second stage below. Nb The agnolotti cooking time depends on how dry the pasta has become.

Meanwhile add the butter into a hot frying pan over a medium-high heat until it sizzles and foams to a golden-brown colour. Stir in the capers and sage and turn off the heat. Add a little lemon juice to arrest the cooking process. Carefully tip in the drained agnolotti, toss gently and serve with Parmesan and black pepper.

Tandoori chicken tikka

A favourite from our Indian pop-up menu, cooked in our charcoal tandoor, we use Howard's of Gayton free-range Norfolk chicken for this. Pictured with a masala sauce, kachumba salad, mango chutney and our own puffy naan. (Serves 4)

675g chicken thighs, boneless
One generous tsp salt
3 tbsp lemon juice
1 tbsp fresh ginger,
peeled and finely grated
2 cloves garlic, peeled
and minced
1 tsp ground cumin
1 tsp paprika or smoked
paprika
½ tsp cayenne pepper
6 tbsp whipping cream
½ tsp garam masala

Prick the chicken all over lightly with a tip of a knife and place in a bowl with the salt and lemon juice. Rub in well. Add in the ginger, garlic, cumin, paprika cayenne, cream and garam masala. Mix well, cover and refrigerate for 6-8 hours, preferably overnight. Pre-heat your grill as hot as possible. Thread meat onto metal skewers. Grill for about 6 minutes on each side, until well-coloured and cooked through.

Argentinian-style rose veal Jacob's Ladder

This free range Norfolk veal short rib dish is good with our Dutch oven bacon beans, oven-roasted vegetables and smoky BBQ sauce. Also works well with beef brisket. It starts in a very hot kettle barbecue or clay oven, heated to 250c but allowing the coals to then die out. (Serves 6+)

1 Jacob's Ladder or short
rib of free range rose veal
1 bottle good Malbec red wine
6 fresh bay leaves
1 head of garlic cloves,
peeled and minced
220g flat parsley leaves,
finely chopped
220g oregano leaves,
finely chopped
2 tsp crushed chilli flakes
50ml cabernet sauvignon
vinegar
100ml olive oil
1 tbsp sea salt dissolved in
200ml water and cooled

Marinate the meat overnight in the wine and bay leaves.

For the chimichurri, mix together garlic, parsley, oregano and chilli. Whisk in the vinegar and olive oil, followed by the brine.

Heat up your barbecue or clay oven to 250c. Remove meat from the marinade and reserve wine and leaves. Pat the meat dry and coat with 200ml of chimichurri. Place meat in a roasting dish and add the wine. Wrap with foil. Bake, with the oven or BBQ sealed for about 8 hours or until very tender. Serve with more chimichurri on the side.

Torta di nocciole

We serve this Piedmontese hazelnut cake alongside glazed limoncello zabaglione and fresh berries. (Serves 6+)

1 tbsp baking powder
3 eggs, separated
200g granulated sugar
125g butter, melted
200g plain flour
200g hazelnuts without skins,
toasted and roughly chopped
I lemon, grated rind only
4 tbsp milk

Pre-heat the oven to 180c. Beat the baking powder with the egg yolks, then thoroughly mix in the sugar, melted butter, flour, hazelnuts, zest and milk. Whisk the egg whites with a pinch of salt to stiff peaks and fold into the mix with a metal spoon. Pour into 20cm buttered, floured cake tin and bake for approx. 35 minutes until browned and a skewer comes out almost dry. Allow to cool.

UNFULFILLED AMBITIONS?

I would like to develop the smallholding to become even more self-sufficient. I would also like to open a bed and breakfast here - but with a little bit extra, serving great food as well. At the moment, I am still developing the pop-up to be exactly how we dreamt it would be.

FAVOURITE LOCAL FOODIE PLACE?

The Spice Market in Gaywood on the outskirts of King's Lynn is amazing. They stock just about any spice you could want.

BEST DISH EVER EATEN?

At Sa Foradada in Deia, Mallorca. We had to take a boat to reach the restaurant which sits on top of a steep rock face. It was the best paella I have ever eaten, it was cooked on an open fire, over grape vines.

WHAT IS YOUR BIGGEST EXTRAVAGANCE AS A CHEF?

Caviar: I know it's not sustainable and is completely naughty, but I love it and so do the rest of the family. It is a rare treat, maybe at Christmas.

LUCKY DAY OFF?

I like getting in the camper van and just shooting off somewhere to explore. We might go up to the Lake District or the Outer Hebrides. Or we might just trundle along the coast to Stiffkey. I do like to get the boat out too.

MATTHEW ON HIS...

QUICK SNACK OR MIDNIGHT FEAST?

I don't really snack, honestly I don't, [at this point Caroline raises an eyebrow]. I suppose if I did it would be one of those Argentine choripan – a baguette stuffed with chorizo, avocado and grilled vegetables.

WELL-THUMBED COOKBOOKS?

Anything by Yotam Ottolenghi, anything by Hugh Fearnley-Whittingstall. anything by Madhur Jaffrey, anything by Diana Henry. And at the moment, I am dipping into Francis Mallman, a chef who specialises in Argentinian cuisine.

FAVOURITE BIT OF KITCHEN EQUIPMENT?

My clay tandoor oven. We spent some time in India and it is a cuisine I love to cook. I am never happier than when making a curry.

MUSIC TO COOK TO?

Funk, any funk!

SIGNATURE DISHES

Starters

Our own oak-smoked salmon, blinis, celeriac remoulade, herby salad

Yemeni falafel, sesame seeds, cardamom, coriander, green chilli, broad beans, lemon, tahini, minted yoghurt

Home-made porcini, ricotta & spinach tortellini, sage beurre noisette

Mains

Slow-cooked whole lamb, rosemary & garlic marinade, caponata, new potatoes

Rare breed brined and roasted pork belly, crackling, cavolo nero, braised puy lentils, salsa verde

Houghton Hall venison Wellington, celeriac purée, wild mushrooms, juniper gravy

Puddings

Apple tarte fine, salted caramel ice cream

Fairgreen Farm blueberry tart, blueberry ice cream

Banana & passionfruit soufflé

FOOD HEROES?

I have a lot of chefs I admire, but my top three would be Rick Stein, Henry Harris and Madhur Jaffrey.

COOK'S TIP?

When using a clay oven, fire pit or barbecue, always make sure your wood is as dry as possible. And hard wood is definitely best – it burns better and for longer.

Time for Tipi

The Tipi in the Paddock became a reality in 2015. It's not been an easy dream to bring to fruition. But now the Owsley-Browns' lavish, soulful pop-up supper venue in the hidden paddock of their bucolic smallholding draws in guests from far and wide to experience their unique River Cottage-style dining experience and Matthew's relaxed, tasty food. "It has been a slog at times to create exactly what we envisaged," Caroline explains. That tireless vision was rigorously trialled in getting the temperature inside just right whatever the time of year; battling with yards and yards of canvas to move the Tipi's entrance; harnessing some slightly Heath Robinson techniques to prevent smoke blowing back inside; and struggling with the elements to perfect cooking outside, the smart field kitchen being the inspired result.

Matthew and Caroline have decked their Tipi – imagine a grand, welcoming wigwam – with an eclectic mix of tables, chairs, furry rugs, lanterns and sofas; in situ year-round and seating fifty diners comfortably, it's toasty and snug come winter by the central open fire, in summer open sides bring the al fresco in, along with the gorgeous views across the meadow to the lush woods around.

Matthew and Caroline might have left the world of traditional restaurants behind but their reputation precedes them. They owned Fishes, their fine dining seafood restaurant in Burnham Market, for eight years, rightly lauded by the likes of *Harden's* and *The Good Food Guide*. Matthew's 25-year kitchen career started in London, with Anton Mosimann, then travelling onto Cornwall to work with one Rick Stein, later becoming head chef at Mayfair's Noble Rot and Harvey Nichols' Fifth Floor Café. The Owsley-Browns' track record is evident in their gift for hospitality; as guests arrive, Caroline swooshes effortlessly into hostess mode, guests treated as friends, dishes arriving seamlessly, proceedings directed with aplomb; meanwhile, in the kitchen a whirling dervish creates magic with simple ingredients, only surfacing, a large glass of wine in hand, when the last plate reaches the tables.

When not 'popping-up', Matthew and Caroline are in demand for their stylish outside catering, the same culinary pedigree given to weddings and party clients with everything home-made from scratch, using fabulous local ingredients – you would expect nothing less.

Tipi in the Paddock & Owsley-Brown Catering
Conkers, Common Road, West Bilney,
King's Lynn PE32 1JX
W: www.owsley-brown.com
T: 01553 840190
E: info@owsley-brown.com
[f] /owsley-brown
[t] @owsleybrownfood

Covers: 50

Cost: average set Tipi menu £30

Open: regular themed pop-up suppers, dates via newsletter and on social media; private parties

Details: BYO wine (£5pp corkage); wine tasting events; cookery workshops; outside catering for weddings and bespoke dinner parties

Bird perfect

Eric Snaith's acclaimed, adventurous cooking is a natural fit with versatile Norfolk quail

TITCHWELL MANOR ERIC SNAITH

Y ou could be forgiven, driving through Titchwell from Thornham, for missing Eric Snaith's restaurant: the view over the bird-busy marshes towards sandy Brancaster Bay where dots of people walk dogs and fly kites, and a strip of North Sea glints, is likely to have your eyes glued left. But turn round, because Titchwell Manor, the Victorian pile on the landward side of the coast road – and Eric's cooking in particular – is worth a visit.

"We take that view for granted," Eric shrugs. That too is forgivable; Eric has been part of the business ever since his parents bought the property in the late 1980s. It's the place he played as a child, pot-washed as a teen, "not cut out for A levels", learning to love the buzz of a professional kitchen until, some 13 years ago, his parents entrusted the kitchen to their self-taught chef son. He has since honed skills formidable enough to earn three AA Rosettes and a slew of awards including *Eastern Daily Press* Norfolk Chef of the Year 2012. The latter is a catching habit: Eric's right hand chef for the past seven years, Chris Mann, won the same title in 2015, something of which Eric is justifiably proud.

The pair work closely together in a calm, ordered space, running a brigade of seven. "It's a great kitchen," says Chris. "There's so much creativity; Eric and I are always bouncing ideas off each other."

This is indeed a kitchen that innovates constantly, it seems, if not on the stratospheric levels of Heston Blumenthal or Grant Achatz (Eric admires both these avant-garde chefs) then at least with more than a passing nod to their approach. "I don't want people to eat food here that they could cook for themselves. I want them to be excited, surprised" says Eric. "I want to challenge, push boundaries, take risks."

He especially loves doing savoury versions of sweet dishes, creating something that is different but still somehow familiar. Eric indicates a 'custard', classically made with cream and egg but with less sugar and more salt, and infused overnight with toasted hay. It will be the base of a popular quail dish that he serves with boned leg schnitzel, coddled egg, Japanese mushrooms and chard.

"I like acidity, saltiness, freshness, sweet/sour," he continues, on a flavourful roll. "My lemon miso curd is a bit of a signature dish. It looks like lemon curd but there's less sugar. I just stir in some white miso paste at the end to give a fantastic umami taste; it really is moreish!" He might serve the curd with confit smoked salmon, cucumber and turnip, or with lightly-cured and blow-torched mackerel.

It's not always to everyone's taste. Eric recalls a Brie de Meaux crème brûlée that divided opinion. "Some people loved it, others

were less keen! But I'd rather cook food that prompts reaction than be bland. Food has got to have oomph; if it is always just middle of the road you'll never hit those highs!"

He talks while keeping an eye on the quail, poaching gently – just five minutes is enough – in stock that is fragrant with mirepoix, coriander seeds and thyme. Next to this he deftly cracks tiny mottled quails' eggs into silicone poaching moulds; they cook in minutes. He lifts the quail out of the stock, takes off the breasts, setting them aside to be pan-finished.

The birds are from John and Ellie Savory, the couple responsible for putting ethically-reared British quail onto restaurant menus around the country. The Savorys launched Norfolk Quail back in 2011, testing the water with twenty birds reared in an old stable on their arable farm near Fakenham. "We now have several thousand," Ellie explains. "We manage every stage here, from hatching to ensuring the dressed birds reach customers in perfect condition. It's a fully traceable operation."

The birds live in airy, heated sheds where light levels mimic natural rhythms and – even though quail are ground-living birds – there are perches and enough height to fly and express natural behaviour. Processed to order at 16 weeks, they are sent, oven-ready, to chefs as far as away as Nathan Outlaw's renowned Cornish restaurant, to places in the Scottish Highlands, and even customers in the Far East. "I love the fact that the birds are available year round and that it's a consistent product," says Eric. "It's versatile and healthy, and particularly good in spring and summer when it's great with fresh peas and beans. We've also done it on the barbecue with watermelon or paired it with lobster."

Eric's is a thoughtful style of cooking. "I used to have a 45-minute commute to work and I'd lock onto a dish, really think about it and focus on how to improve it. I love using the Internet and Instagram; it's so easy to see what's happening in kitchens round the world and I really enjoy picking up new techniques or inventive presentation."

For all that, Eric remains grounded, alive to the fact that he has to balance ingenuity with convention. Guests can immerse themselves in the full creativity of the seven-course 'Conversation' tasting menu, or choose the more predictable à la carte and eat line-caught fish and chips or a Dexter cheeseburger. "I want to cook for my customers, but I also want Titchwell Manor to become a destination for food that's a bit different. I don't want to be middle of the road."

Norfolk quail, schnitzel leg, hay custard, oriental mushrooms, coddled egg, hedge garlic and rainbow chard

We are so lucky to have John and Ellie Savory farming quail just a few miles from Titchwell at Great Ryburgh – their product really is second to none. This elegant dish works well as a light main course or as a starter. The chard and hedge garlic can be substituted with interesting, seasonal greens throughout the year. (Serves 4)

Hay custard

- 1 handful of hay, toasted to light-brown in a medium oven
- 300g double cream
- 100g egg yolks
- 15g caster sugar
- 2.5g salt

The day before, bring the cream and hay to low simmer in a deep wide saucepan. Remove and decant contents to a container before cooling and chilling overnight.

The next day, strain the cream and reheat to a low simmer. Remove from the heat while you whisk the yolks and sugar together until pale in a separate bowl. Whisk in the cream and pour into a deep saucepan. Cook over a low heat, stirring till thickened. Whisk in the salt, pour into a bowl, cover with clingfilm touching the custard surface to prevent a skin forming, then cool before refrigerating if necessary. Allow to come to room temperature before serving.

Quail crowns

- 1 cup chopped carrot, leek, celery and onion
- 1 sprig thyme
- 1 bay leaf
- 8 black peppercorns
- 8 fennel seeds
- 4 oven ready quail, legs removed and set aside

Place the vegetables and aromatics in a medium pan of water, cover and bring to a simmer, season with salt to taste. Poach the quail crowns on a low simmer for 5 minutes, remove the birds and allow to cool at room temperature.

Chard

- 4 leaves of rainbow chard
- 200ml orange juice

Remove the green leaves from the chard and set aside. Cut the stems into 5cm lengths and bring up to the boil in the juice, remove with a slotted spoon to iced water. When cold, drain and set aside.

Schnitzel legs

- 4 tbsp plain flour
- 1 hen's egg, lightly beaten
- 4 tbsp panko breadcrumbs (from good delis)
- 1 lemon half

Carefully remove the skin and bones from the quail legs, keeping meat as a whole piece. Place between oiled clingfilm and beat gently until they are very thin (3mm is ideal). Chill until required.

To finish

- 4 quails' eggs
- Unsalted butter
- 12 leaves of hedge garlic, washed
- 1 punnet shimeji or other oriental mushrooms, cleaned
- Rapeseed oil

You might need another pair of hands here as there is some pan-juggling with the egg poaching, browning the butter, pan-frying the breasts with the chard and mushrooms and deep-frying the legs.

Pre-heat your deep-fryer, with appropriate level of vegetable oil. Dust the leg meat in the flour, followed by the egg, and then the breadcrumbs. Carefully lower into the deep-fryer and cook until golden-brown. Allow to drain before removing and then season to taste and spritz with lemon juice.

We bake our eggs in baby silicone moulds but simply poaching them will work fine. Meanwhile heat a few knobs of butter in a frying pan over a medium heat until light brown. At the same time, remove the quail breasts from the crowns and pan fry in a hot pan over a high heat with a little more butter and rapeseed oil. When they are brown, remove to a warm plate while sautéing the chard leaves, stems and mushrooms to heat through.

To serve, spoon the custard onto plates, followed by the chard stems and leaves, the crispy legs, the breasts, garlic leaves and mushrooms, ending with the eggs, brushed with the brown butter and seasoned.

38

Thornham apple

We are spoilt with the heritage apple varieties at Drove Orchards in nearby Thornham, where we source our fruit and juice for this dessert. The garnishes here are unbaked Italian meringue, using hot sugar, which we pipe on the plates and malto olive oil pebbles. If you search online, you will find recipes for these two elements easily. (Serves 6)

Apple sorbet
750ml local apple juice
Juice of 1 lemon
50g glucose

Warm the apple juice and then combine with the lemon juice and glucose in a food processor, blend, sieve and churn in an ice cream machine before freezing.

For the apple pearls
3 large apples, Granny Smith or Braeburn etc
50g white wine
125g apple juice
13g lemon juice
25g caster sugar

Peel the apples and using a melon baller, make 24 pearls and set aside.

Put the other ingredients in a pan and bring to a gentle simmer. Add the pearls and poach, as gently as possible, for 7 minutes. Remove from the heat and cool in the liquor.

Frozen apple
1 apple, peeled and cored

Peel and cut into 3mm dice before freezing.

Quenelle the sorbet using two spoons and scatter with the diced apple and poached pearls.

Charred onion, potato gnocchi, avocado, brazil nuts, burnt onion crème fraîche

Home-made potato gnocchi dumplings are very easy and well worth making but equally accessible in good delis. (Serves 4)

Onion elements
2 large white onions
100g butter
150g crème fraîche

On a very hot griddle pan or barbecue, char the onions with their skins on until black, allow to cool, then halve and remove the skins to one side. Brush the onion centres with butter and season with salt, and char again along with the skins. When onions are soft, remove and set aside. When the skins are black and crispy, remove, cool, process to a powder and fold into the crème fraîche, then chill.

For the avocado
1 ripe avocado
Lemon juice and salt
50g crème fraîche

Purée the avocado and crème fraîche until smooth, adding lemon juice and salt to taste.

To serve
Home-made or good gnocchi
Brazil nuts, roughly chopped

Warm the onions as required in a medium oven. Sauté the gnocchi in a hot frying pan with a little olive oil until starting to crisp, then finish with butter. Place onion on the plates, scatter around the gnocchi, spoon on the onion crème fraîche before garnishing with the avocado and nuts to finish.

Fillet of brill, lavender, oyster and samphire

This elegant dinner party starter or fish course is a true expression of the Norfolk coast. (Serves 4)

6-8 lavender sprigs, tips reserved
200ml buttermilk, warmed
2 oysters
Olive oil
1 large beetroot
4 brill fillets
Milk
Small handful of samphire, trimmed and blanched
4 sorrel leaves

Infuse the lavender with the warmed buttermilk and set aside for 1 hour before sieving, retaining the milk.

Open the oysters and sieve the juices into a bowl, chop up the flesh and mix with two tablespoons of oil to make a dressing. Pre-heat the oven to 180c and bake the beetroot in a loose foil parcel for 2 hours until tender. Remove and refrigerate when cool. Thinly slice into discs, place flat on a tray, brush with a little oil and set aside.

When ready to serve, reheat the beetroot in a 200c oven until hot. Meanwhile poach the brill in a snug lidded saucepan, covered with milk and gently simmer until just cooked. Drain fish, season to taste and keep warm.

To serve, place a good spoonful of the lavender buttermilk in the centre of each plate, scatter on the warm samphire and top with the fish, a sorrel leaf, the lavender tips and the oyster dressing around.

FOOD HEROES?

Heston [Blumenthal]. It's amazing what he's achieved. It's also brilliant what the team at Norfolk Quail have created – it would be so easy to cut corners but they never do and the quality of their product is amazing.

INSPIRING NORFOLK VIEW?

I've grown up with the view from the front of Titchwell Manor but I still love it, it's unspoilt and very Norfolk! Our sunsets are as good as anywhere in the world but photographs always look rubbish, so it's best to stop the car and just soak it all up!

SIGNATURE DISHES

Starters

Brancaster lobster, heritage tomato, pear, vanilla

Brancaster cockles, shallot, white wine

Cauliflower soup, truffle bread & butter pudding, confit yolk

Mains

Salt-baked celeriac, fresh walnuts, Lincolnshire Poacher, onion jus

Halibut, smoked potato, white bean, confit lemon, rainbow chard

Local lamb loin & belly, Jersey Royals, wild garlic

Puddings

Lemon & cucumber tart, burnt lemon ice cream, gin

Dark chocolate delice, passion fruit, olive oil, pastry

Granny Smith apple & celeriac terrine, pistachio, white chocolate

FAVOURITE BIT OF KITCHEN EQUIPMENT?

My Thermomix. I'm a big fan. Among other things it means you can make custards easily, quickly and consistently well. It's like having an extra chef!

FOODIE NOSTALGIA?

I love the smell of cooking over charcoal. It brings back family holidays in the Algarve in my early teens, especially the chicken piri piri we used to have.

ERIC ON HIS...

FAVOURITE TIME OF YEAR FOR FOOD?

Spring and summer when all the fresh greens, peas and beans are out, there's crab available and the berries are local. If you cook with the seasons, food retains its specialness throughout the year and you find yourself always looking forward to the next ingredients as they come in.

FAVOURITE LOCAL PLACES TO EAT?

Am I allowed to say Eric's Fish and Chips at Drove Orchards in Thornham?!

WELL-THUMBED COOKBOOKS?

I use recipe books less and less these days but I've had the *Alinea* book [Grant Achatz's three Michelin-starred Chicago restaurant] for the past 12 years or so, and still think he's the most inventive chef out there.

CHEF'S TIP?

When you're picking down crab, drop the crab from a height onto a metal tray – that way you'll spot the scraps of shell.

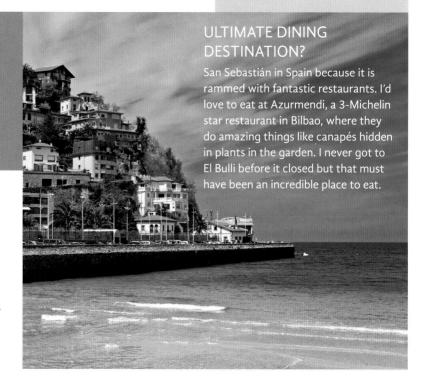

ULTIMATE DINING DESTINATION?

San Sebastián in Spain because it is rammed with fantastic restaurants. I'd love to eat at Azurmendi, a 3-Michelin star restaurant in Bilbao, where they do amazing things like canapés hidden in plants in the garden. I never got to El Bulli before it closed but that must have been an incredible place to eat.

Style and substance

Titchwell Manor is more vibrant Shoreditch funk than bleached seaside cool – and deliberately so. Eric and his wife Lydia have eschewed the muted colourways popular in many coastal spots in favour of a bold, urbane, contemporary style for their boutique hotel and restaurants, a look honed with guidance from east London designer, Shaun Clarkson.

It's nonetheless very comfortable. This is a place to relax in vibrantly pink velvet armchairs, or on the vast yellow leather sofa that fills the bay window in the bar area. There's a dramatic starburst-patterned rug, proper fires are lit in season, there are huge lamps, and wallpaper that makes you stop and look rather than drift on by. It creates a unique setting, an appropriately show-stopping backdrop to Eric's adventurous cooking.

Eric's parents, Margaret and Ian Snaith, bought the property in 1989 when Eric was just nine years old. The younger generation is now in charge, Eric of course in the kitchen and Lydia managing the accounts in between caring for the

couple's two young daughters, Jemima and Verity.

Together, they have brought the property bang up to date. There are now 27 en suite bedrooms between the main house and converted adjacent buildings, and the two separate dining areas enable guests to choose between the fine dining atmosphere of the Conservatory or the less formal Eating Rooms. Dishes evolve constantly on all the menus, and diners can enjoy the full seven-course tasting experience, choose from a more conventional à la carte menu, or go for simpler brasserie-style options such as mussels or French onion soup in any of the dining areas.

Eric's Fish and Chips at Drove Orchards in nearby Thornham (www.ericsfishandchips.com) is a recent departure from the conventional restaurant scene for the Snaiths. The retro-styled diner with its eat-in and takeaway menus featuring line-caught fish is proving extremely popular with upwards of 500 portions served on the busiest days.

Titchwell Manor Hotel and Restaurants
Titchwell, Brancaster PE31 8BB
W: www.titchwellmanor.com
T: 01485 210221
E: info@titchwellmanor.com
 /titchwellmanor
 @TitchwellManor
 /ericsnaithchef

Accolades: Waitrose *Good Food Guide 3*; AA Three Rosettes; Winner – 'Best Restaurant and Pub Dining' 2013, Winner – Chef of the Year 2012 (Eric Snaith), Winner – Chef of the Year 2015 (Chris Mann) *EDP* Norfolk Food and Drink Awards; Masterchef of Great Britain (Eric Snaith); Winner, Best Independent Hotel, *EDP* Visit Norfolk Tourism Awards 2012

Covers: 65 seats in Conservatory, 40 in Eating Rooms; 20 outside

Cost: carte average £32; tasting menu £55 (five courses) or £65 (seven courses); set lunch two courses £15, three courses £20; wine from £19

Open: all week L 12-5 (Sun 12-2.30); D 6-9:30; afternoon tea 12-5

Details: al fresco dining; children's menu; civil-licensed and wedding catering for 85; 27 en suite bedrooms in the main house and in outside converted buildings; dogs welcome in certain rooms; parking

Lettuce and lovage

Herbs, picked from Congham Hall's stunning gardens,
take centre-stage on Nick Claxton-Webb's
menu of modern classics

CONGHAM HALL NICK CLAXTON-WEBB

It is not difficult, as you walk through the herb garden at Congham Hall, to be transported. This is the sort of place that, in your mind's eye, a winsome Jane Austen heroine will float into view, plucking rosemary leaves as she drifts between the box-edged beds and around gnarly old apple trees, or bends to smell fragrant, frothy meadowsweet and run her fingers through swathes of mint. She may have a wicker basket to collect aniseedy sweet cicely, pale green lovage or pungent clary sage.

But snap out of the reverie, because the Congham Hall herb garden – as well as being an extraordinary public collection of herbs – is a practical, working space. You are more likely to meet head gardener Philip Bailey digging over a patch of earth or head chef Nick Claxton-Webb picking herbs for a lunchtime menu, than anyone dressed in layers of chiffon.

The internationally-renowned herb garden was created by Christine Forecast who, together with her husband Trevor, turned Congham Hall into a hotel in 1982. It was Christine's passion for herbs that led to the vast collection there is today. And it is something that still enthuses Nick, even four years into running the kitchen. "To be able to step out and pick fresh herbs like this is amazing. In the height of the season we'll have a 10am herb run, and if you go earlier on a summer's morning, maybe after some rain, it is incredibly fragrant."

Many of the herbs are eminently recognisable, not just because of their careful labelling. There are chives, their purple flowers about to open, blue-flowering rosemary, woody thyme, numerous takes on

mint contained under a rose trellis, dwarf oregano and broad-leafed sorrel. Others are unexpected and evocatively-named: madder, traditionally used as a dye, and alecost, an ancient flavouring for ale, sit alongside betony, bistort, horehound and spinach-like good King Henry, plants favoured by medieval cooks.

The kitchen is self-sufficient in salads for about six months of the year too and has squash and apples (Laxton's Superb and Cox's Orange Pippin) aplenty come autumn. Some crops are grown in protective polytunnels and all are sown in succession, a couple of rows at a time. "That gives me a manageable flow and means we don't have a glut and get fed up!" says Nick. "Tomatoes and courgettes are the usual culprits, beetroot too." Any over-abundance is turned into chutney or put through a dehydrator and used perhaps to flavour biscuits, or placed in a basket by the front door for departing guests to help themselves.

Nick finely chops sorrel leaves for his popular Norfolk shorthorn beef dish. He works methodically; there's a sense of serenity in this kitchen, an atmosphere that Nick has cultivated instinctively and that he believes is essential for a productive workplace. "He is the most chilled chef I've ever worked with," confirms senior sous Dan Herbert, whom Nick has nurtured from his early days as a commis. Dan picks over the wild garlic just gathered in a nearby wood, selecting the prettiest flowers as garnish while Nick warms the beef cheeks in a rich sauce, a sprig of rosemary flavouring the contents of the pan.

At the pass, he places some of the last of the winter's cavolo nero, still darkly glossy, centre-stage on the plate, arranging slices of tender beef rump – the cattle graze the picturesque fields around the Hall – and nuggets of cheek alongside. Broad sorrel leaves, dots of wild garlic purée and the shiny sauce bring the plate to life.

Nick's classically-inspired menus are rooted in a career that has seen him cook for ten years in France before immersing himself in the East Anglian scene: he's headed up the kitchens at the Ickworth House hotel and Leaping Hare restaurant, both near Bury St Edmunds and places with similar abundance on their doorsteps. His understanding of local ingredients celebrates Norfolk with the likes of Holkham Estate venison, Cromer crabs, mussels and oysters from Brancaster and outdoor-reared local rare-breed pork.

When it comes to pairing ingredients with herbs, he looks for natural bedfellows and works with what's available. He'll pick Russian or French tarragon for a classic béarnaise to accompany beef, or parsley, mint and basil for the dollop of salsa verde that goes with a piece

of lamb. Delicate bronze fennel works with an orange and Grand Marnier salmon tartare, served with a fennel salad, citrus labne and beetroot. Puddings get the same treatment, Nick infusing a pannacotta with lemon verbena – one of his favourite herbs – to give a fresh, citrussy tang.

Back in the glasshouse, a tumbling Victorian building with ivy creeping through cracks, Philip casts an expert eye over trays of tender squash, cosmos, runner beans, tomatoes, courgettes. It's been a slow start to the season, but he plans to prick out the young celeriac seedlings later today. This may be a garden that's as pretty as a Georgian picture, but it works very hard too.

Rare-roasted rump of Shorthorn beef, slow-cooked cheek, Smoked Dapple gratin, cavolo nero, sorrel and wild garlic

We are often lucky enough to see the Shorthorn herd grazing happily on the lush parkland around Congham Hall. Good beef is all about being well-bred, well-fed and well-hung – the beef we use is 28 days' maturing. We use smoked garlic for the cheese potato gratin but plain cloves work fine. Start the dish the day before serving. (Serves 4)

Rump steaks

- 5 tbsp local rapeseed oil
- 4 garlic cloves, peeled
- 1 large sprig thyme
- 4 rump steaks

In a food processor, blend the oil, garlic and thyme before straining into a bowl. Place in the steaks, mix around, cover and leave to marinate in the fridge overnight.

Braised cheeks

- 200g beef cheeks, well-trimmed
- 1 large onion, diced
- 2 celery sticks, chopped
- 1 sprig rosemary
- 4 garlic cloves
- 375ml rich red wine
- 1 litre good beef stock

Pre-heat the oven to 160c. Cut the cheeks into large pieces and seal in very hot oil on all sides. Put them into a flame-proof lidded casserole with the other ingredients and bring to a simmer. Cover well and braise in the oven for 2½ hours or until tender.

Carefully remove the meat and strain the liquor through a fine sieve before combining in a snug lidded container, then cool and refrigerate overnight. Reheat gently over a low heat before serving.

Cheese potato gratin

- 300ml double cream
- 6 cloves of smoked garlic, crushed
- 1 tsp English mustard
- 1 sprig thyme
- 500g Maris Piper potatoes, peeled and thinly sliced
- 100g grated Smoked Dapple cheese

Pre-heat the oven to 180c. Line the sides and bottom of a gratin dish with silicone paper. Bring the cream, garlic, mustard and thyme to a gentle simmer and then strain. Carefully build layers of the potatoes, grated cheese, seasoning and the cream mixture. Top with another piece of silicone paper and gently press to ensure the contents are levelled and well-covered with cream. Bake for around 40 minutes or until the potatoes are cooked when pierced with the point of a knife.

Allow to cool, preferably weighted down and then refrigerate overnight. Remove and cut into portions before reheating in a hot oven.

Sorrel crème fraîche

- 100g sorrel
- Pinch of lemon zest
- 50g crème fraîche

In a processor, blend together the sorrel, crème fraîche and lemon zest. Season to taste.

To serve

- A little red wine
- Sprig of fresh rosemary
- 200g cavolo nero or kale, blanched
- Unsalted butter
- 50g wild garlic

First re-heat the gratin portions in a oven and gently warm the cheeks through on a low hob setting.

Season the marinated steaks (at room temperature) and sear in a very hot frying pan. When well-coloured, add a large knob of butter and baste on both sides. When cooked to your taste, remove steaks from the pan. Deglaze the pan with a splash of red wine and add in the liquor from the hot cheeks pan. Stir and season to taste. Transfer back to the cheeks pan with the rosemary sprig.

In a hot frying pan, gently wilt the cavolo nero with a knob of butter and a little boiling water. Add in the wild garlic leaves to soften. Arrange both on hot plates and place on the gratin portions, top with sliced rump steaks and pieces of cheeks, before finishing with the crème fraîche. Spoon around some sauce.

Pan-roasted fillet of local rainbow trout, sweet potato and pickled vegetables

We make this a colourful dish with wilted garden greens and a vivid beetroot and Pernod sauce. (Serves 6)

1 large carrot, peeled
2 baby beetroot, peeled
200ml white wine vinegar
5 white peppercorns
1 orange, peel only
10ml runny honey
4 sweet potatoes
6 rainbow trout fillets
Unsalted butter
Lemon halves

With a potato peeler, cut long strands of carrot and place into a zip-lock bag. Very thinly slice the beetroots and place in another bag. Gently warm the vinegar, white peppercorns, orange peel and honey. Pour half the liquor into each bag and seal well. Leave to pickle for at least 1 hour.

Pre-heat the oven to 180c. Bake the sweet potatoes whole for 1 hour or until well-softened. Split the potatoes and scoop out the flesh, blend to a purée and season to taste.

Place the seasoned fish into a hot oiled heavy frying pan over a medium heat and cook for 2-3 minutes. Add a knob of butter and a squeeze of lemon juice. Carefully turn the fish over, remove from the hob and continue to cook with the residual heat for a further 1-2 minutes, before serving with the potato and pickled vegetables.

Maple and pecan brownie

This is made extra special, if served warmed alongside rich caramel ice cream and chocolate rocks for crunch. (Serves 6+)

100g plain flour
10g good cocoa
4g baking powder
90g butter
3 eggs
140g caster sugar
1 pinch of salt
60g maple syrup
300g dark chocolate, melted
80g chopped pecans

Pre-heat the oven to 180c. Line a 20cm square tin. Sieve together the flour, cocoa and baking powder. Melt the butter. Whisk up the eggs and sugar until light and fluffy. Mix the dry ingredients with the butter, egg mixture, salt and maple syrup until smooth. Beat in the melted chocolate and fold in the nuts. Pour into the tin before baking for 35 minutes or until just firm and cooked through in the centre.

Roasted pumpkin, wild mushroom and Jerusalem artichoke risotto

A flexible recipe for whatever seasonal garden produce you have to hand. As the rice starts to soften, you need to sauté the raw mushrooms and heat up the other vegetables. (Serves 6)

50g dried wild mushrooms
1 litre good chicken or vegetable stock
1 large white onion, peeled and chopped
2 garlic cloves, peeled and chopped
50ml dry white wine
Rapeseed oil
400g arborio rice
Good pinch fresh thyme, chopped
300g raw mushrooms, cleaned and sliced
300g pumpkin, peeled, diced and roasted
50g roasted Jerusalem artichokes, sliced
30g unsalted butter
Handful of Parmesan cheese shavings
25g rocket leaves
White truffle oil, to drizzle

Rehydrate the dried mushrooms in the simmering stock until softened. Strain off the mushrooms and reserve. Sieve the stock to remove grit and keep hot.

In a processor, blend the onion, garlic and white wine. In a hot deep frying pan over a medium heat, sweat the onion purée with a dash of rapeseed oil until cooked but not browned, add the rice and keep stirring. When it starts to dry out, add the thyme, followed by a ladleful of simmering stock, stirring until the liquid is absorbed over a low-medium heat, repeating ladle-by-ladle, stirring until absorbed before the next. Cook until the rice is just al dente.

Meanwhile start sautéing the raw mushrooms in hot rapeseed oil until cooked. Separately warm up the pumpkin, rehydrated mushrooms and artichokes in any remaining stock. When the rice is cooked, strain off the vegetables and mushrooms before folding into the risotto with the butter and most of the Parmesan. To serve, spoon out the risotto and garnish with rocket, a drizzle of truffle oil and the remaining cheese.

FAVOURITE TIME OF YEAR AS A CHEF?

Autumn/winter. I love squash, mushrooms, hearty, wholesome flavours, log fires, making a cosy daube using shin of beef.

A 'TAKE 5' RECIPE?

Lemon posset is my 'go-to' dessert. Bring 600ml double cream and 200g sugar to the boil, remove from the heat and add 75ml lemon juice and the zest of three lemons. Divide between six bowls and leave to cool, easy! I usually serve it with shortbread and any good ice cream.

QUICK SNACK OR MIDNIGHT FEAST?

Millionaire's shortbread! I have a sweet tooth so I'll quite often buy a packet and eat them on my way home. If not, one of our home-made brownies does the trick.

SIGNATURE DISHES

Starters

Asparagus velouté, ransoms, girolles

Roasted pumpkin & cep risotto, wild rocket, pecorino

Duck & chicken liver parfait, garden chutney, toasted brioche

Mains

Pan-roasted bass, little gem lettuce, caper & saffron velouté

Slow-cooked rump of lamb, pommes Anna, fresh pea & watercress purée, black kale, wild mushrooms

Spiced aubergine, artichoke & roast tomato linguine, red pesto, baby leaves

Puddings

Iced nougat parfait, hazelnut croquant

Glazed lemon tart, raspberry sorbet

White chocolate pannacotta, strawberry consommé, garden mint

DREAM DINNER?

I'd be eating BBQ sardines with Thomas Keller and Ferran Adrià at Thomas' place in the Napa Valley with a glass or two of rosé.

NICK ON HIS...

IF NOT A CHEF, WHAT WOULD YOU HAVE BEEN?

Front man for Scone Direction, the first-ever chef boy band – look out for us, we're going to be big! I don't have music on in the kitchen apart from me singing whatever it was I heard on the radio on the way into work (though it's only ever two lines!). I think only my mum likes my singing...

BEST DISHES EVER EATEN?

Zander at La Bouitte, the three Michelin star restaurant in St Martin in the Trois Vallées ski area. Zander is a freshwater fish, sometimes called pike-perch, and even though it must be 10 years ago that I ate this dish, I can still remember the taste – the delicate flesh, perfectly cooked, the crispy skin.

LUCKY DAY OFF?

I'd go kite-flying on Hemsby beach with my boys. We have four – Ollie (16) Zachary (12) Seth (9) and Noah (6).

RECENT FOODIE DISCOVERIES?

Clean cooking. A friend of mine is a personal trainer and we talk a lot about diet and nutrition. I like the idea of trying to eat foods you can either shoot, fish or pick – the paleo diet essentially. We have a spa at Congham, so while we are not a health retreat lots of guests ask for healthy options and I often use sweet potatoes instead of potatoes, pearl barley or quinoa instead of white rice. I now make my porridge with coconut or almond milk and sweeten it with honey and add berries and bananas.

Lucky for some

Congham Hall is hotel number thirteen for Nicholas Dickinson – and it is the one he has most enjoyed creating.

He determinedly avoids the title 'country house hotel' for Congham Hall, the Georgian mansion near King's Lynn, starved of investment, that he and a team of investors bought in March 2012. "It suggests something stiff and starchy, a bit Downton Abbey. We are not like that." He should know: his career in provincial hotels started at Chewton Glen and took him to the helm of Le Manoir aux Quat' Saisons, Martinhal (the luxury resort in Portugal that he created) and the Luxury Family Hotels portfolio that he set up – then sold – with business partner Nigel Chapman.

"Congham is a country house which happens to have a spa, a restaurant and bedrooms, while providing a range of other leisure pursuits – tennis, falconry, walks. It's a place people visit to relax." Nicholas likes that it is only thirty minutes from the sea, but not competing for space on the well-trodden Norfolk coastal scene. "That's a selling point! It makes it more peaceful." Guests often visit

Sandringham, Houghton, Oxburgh and Holkham Hall, and wander down to the Three Horsehoes, the local village pub owned and refurbished by Congham Hall.

Nicholas and his team have transformed the 26-bedroom hotel into a serene, comfortable place. Limestone floors, warm rugs, shades of violet, sage green, gentle raspberry-red are order of the day, tall sash windows let light flood in. Outside, Bryone Dillow is the creative mind behind stunning displays of tulips, swathes of purple and red-orange blooms in pots or beds underplanted with wallflowers.

The team is not sitting back, though; a second five-year plan includes more accommodation – maybe some self-catering – and extended spa facilities. There will be a second restaurant too, though for now guests eat in an elegant dining room, tables laid with white cloths, gleaming crockery and a pot of fragrant herbs for decoration. Looking out onto beautifully-kept lawns and flowerbeds, it is a seductive place – a perfect setting for Nick Claxton-Webb's tasty menu.

Congham Hall
Grimston, King's Lynn PE32 1AH
W: www.conghamhallhotel.co.uk
T: 01485 600250
E: info@conghamhallhotel.co.uk
f /ConghamHallHotel
🐦 @Congham_Hall
📷 /Congham_hall

Accolades: AA Two Rosettes; AA Three Red Stars for accommodation; Winner, 'Best Hotel – East of England' 2015, *Best Loved Hotels*; Winner, 'Best Adult Leisure Break' 2015 & Winner, 'Best Independent Hotel' 2013, *EDP* Visit Norfolk Tourism Awards; 'Editor's Choice – Family Friendly Hotel', *Good Hotel Guide* 2016; *Sawday's*

Covers: 80 inside; 20 on the terrace

Cost: carte average £45; Sun L £27.50; full afternoon tea £20 (£30 with a glass of fizz); wine from £22

Open: all year, L 12-2; D 6.30-9.30

Details: private dining; 26 bedrooms in main house and garden rooms; indoor swimming pool; outdoor hot tub; spa treatments; croquet lawn; putting; tennis court and equipment to hire; trampoline; herb garden; walks from the hotel; falconry; wedding licence; meeting rooms; wheelchair accessible; dogs welcome in certain rooms (£10/night); parking

Simple pleasures and seafood heaven

Gemma Arnold enjoys the
rich pickings offered by the coastal
larder around this thriving foodie
enterprise in Thornham

"**G**lad it's a calm sea and good weather, not sure I'd be doing this if it was blowing a gale, Simon," Gemma Arnold admitted as we climbed aboard the rickety wooden skiff that had chugged up the marsh to find us. Setting off inches above the gentle swell, it was just the necessary means to get to Simon Letzer's fine sea-going twin catamaran lying midstream off Brancaster Staithe harbour, a very reassuring sight to us landlubbers not relishing our current vessel.

There was a calm assured face and wry smile on well-known fisherman Simon's face. "Don't worry, this old girl has served me well for decades, she was the first boat I started on, believe or not, she's just about holding up," Simon explained as he tapped a loose plank in the bottom with his trusted welly, "but now after three years of hard work fitting her out, we've ended up with the *Speedwell*". He gestured high above as he moored us in the shadow of his very large and welcome modern boat. After clambering aboard rather inelegantly, we were much happier reflecting nostalgically with him from this more reassuring, sturdy vantage point.

Well-acquainted as they are, Simon and Gemma's long-standing chef-local producer relationship – like all fruitful interactions at kitchen doors up and down the coast around here – is clearly one of trust and confidence, not least out on the ocean waves, Simon having Gemma jumping up and over from one boat to another.

But this is nothing for Simon, as coping with high tides, the rigours of the raw elements, the sheer hard graft and the rollercoaster of not knowing what fruits of the sea Mother Nature will give up each day is the norm for a fisherman like him. "We give so little thought to the struggle it takes to get this fabulous fresh seafood on our plates, don't we?" mused Gemma aloud. "This hardship is a world away from my warm kitchen and the happy diners tucking into lobster back at Thornham Deli. I'm glad I'm a chef!"

Gemma and Simon were soon in deep conversation about the state of the harvest off their beloved coast. "We head out about 15-25 miles typically to our secret hotspots, often far out into The Wash. The best places change with the months and the temperatures and of course, crabs and lobsters favour different types of seabed, so we have to juggle where we drop our pots. The lines are down there about 20 to 40 metres deep depending on where we anchor up." Inside the first baited pots were not just a few delicious brown pie-crusted crabs but exactly what we had come for, a couple of big blue-shelled lobsters, their prehistoric appearance and menacing claws befitting a creature from the deep as they emerged from the clean green waters.

For a local lass like Gemma, who has grown up close to the coast all her life and cooked more lobsters than she would care to remember, these scary crustaceans posed little fear. Soon removing them two at a time, she and Simon set to, slipping rubber bands on their vicious pincers, as he explained, "they are territorial and will readily attack each other".

Soon it was time to head to shore, dropped back in the shallows from Simon's old faithful, right by the Letzer family's Crab Hut on the harbourside car park at Brancaster Staithe. This was a delicious shop window on what they had been hauling aboard the *Speedwell*, locals and visitors tucking into the freshest local seafood, clearly as wise to the source as Gemma was, who was now heading back to Thornham with a crate of lobsters in hand.

Cleaned up in her whites in the Deli's kitchen and wielding a very sharp cleaver, Gemma swiftly despatched the semi-frozen lobsters. "Chilling first anaesthetises them, so it's more humane," she explained as she halved the lobsters, before pan-frying them over a scorching heat with some aromatic oriental-spiced butter. "I love local ingredients, especially seafood, and lobster is the ultimate treat for me. We are blessed with some of the best farmers and fisherman on our doorstep." She explained her ethos: "good food depends on great relationships with my suppliers, getting the best produce at an affordable price for the diners and it not costing the earth in every sense." Back to the lobster, now bright red after cooking, its caramelised sweet meat delicately balanced with a simple stir-fry from the wok and more of that delicious fragrant herb butter on top as Gemma plated it up "Fresh, simple, local, ethical, landed two miles down the coast; it's doing something different but not messing around with a great ingredient, just a hint of Thai flavour to interest the palate, exactly how I like my lobster. Well, that's if it's not lobster salad, a ravioli filling, a thermidor gratin, or just with chips and garlic mayo. Can you have too much of a good thing?!" Every day is clearly an indulgence for Gemma and her diners at Thornham Deli.

57

Thai-buttered Brancaster lobster, Asian noodle stir-fry, sweet chilli dipping sauce

A taste of the Orient brightens up any gloomy day and gives a sense of the tropics when eating outside on a sunny day. This works well with local salads and greens for more Norfolk flavour alongside the Asian spices. (Serves 4)

Sweet chilli dipping sauce
125ml white wine vinegar
125g sugar
1 tsp tomato purée
2 red chillies, finely chopped
1 stick lemongrass, finely chopped
3 garlic cloves, finely chopped
4 lime leaves, finely chopped
Knob of ginger root, peeled and grated
1 lime, juice & zest
Splash of nam pla fish sauce
Small handful of coriander leaves

Bring vinegar, sugar and purée to a simmer, add in the remaining ingredients, except the coriander, boil gently and reduce to a rich consistency. It will thicken as it cools. Finish with the shredded coriander.

Thai butter
250g butter
3 red chillies, finely diced
Knob of ginger root, peeled and grated
2 sticks of lemon grass, finely diced
4 garlic cloves, finely chopped
Splash of nam pla fish sauce
1 lime, juice & zest
Splash of the home-made chilli sauce
Small handful of coriander leaves

Blend all the ingredients (except the coriander) together and finish by pulsing in the coriander at the end. Decant onto a double sheet of clingfilm, wrap up whilst shaping into a cylinder and refrigerate until required.

Asian noodle stir fry
1 packet egg noodles, rice or wheat
Groundnut oil
1 red onion, finely sliced
2 pak choi, shredded
1 large carrot, grated
1 bunch spring onions, shredded
1 courgette, finely sliced
1 red pepper, finely sliced
1 packet of baby corn, sliced lengthways on a diagonal
Sesame oil
Splash of nam pla fish sauce
I lime, halved

Start this when the lobsters are baking. Cook the noodles in boiling water, drain and glaze with a little oil. Meanwhile, heat up a wok over a very hot heat, carefully add a splash of oil and fry the vegetables together for a few minutes until al dente, at the end adding a slice of the Thai butter and the hot noodles. Heat through and finish with a drizzle of sesame oil, fish sauce and lime juice to taste.

To serve
4 whole cooked lobsters
Sesame oil
Thai butter

Pre heat oven to 180c. Cut the lobsters in half, remove the stomach parts and crack but do not break the claws. Add a small amount of sesame oil and a slice of Thai butter to a hot wide ovenproof frying pan, place the lobster meat-side down in the pan and cook over a high heat for 5 minutes, turn over, add a slice of Thai butter onto each and bake in the oven for a further 15 minutes. Start the noodle stir-fry. Carefully remove the lobsters to plates, drizzle with cooking juices, before serving the noodles and sweet chilli dipping sauce alongside.

60

Binham Blue crème brûlée

Not a dessert but a delicious light starter or savoury, made with Mrs Temple's superb cheeses. We serve this with Parmesan & olive biscotti and a balsamic pecan salad. (Serves 6)

400ml double cream
180g grated blue cheese
5 egg yolks
30g caster sugar
Granulated sugar

Pre-heat the oven to 110c. Simmer the cream and slowly beat in the blue cheese. Blend the yolks and caster sugar in a food processor and slowly mix into the cream mixture. Pour into ovenproof ramekins placed in a bain-marie halfway up the sides before baking for 15-20 minutes until set. Remove and cool.

To serve, sprinkle the tops with granulated sugar before caramelising with a cook's blowtorch.

Pork tenderloin ballotine with sage and shallots

This eats well as a hearty main course with simple fondant potato, apple purée, crispy sage and a cider jus. (Serves 4)

2 pork tenderloins
2 shallots, finely diced
Unsalted butter
Rapeseed oil
6 sage leaves, finely shredded
150g sausagemeat

Slice the tenderloins lengthways, place individually between clingfilm sheets and flatten until thin with a wooden mallet or rolling pin.

Soften the shallots in a frying pan with a little butter and oil over a medium heat. Remove to cool. Add the sage and sausagement, season to taste, mix together and chill. Once cold, make sausagemeat cylinders for the centre of two tenderloin pieces, top with the other two, tuck in and wrap the outside around into neat parcels. Tie securely but gently and steam for 45-60 minutes until very hot, cooked through to the centre.

Sharrington strawberry trifle

We make a simple vanilla sponge and whipped sweetened chantilly cream for our trifles with our home-made anglaise custard and jellied strawberry consommé. (Serves 2)

Strawberry consommé jelly
1 punnet of strawberries, de-stalked and sliced
25g icing sugar
Half a gelatine leaf
Handful of strawberries, diced

Place the strawberries and the sugar into a bowl, cover with clingfilm and put somewhere warm for an hour. Soften gelatine in cold water for 15 minutes. Strain off the fruit and keep the liquor. Warm the juices and whisk in the gelatine. Pour into four wine glasses with the diced strawberries. Chill to set.

Custard
2 egg yolks
30g sugar
1 vanilla bean, pod split and seeds scraped
100ml milk, simmering
20ml sweet sherry

Whisk up the egg yolks, sugar and vanilla until the ribbon stage, pour in the milk while stirring. Strain into a clean saucepan. Return to a low heat and stir until thickened. Finally whisk in the sherry before cooling and refrigerating.

To serve
Good sponge cake
Sweetened chantilly cream

Top the jelly glasses with sponge cubes, chantilly cream and the custard.

COOK'S CHEATS OR CHEF'S TIPS?

When separating an egg, if some yolk mixes with the white, swirl an empty eggshell in the white and it will collect the unwanted yolk.

FAVOURITE TIME OF YEAR FOR FOOD?

Summer of course for the local seafood, all those lobsters and crabs.

FAVOURITE BIT OF KITCHEN EQUIPMENT?

My Rational combi oven – allows me to control my kitchen environment, I would say, calmly... the rest of the team might disagree!

FAVOURITE LOCAL PLACES?

The White Horse at Brancaster, just paradise sitting on the terrace overlooking the marshes on a summer's evening.

RECENT FOODIE DISCOVERIES?

A macaroon tray, finally they come out all baked, crisp and even.

'TAKE FIVE' RECIPE?

Norfolk asparagus, olive oil, Parmesan cheese, parma ham and a poached egg.

MUSIC TO COOK TO?

In The Deli kitchen, we have *Kisstory*, the online music stream blaring out to keep us going.

QUICK SNACK?

Crisps – plain and simple!

GEMMA ON HER...

SIGNATURE DISHES

Starters

Asparagus, parmesan and poached egg

Chicken satay salad

Smoked haddock kedgeree scotch egg, coronation sauce

Mains

Marinated duck breast, vegetable spring roll and oyster sauce

Beer-battered fish & chips with mushy peas

Baked cod, roast cherry tomatoes, pesto mash, ratatouille and balsamic glaze

Puddings

Lemon curd cheesecake, Sharrington raspberries

Deli summer pudding with brioche, berries and sloe gin

Sticky toffee pudding, pecan caramel and vanilla ice-cream

FOOD HEROES

Rick Stein. Oh, and honey bees, no bees, no food, simple.

DREAM DINNER?

A perfect Thai banquet out there on the beach as the sun sets, just the two of us, Baxter the dog can stay at home.

BEST DISHES EVER EATEN?

Pierre Koffman's squid Bolognese – the kitchen tour was awesome too.

FOODIE NOSTALGIA?

Phil Milner's Fairground Assiette dessert, so evocative of the annual King's Lynn Mart, almost smelt the dodgems as you tucked in!

WHERE ARE YOU HAPPIEST?

Asleep, love my bed, so I need the alarm clock set to 5.30am every morning!

62

One for all, all for one

Café-restaurant, food hall and lifestyle store, Thornham Deli is far more than a simple delicatessen. This rather delicious and chic expression of both north Norfolk character and London style has been cleverly designed to be many things. It wears several hats with equal pride, a lovely stop-off for great coffee and home-baked cakes, a bolthole for a light brunch or leisurely lunch, a bulging larder of artisan ingredients and local produce, and a stylish retailer of homewares and foodie accoutrements to tempt the most reluctant shopper.

Jeanne Whittome (a very familiar face in these parts after two decades at the well-known Hoste Arms in Burnham Market) and her co-owner Janie Thompson are passionate about The Deli, their aim being "to seek out beautiful, sustainable products and provide memorable experiences for all who visit. This includes of course what we do with the Café-Restaurant, it's about being both a destination and a neighbourhood hub for our village community. We all share and relish this special part of the North Norfolk coast, it's about making something enduring."

With a background as one of Norfolk's leading hoteliers, it is no surprise to hear that upstairs are two very special suites providing luxury bed and breakfast. Named No33 Thornham, it follows on in the style of its namesake, the original No33 in Hunstanton. Jeanne describes it as a "chic, stylish, yet relaxing boutique bed and breakfast and self-catering accommodation where guests can really feel at home."

Recent additions to the Deli business are the two converted cottages opposite, finished with all the No33 comforts. If more reasons for lingering over Gemma's simple, seasonal, local cooking were needed, a few nights of luxury are a great excuse.

Thornham Deli has been an eating place in the village for a number of years, first as a café and then as a restaurant but it has been the arrival of Jeanne and Janie that has seen it flourish.

Thornham Deli
High Street, Thornham PE36 6LX
W: www.thornhamdeli.co.uk
T: 01485 512194
 /thornhamdeli
 @Thornham_deli

Cost: breakfast average £7.95; main course average £10.95; craft beer £3.95; wine by glass £4.50 or available by the bottle from store (corkage £4.50)

Open: every day 8-5. Breakfast served all day; occasional culinary themed evenings

Details: restaurant; coffee bar; outside seating; picnic hampers; home-made meals to go; private parties; outside catering; boutique B&B accommodation; play area; parking

Back to black

Rock 'n' roll fun and flamboyance is teamed at Strattons
with unshakeable environmental credentials,
a commitment to local producers, and particular devotion
to Scotts Field Large Black pork

t's hard to believe that the Large Black breeding sows, snuffling, in the sandy Breckland soil near Oxburgh Hall, are rarer than Siberian tigers; they seem so familiar, so ordinary, such an essential part of the landscape.

Rob Simond of Scotts Field Pork owns a third of the 300 or so registered sows left in the UK, caring for his precious free range herd and their offspring on the dry, light land – it's ideal for keeping pigs – which is typical of this part of Norfolk. This is where the sows, pregnant for the statutory three months, three weeks and three days, have their litters (usually around nine offspring), where the piglets suckle, are weaned at six weeks and live for six months or so happily nourished on a bespoke cereal feed.

Rob's careful system means he has a year-round supply of pork that he sells to retail and restaurant customers in East Anglia and further afield. "Large Blacks are a slow-growing breed, very maternal, milk well and have a nice temperament," he says, clearly fond of his giant, lop-eared, animals. "And the meat they produce is succulent and tastes fantastic."

It's their slow-growing tendencies that have led to their scarcity, however. "The Large Black used to be the most common pig in Britain but they couldn't be brought-on fast enough after the Second World War when farmers needed to produce food very quickly. That's how

intensive farming started of course," Rob adds, a tad ruefully. He is clinging on to the belief that gradually, the British public is embracing the better taste and ethical credentials of carefully, slowly-reared meat.

His Scotts Field Pork brand is sold directly to local butchers' shops. "With the brand, butchers and consumers know the food is safe, that it's been reared with care and that the animals have had a happy life. I take the pigs to slaughter – it's just me and a part-time helper on the farm – and the meat is butchered at Impson's in Swaffham. It's totally traceable."

Unsurprisingly the Scotts Field Pork ethos chimes with Vanessa and Les Scott. The owners of Strattons Hotel in Swaffham have been pioneers of the local food movement, champions of careful, local sourcing and environmentalism from the word go, winning widespread recognition and industry awards over the years. Vanessa, everyone knows her as Ness, is a patron of the renowned Norfolk Food & Drink Festival, is a die-hard champion of Breckland producers in particular, to the point of setting up in 2011 the Brecks Food Festival, an event now established on the county's food and drink scene.

"I love buying from local producers and farmers like Rob who care how their animals live," she says. A self-taught chef, she oversees the kitchen at Strattons, working with head chef Jules Hetherton, who has been in post since 2013, sous chef Daniel Freear and Maggie Cooper who heads up the kitchen at the adjacent café-delicatessen, CoCoes.

Ness and Jules invariably put Rob's pork on the Strattons menu as belly. "We still get the odd customer complaining because a piece of belly pork is 'too fatty'," Ness says, eyes rolling, "but an understanding of ingredients is happening – slowly! – and pork belly is a dish I don't think we could take off now." The meat is confited to tenderness for 12 hours in a very low oven, the skin crisped up at the end; it's often served with hasselback potatoes, broccoli and cauliflower cheese, roasted carrots and apple sauce. She takes the same slow-cook approach with lamb shoulder or beef brisket, putting new potatoes, horseradish dumplings and tarragon mayonnaise alongside the meat. Trotters – another 'unloved' part of the pig – are used for a popular ham hock terrine, while other cuts are used in sausages made by Impson's, or into home-made sausage rolls and dumplings. "It's important to support dying breeds; that's why we buy from our local butcher," she laughs.

Jules brings out a stunning plate of pâtisserie as we talk. White chocolate and lemon meringue spheres are topped with chantilly cream and filled with a light sponge and lemon syrup; a hazelnut dacquoise has mini layers of meringue with almond and hazelnut buttercream filling; and a blueberry and banana mini loaf is moist and fruity. The cakes are this month's afternoon tea line-up and all made by Jules, a talented pastry chef. She also bakes for CoCoes, adding to the delicacies created by the café's own chef and fellow baking talent, Maggie. Conventional bakes are popular of course, but there is plenty on offer for diabetics, vegans, customers with coeliac disease or allergies. "Maybe that's why CoCoes is so busy," says Ness. "Maggie does a lovely fruit and nut bar that's become known as a 'yogi bar' by a local yoga teacher and her class, now regular visitors." In fact, the café is soon to move to a new, larger location closer to the hotel where it will be capable of seating forty customers inside and out.

The ethos at Strattons is a simple, rooted, one: to source locally, organically if possible, and to prepare a fresh, seasonally-changing menu. Ness brings produce from her own nearby vegetable garden whenever possible – yellow and purple carrots, herbs, Jerusalem artichokes, eggs laid by her hens – and scours the immediate area for the likes of asparagus, blueberries, foraged mushrooms and locally-shot game. She goes to William Gribbon at Heygate Farms, Swaffham, for flour and Norfolk Peer potatoes and buys trout to smoke on site from Westacre. It is as deeply rooted in its location as a place could ever hope to be.

67

Honey-roast ham hock terrine with apricots and black pudding

This is a great staple to have in your fridge, it keeps for a long time being cured meat and is an excellent standby for a light lunch or dinner party starter, whatever the season. We like to serve this with the sweet crunch of a pecan nut and apple salad and a sharp mustard dressing but it also eats well with anything fruity such as pears, tangy pickles or relishes and bitter, peppery leaves. (Serves 6+)

3 or 4 ham hocks (smoked or green)
200g carrot, peeled and chopped
1 large onion, peeled and chopped
1 large bouquet garni with plenty of thyme
6 cloves
1 tbsp black peppercorns, crushed
1 bottle dry chardonnay eg white Burgundy
100g clear honey
150g black pudding, we use Fruit Pig Co.
150g dried apricots

Preparing the hocks
Cover the ham hocks with cold water and leave to soak overnight to remove excess salt. The next day, discard the soaking liquid and refill the pan with fresh water. Bring the ham hocks slowly just up to a simmer in a very large lidded saucepan, cook very gently for 30 minutes, skimming the surface as much as possible, then add the carrots, onions, bouquet garni, cloves and peppercorns. Simmer for 2 hours, add the wine and continue to cook for another hour, until very soft (testing if the bones come away easily). Remove the hocks from the liquid and leave to cool. Sieve the stock and boil strongly in a saucepan to reduce by half. Leave to cool.

Roasting the ham
Pre-heat the oven to 200c. Place the hocks on a roasting tin and pour over the honey. Bake for 20-30 minutes, basting regularly after 15 minutes until the hocks have lightly-caramelised, then remove to a board. Pour some of the stock reduction into the tin and boil over a high heat, scraping to deglaze while simmering. Strain tin contents through a sieve back into the remaining stock.

Once cool, using your clean hands and forks, flake the meat, removing any fat and sinew as you go. Crumble the black pudding and cut the apricots into halves. Combine the meat with the apricots, pudding and seasoning to taste (easy on the salt) and use to fill a 1kg mould, lined with double clingfilm. Press down well and pour over the reduction to near the top. Chill in the fridge overnight until set, topping up every 15 minutes for the first hour with the reduction.

Pumpkin and cheese gnocchi

A great store cupboard supper, for the cooler months, these gnocchi make a delicious vegetarian treat and work well with most pasta sauces. Here they are served in a creamy roast garlic and white wine sauce, topped with crispy sage, butternut & Alpine cheese breadcrumbs, alongside wilted spinach and local asparagus. (Serves 4)

1kg peeled pumpkin, roasted and puréed
100g plain flour
90g Mrs Temple's Wells Alpine cheese, grated

In a food processor, mix the pumpkin and flour slowly until it becomes a thick stable 'roll-able' consistency. Now add the cheese and seasoning to suit.

Test that a piece of the gnocchi dough does not disintegrate in boiling water. Add more flour if it does. If not, roll into finger-thick cylinders, refrigerate and cut into inch pieces before dredging in more flour.

Cook the gnocchi by dropping into boiling salted water in small batches for 3-5 minutes, removing when they rise to the surface, before draining on a clean tea towel. If storing them for any length of time before finishing or serving, gently toss with a little rapeseed oil and keep warm.

Miniature dacquoise sponges

We are well-known at Strattons for our rather grand afternoon tea and the home-baked cakes at CoCoes Café-Deli. These French fancies, usually sandwiched with a toasted hazelnut buttercream, are a favourite choice of our pâtissière, Jules. (Makes 12)

25g plain flour
125g ground almonds
125g icing sugar
4 egg whites
50g caster sugar
A few drops of vanilla extract
Chosen cream filling

Pre-heat the oven to 170c. Line two baking sheets with parchment and draw 24 x 5cm circles onto each, 1cm apart. Turn the parchment over. Mix together the dry ingredients.

Whisk the egg whites and caster sugar together in a food mixer until a meringue forms. Remove and fold in a third of the dry ingredients at a time and finish by mixing in the vanilla.

Pipe the mixture into spiral discs on top of each of the parchment circles. Bake for 20 minutes until golden brown. Remove to cool. Once cold, sandwich the underneaths of the discs together into pairs, with your chosen filling. Refrigerate for 20 minutes to firm up.

CoCoes beetroot falafel

A great summer lunch dish, full of Middle Eastern sunshine, we stuff these into split and warmed pitta breads, with zingy slaw, wild rocket, red onion and shredded mint or coriander. (Serves 6)

1 onion, finely chopped
1tbsp light rapeseed oil
500g raw beetroot, peeled and grated
2 tsp cumin seeds, roughly crushed
1½ tsp ground ginger
300ml soya milk
115g chickpea flour
450g cooked chickpeas
Rapeseed oil for frying

Fry the onion in the oil, stirring over a medium heat for a few minutes until just beginning to soften. Add the beetroot and fry for 5 more minutes, stirring occasionally until tender. Add the cumin and ginger and cook for another minute.

Bring the soya milk to a simmer in a saucepan, stir in the chickpea flour and cook over a medium heat, beating thoroughly until very thick and smooth. Season generously and

fold in the beetroot mixture and the whole chickpeas thoroughly. Allow to cool and divide into 24 portions of about one dessertspoonful onto a chopping board. Chill for 15 minutes.

Heat up your deep fryer with rapeseed oil to 170c and deep fry the falafel in batches until browned and crisp. Lift out to drain and keep warm between kitchen paper.

LUCKY DAY OFF?

I'd walk a bit of the Peddars' Way with Les and our three dogs, Dolly the long-haired dachshund, Goose the lurcher and Tilly the whippet. We'd always aim for a pub. It's not on the Peddars' Way, but we do like the King's Head at Shouldham.

CHEF'S TIPS?

Conserve, compost, and recycle, and eat locally, sustainably and seasonally! And plant a garden – if you've grown something yourself, you'll always value it more.

WHAT AMBITIONS DO YOU STILL HAVE?

To write another book! I co-authored *Norfolk's Own Cookbook: Everything Stops for Tea* in 2015, a collection of recipes from Norfolk chefs and producers. I'm very proud that it raised £100,000 for Marie Curie Cancer Care.

MUSIC TO COOK TO?

Nina Simone, David Bowie, Vivaldi... I like the Buddha Bar mixes too for the diverse world music vibe.

CHILDHOOD AMBITIONS?

I always wanted to be a show jumper! I ride a bit now, but not as much as I'd like.

INSPIRING NORFOLK VIEW?

The woods and heathland along the so-called 'yellow brick road' between Beachamwell and Swaffham. It's pure Brecks!

FAVOURITE TIME OF YEAR FOR FOOD?

Spring. It heralds things to come and I find it exciting every year: the arrival of the first wild garlic, early rhubarb, asparagus, lambs in the fields and my hens starting to lay in earnest.

NESS ON HER...

ULTIMATE DINING DESTINATION?

Les and I won a food trip to San Sebastian in 1997 and had a wonderful meal, one of the best we've ever had, at the three Michelin star restaurant, Arzak. Eating at Chez Panisse, Alice Waters' restaurant in Berkeley, California, was another amazing experience.

SIGNATURE DISHES

Starters

Baked celeriac with smoked Pinney's trout, caper salsa, horseradish cream

Cumin hummus, chargrilled cauliflower, hazelnut brittle, coriander & curry oil, crispy shallots

Pressed Cornerway's tomato cake, peppered Ellingham goats' cheese, shallot, parsley & lemon dressing

Mains

Beef & lamb meatballs, broad beans, lemon, garlic mashed potatoes, mashed young carrots, pistachio, cardamom

Mrs Temple's mozzarella pie with peas, herbs, green salad, roasted Maris Peer potatoes

Salmon & fennel en papillote, wilted summer greens, Venetian potatoes

Puddings

Jam doughnuts, sea salt praline ice cream, peanut brittle

Chocolate and caramel tart, strawberry & black pepper ice cream

Raspberry sorbet, crème fraîche, shortbread

WHERE ARE YOU HAPPIEST?

At home and in my kitchen or garden surrounded by friends and family. We live in a 200-year old cottage, very much a work in progress, on the edge of Swaffham, and have a flock of hens and geese, and an orchard with old fruit trees. It's a very special place.

Brecks and mortar

Vanessa and Les Scott have always loved a project. "We jacked in art school to buy a cottage to renovate, and went on buying ever bigger properties to do up, until we found Strattons in 1990."

The couple have created a quirky boutique hotel-restaurant-café-deli with two self-catering apartments in the heart of the Breckland town of Swaffham. "I wanted somewhere for people to come and eat my food – I've always loved catering for lots of people – and Les wanted a big renovation project, so this was perfect." The business now involves the couple's daughter, Hannah, and her husband Dominic, who bring their organisational, marketing and financial skills.

Strattons is nationally recognised for its firm environmental principles. "It wasn't something we really thought about," Ness says. "Turning off lights and heating when not needed, and saving water for plants or to wash the car, or keeping hens for eggs and meat, were second nature to us and it seemed natural to apply our domestic values to a commercial operation."

Everything that goes out of the back door is weighed, the Scotts harvesting 250,000 litres of water a year, and recycling more than 90% of waste. "As a result, on average we spend 70% less than the industry norm on energy bills," she says.

The couple's artistic talents come to the fore throughout the hotel. It is a rich treasure trove of eclectic art finds, funky colour schemes and bold paintings, sculpture and textiles. A pink bust lights up above one table, a magnificent chandelier hangs in the reception area, the bedrooms are sumptuous and exotic: one has a magnificent mural, another a four-poster bed, and all have luxurious fabrics and finishing touches. For those who prefer a more conventional style, there are sleek modern rooms in stables, outbuildings and the town's old print workshops.

Strattons Hotel
Ash Close, Swaffham PE37 7NH
W: www.strattonshotel.com
T: 01760 723845
E: enquiries@strattonshotel.com
 /Strattons-Hotel-Restaurant-Café-Deli

 @strattonshotel @eatatstrattons
 /strattonshotel

Accolades: *Waitrose Good Food Guide* 2; Winner, 'Top Green Hotel' Good Hotel Guide 2014; GoldStar, 'Green Tourism Awards' 2014; Finalist, Customer Service award, *Eastern Daily Press* 'Business Awards' 2014; Finalist, Front of House Manager, Hotel Cateys 2014; Green award, Cateys 2008; *Sawday's*; *Mr & Mrs Smith*

Covers: 40 inside; 12 outside; 40 in CoCoes inside and out

Cost: carte average £32; wine from £20.50

Open: Mon-Sun D from 6.30; Sun L 12-2.30; lunch by arrangement on other days; afternoon tea 12-5, booking essential. CoCoes café Mon-Sat, closed Sun

Details: afternoon tea; children's portions available, or children's menu to pre-order; parties up to 40; 14 rooms in the main building and adjacent converted barns including two self-catering apartments; family-friendly rooms; free wifi; dogs welcome in certain rooms (£10/day per dog)

Jewel in the King's Lynn crown

With a wealth of ingredients at his fingertips,
Richard Golding brings a midas touch to dishes
at his family-run restaurant

The heart of King's Lynn is a gem. Imposing merchants' houses, memories of the town's prosperous maritime trading history, line cobbled streets that lead to the waterfront where the Great Ouse flows widely into the Wash. Among the elegant Georgian architecture, is quirky medieval wonkiness, and – such was the town's 12th century wealth – a church built on the theatrical scale of a cathedral.

In the shadow of St Margaret's Minster, on Saturday Market Place, is Market Bistro, the neighbourhood restaurant owned by Richard and Lucy Golding. Like many of the buildings around it, it is a gem.

"When we took over here in 2009 leaving our country house B&B in Wales behind us, we decided to carry on running the restaurant as a 'lasagne and salad' Italian until we'd developed our own style," says Richard. "As we started to realise what wonderful ingredients we have round here, we understood that the only way to ensure the region's farmers flourish is for people like us to support them." The couple embraced local, ethical and sustainable sourcing wholeheartedly, to the extent of winning a three star award from the Sustainable Restaurant Association. "That's the same rating as Le Manoir [aux Quat' Saisons, Raymond Blanc's famed Oxfordshire restaurant] and we're very proud of it. It obviously costs more to put free range and organic produce on the menu – but I think we are slowly getting the message across that it's worth the extra."

So how do they do it? Moments away from the restaurant is the Goldings' vegetable patch, a place tended with meticulous care by passionate gardener and forager, Tom Turnbull. When not tending the vegetables, Tom will scour the riverbank for coastal greens – sea beet, samphire, sea purslane and sea aster growing in spring abundance on the salty foreshore – and bring basketfuls to Richard.

In the garden, Tom grows specialist produce and herbs for Richard. "I do grow some things to order, but I prefer to tell Richard what's available and for him to work out a menu on that basis." Richard's happy with that. "It means we have a 'when it's gone, it's gone' approach, and a concise menu which we tweak daily and which really does reflect what's in season," he says.

There's an order about Tom's garden. Pots are stacked, propagating trays clearly labelled, rows of fledgling plants set in tidy rows in a polytunnel waiting for the fear of frost to pass before being planted out. The last of the robust cavolo nero still looks perfect, and there's rhubarb in abundance, soon to be joined by beans, peas, heirloom courgettes and Jerusalem artichokes. Strawberries, tomatoes (Tom is growing Red Pear, stripy Tigerella, and Principe Borghese this year) and sweetcorn will all soon have their moment.

Various mints, fennel, oregano, chives, sage, and edible violas fill pots and Tom regularly brings living trays of peppery salad leaves for Richard to pick as needed. "It can be so expensive to buy enough fresh herb – this is really where the garden makes a difference to our business." He crouches down to pick tender viola petals, placing them in a trug – they'll be used to give a colourful finish to a popular dish of home-smoked salmon with crab cannelloni.

Back at the restaurant, Richard gets to work on a dish of white-gilled St George's mushrooms (so-called because they first appear around our patron saint's day, 23 April), picked that morning by Tom.

Garlicky, earthy aromas fill the small kitchen as the fungi are tossed in hot butter then tumbled onto a slice of toasted enriched bread. He pours round a mushroom velouté, a deeply flavoursome combination of ceps, chanterelles, shallots and garlic and places a pair of soft-poached, panéed quails' eggs, golden yolks spilling from the white, on top. A scattering of peppery foraged miner's lettuce (winter purslane) finishes the dish.

"I love that these mushrooms are so seasonal and their flavour is superb. If I don't put them on the toast we might use them with pancetta in a savoury custard."

Spring clearly fits with Richard's rooted style of cooking. "Local asparagus, Cromer crab, sea vegetables from the banks of the Wash, everything fresh, new, not yet maincrop... I love this time of year!" Other delights are available year round of course: Richard smokes his own fish and meat, bakes bread daily, and supports local suppliers such as Mrs Temple for cheese, Burnham Market-based butcher, Lisa Scothern for charcuterie and the Fruit Pig Company for black pudding and pork. "Matt [Cockin, owner of Fruit Pig] does all sorts of different flavours for us, all from fresh blood. Their products are amazing."

Black pudding is an essential element of a deliciously tender pork dish, a popular main course. The pork has been brined for two days, cooked for another two at 65c, and is served with an unashamedly generous layer of syrupy fat, the sweetness balanced by squeaky-fresh watercress and a puck of beetroot. It's a delicious gem of a dish.

77

St George's mushrooms on toast with mushroom aioli

This is a simple and tasty dish, a lovely expression of wild fungi, in this case the delicious summery St George's. The recipe can be adapted to make use of whatever is in season and good eating, so long as you have legally and sustainably gathered them and most importantly, you are certain your harvest is safe to eat. If in doubt, do not eat foraged mushrooms without getting personal advice from a fungi expert about their edibility.

Pictured is the dish as a warm salad with other mushroom garnishes of a rich marmalade, a velouté-style dressing and gel cubes, plus crispy quails' eggs and simple leaves. (Serves 4+)

Mushroom aioli
200g dried bay bolete (or porcini/ceps)
600ml good rapeseed oil
4 egg yolks
1tsp lemon juice
Salt
Sherry vinegar

Blend the dried mushrooms with the oil in a food processor for 8 – 10 minutes until smooth. Transfer the mushroom paste to a saucepan and heat on a low heat to 78c (using a digital thermometer). Remove from the heat and transfer to a heatproof bowl and allow to cool to room temperature. Once cooled, pass the mix through a fine sieve. You can now discard the mushrooms left behind in the sieve, they have done their job.

To make the mayo, measure out 400ml of your mushroom oil. Place the egg yolks and lemon juice in a food processor and blend for a minute until pale in colour. Keeping the machine running, blend in your measured oil a few drops at a time to begin with, this will help to prevent the mixture splitting, and then add it faster in a fine trickle. Once half the oil has been mixed in, you can add the rest as a steady stream and then continue to blend for a further two minutes. Season to taste with ground sea salt and sherry vinegar.

Enriched loaf
1080g bread flour
80g caster sugar
110g unsalted butter
22g salt
11g quick action dried yeast
2 eggs
600ml whole milk (at room temperature)

Combine all the ingredients with a dough paddle or bread hook, mixing until it is elastic and can be stretched sufficiently to be thin enough to see through, without it breaking. Place in a bowl somewhere warm, covered with greased clingfilm, until proved and doubled in size. Pre-heat your oven to 180c. Knock the dough back for a few minutes and then place into your chosen loaf tin, before proving once again until it has doubled in volume and is well-risen. Bake for 30 minutes until golden.

To serve
2 good handfuls of St George's mushrooms or other seasonal safe edible fungi
1 tsp garlic purée
Good rapeseed oil

Take an oiled hot sauté pan, add the mushrooms and garlic purée, turn down the heat to a low-medium setting and sweat until lightly coloured. Season to taste.

Place the mushrooms on slices of the loaf and garnish with the aioli (and other chosen garnishes, if used).

Spiced home-cured salmon

Here pictured with Cromer crab cannelloni, carrot slaw, horseradish and keta caviar, the cured salmon is also delicious on its own. It also makes a great base for smoked salmon if you invest in your own home-smoking kit. It's best to use organic farmed salmon (Serves 6+)

1 side fresh salmon, boneless, around 1.4kg
8g white pepper
6g allspice berries
7g dried bay leaves
4g cloves
5g mace blades
12g pink salt
250g coarse sea salt
100g soft dark brown sugar
200g granulated sugar
50ml spiced rum

Grind all the spices together in a spice grinder and mix well with the other dry ingredients.

Put a third of the salt mix into a non-reactive tub, lay the salmon, skin-side down on top of this. Pour the rum over the flesh and then evenly coat with the remaining salt mix. Be careful to make sure there is more salt on the thickest part of the salmon than the tail end and that all the flesh is covered. Seal tightly and carefully place into the fridge for 2 days. Rinse all the salt from the salmon, pat dry, place on a tray and pop it in the fridge uncovered for another 24 hours to firm up. Carve into thin slices away from the skin.

Slow-roast rare breed pork belly

A perennial favourite here, we serve this with other pork cuts, black pudding, beetroot and potato purée. It just calls for apple sauce and wholegrain mustard. (Serves 4+)

2 cloves garlic, smashed
1 sprig rosemary
2 sprigs thyme
2 star anise
4 allspice berries
3 juniper berries
30g coriander seeds
6 bay leaves
5 whole cloves
200g coarse sea salt
1 litre water
1g pink salt
1-1.5kg pork belly, skinless and boneless

Put all ingredients (except the pink salt and pork belly) in a pan and bring to a simmer while stirring. Remove from the heat, cool for 20 minutes and dissolve in the pink salt. Once cold, strain through a sieve into a non-reactive tub, add the pork belly and refrigerate covered for 24 hours. Soak the meat in cold water for an hour, refresh and repeat. Drain and pat dry. Preheat your oven to 120c. Place the pork in a roasting tin with 100ml of water. Tuck in a sheet of parchment over the meat and cover the tin with foil. Bake for 10 hours or overnight. Remove from the tin into a storage container, press down with a board and heavy weights, cool and chill in the fridge. Cut the pork into portions and thoroughly heat through by baking or pan-frying before serving.

Dark chocolate bavarois

An intense but light chocolate dessert is always a treat and we enjoy this with salted caramel, vanilla macaroon and burnt orange. (Serves 4+)

2 gelatine leaves
90ml full-fat milk
1 vanilla pod, split and seeds scraped
3 egg yolks
50g caster sugar
90ml double cream
250g good dark chocolate
200ml double cream

Soak the gelatine in cold water. Warm the milk, vanilla pod and seeds in a saucepan until steaming (do not boil). In a bowl, beat the egg yolks and sugar until thick, pour in the milk and vanilla, return to the pan and heat stirring until 82c or just coating the back of a spoon. Whisk the drained gelatine into the custard and mix in the 90ml of cream. Melt the chocolate over a bain marie and stir into the custard. Cover the surface with clingfilm and cool. Whip the 200ml of cream to soft peaks. Fold into the custard and decant into a suitable serving dish or ramekins, before cooling and refrigerating.

LUCKY DAY OFF?

No question – I'd spend time with the family. We get precious little time together as it is, so I really do value it. It doesn't matter what we do, it's about being together!

WHAT DRIVES YOU?

The prospect of learning something new. And fear; I have to make money, I am the business, it's as simple and scary as that!

MUSIC TO COOK TO?

The original soundtrack to Joseph and the Amazing Technicolour Dreamcoat, and in particular *Any Dream Will Do*!

ULTIMATE DINING DESTINATION

Faviken in the north of Sweden. It's in the middle of nowhere, a real journey, you have to stay overnight, and there are only 12 tables in the restaurant. It would be incredibly exciting. The chef, Magnus Nilsson, pickles and cures ingredients so that he has a year-round supply, all picked, caught or shot on the land around him.

INSPIRING NORFOLK VIEW?

Looking down the Wash early in the morning. The buildings are absolutely beautiful.

FAVOURITE TIME OF YEAR?

Spring and summer. I love the start of the asparagus season, it's a time when you know all the green veg is coming, peas and beans are on the way. That initial ping of spring is so exciting for a chef.

SIGNATURE DISHES

Starters

Truffle custard, peas, bacon

Woodpigeon, beetroot & spelt risotto

Beetroot, goats' curd, walnut

Mains

Venison fillet, celeriac lasagne, cavolo nero

Pollock fillet, potatoes, sea vegetables, mussels

Chicken breast, thigh roulade, celeriac, truffled mushrooms

Puddings

Brown butter sponge, rhubarb, burnt butter ice cream

Carrot cake, yoghurt, gingerbread

Frozen apple crumble, parfait sandwich, duck egg ice cream

RICHARD ON HIS...

CHEF'S TIP?

Pressure cookers save hours of time. They are incredible things, you can cook so much in them – casseroles, sticky toffee puddings – but they're hardly used now. Just one tip: don't break the handles or pressure valve because when they go they really do explode! I've had that happen and you end up with the kitchen sprayed at high pressure with whatever was inside – in my case a brown liquid – and you can't even go near the thing till the pressure drops. Nightmare.

BEST DISHES EVER EATEN?

At Azurmendi near Bilbao in Spain on 16 October 2015, we had an amazing inside-out truffled egg which was absolutely incredible! I also remember a dish Lucy and I had at Abadia Retuerta Le Domaine in Spain's Duero Valley – roast beetroot, red wine glaze and bone marrow.

FAVOURITE PIECE OF KITCHEN EQUIPMENT?

My knives. I even take them on holiday because I can't bear turning up somewhere and the knives being rubbish. They are the one thing I use every single day. I waited 10 months for my lovely Blok knife, handmade to order in Derbyshire, to arrive – but it was worth it.

CHILDHOOD AMBITIONS?

RAF pilot. I've never flown but it's always what I wanted to do at school, to be a jet fighter pilot. I didn't do well enough at school to even have a chance of getting through the selection process.

In the market for good food

Market Bistro is unrecognisable from the hapless days when it starred, then called Rococo, in Gordon Ramsay's Channel 4 series, *Kitchen Nightmares*. And although Richard and Lucy Golding have turned round the fortunes of this unpretentious neighbourhood bistro, cooking wasn't always in the couple's life plan. "I used to make sweets as a child, but never thought cooking could be a real profession," Richard says.

The couple left stable careers with British Gas to pursue the dream. With a bit of help from Richard's father, they bought a country house B&B with a trout lake and spectacular views in deepest Wales. "It was a massive learning curve – eight bedrooms! – and we were novices. We had a 10-week old baby and our second son was born there. But we loved it."

A regular visitor – Phil Milner, then at the Rose & Crown, Snettisham – tempted the couple from Wales to Norfolk where Richard worked at the pub and then at the Orange Tree with Phil. "But when this place came on the market we thought 'if we don't do it, we'll always think what if...' so we took the plunge."

Richard heads up the Market Bistro kitchen working with sous chef Jess Marlow and commis Brandon Allison. Lucy runs the front of house, juggling restaurant commitments with looking after the couple's three children; the eldest of whom, Isaac, aged 16, helps make puddings at weekends.

"There's a lot of multi-tasking round here," Richard says. "I'm head chef but also general builder, electrician, accountant, book-keeper and chief dog-walker!" The family's pug-terrier cross, Dave, enjoys a daily morning walk with Richard after the school run. "I walk with a friend and we laugh from the moment we say hello. That's also my time to plan the day." It's when he'll ponder bigger ambitions too, such as the one to open a pub, an informal 'sausage and mash' place with traditional ales and delicatessen.

Market Bistro
Saturday Market Place,
King's Lynn PE30 5DQ
W: www.marketbistro.co.uk
T: 01553 771483
E: info@marketbistro.co.uk
[f] /Market-Bistro
[t] @Market_Bistro
[i] /marketbistrokl

Accolades: Waitrose *Good Food Guide* 2; Three Stars, Sustainable Restaurant Association; *Michelin*

Covers: 35

Cost: carte average £30; wine from £17

Open: Weds-Sat L 12-2; Tues-Sat D 6-8.30 (9pm Sat); first Sun of every month L 12-3; closed Mon

Details: children's menu; wheelchair access; tables outside on pavement

Of mists and meat

Salty sea air gives a special coastal flavour to the beef
Ben Handley uses on his Duck Inn menu

THE DUCK INN BEN HANDLEY

Try as you might, you won't get Ben Handley to share his scotch egg recipe. The quails' eggs are lightly cooked, then cocooned in a mix of his butcher's Arthur Howell's sausagemeat and black pudding, before being crumbed and deep-fried, very precisely, to order. Slice through the crisp crust, the dark meat and just-firm egg white, and the golden-orange yolk runs out slowly, just as it ought.

'Original Mr H scotch quails' eggs', served with home-made mustard and tarragon mayonnaise, are one of The Duck Inn's most popular bar bites. "They're up there with our lager and lime whitebait, and the scampi," says Ben. "Dishes like this are a bit retro but there's pure pleasure in eating them."

We are in Ben's compact kitchen, a hard-working space from which a six-strong brigade is capable of turning out deeply pleasurable meals – a staggering 300 of them on the busiest days in fact. With the oven under his six-burner stove more useful as storage, and the solid-top constantly rammed with pans, he couldn't manage without a sous-vide water bath. "Everything depends on the quality of the initial ingredient, but you can't get a more reliable end result," he says. With a busy weekend in the offing, Ben anticipates six whole sirloins going into the water bath – and emerging perfectly cooked.

Those perfect sirloins will be from Wells-next-the-Sea butcher Arthur Howell. "I reckon Arthur's is the best beef I've ever cooked with," says Ben, deftly cutting the dark red fillet from a whole sirloin and removing the ribs with a few accurate strokes of a razor-sharp knife. The boned joint is marbled with creamy-coloured fat; even uncooked it looks good.

Little is wasted. Prime steak cuts might be offered (classically) with onions, mushrooms and skinny fries, or as a fillet and short rib dish, richly-flavoured and supremely tender. Cooked for four gentle hours in a 52c water bath before being finished in the pan with butter, garlic and herbs, it sits on a creamy risotto, packed with chanterelles, king oysters, pieds de mouton and wood blewits. Just-wilted spring

onions give the dish a vivid snap of green, there's shine from a glossy beer-honey reduction, and a scattering of onion powder texture.

Brancaster mussels cooked classically with cream, shallots and white wine; fish and chips; and a leek and Norfolk Dapple gratin are among the popular non-carnivorous options, but this is a place to enjoy meat. Ben and his chefs glam up pub staples such as liver, bacon and mash by using ox liver with cubes of Arthur's pancetta, confit onions, and smoked mash, or turn a simple dish of locally-shot pigeon into something special: two breasts, perfectly deep-pink in the middle, are set on a celeriac purée, pieces of butter-fried black pudding scattered round and a jus noisette made with pigeon-bone stock, poured over. "That dish sums us up," Ben says, pushing it across the pass, satisfied. "It's local, flavoursome and uses virtually all the bird."

Arthur Howell is a fifth-generation local butcher (est. 1889, no less), his red-liveried vans familiar in these parts, his trademark scarlet shop coat recognised by many. Like his father before him, he buys cattle from the 25,000-acre Holkham Estate, slaughtering at his on-site abattoir, one of the last remaining small operations in Norfolk. He swings out a carcass from the coldstore. "Look at the fat, just the right amount, and the colour of that meat. That's a well-reared animal." He pats it, and satisfied, shuts it back into the store. "I'm in and out of the estate all the time," he adds. "I see how well-looked after the cattle are, that they have a good life. The North Sea mists give the grass a flavour that you really can taste in the meat too."

Arthur swaps his scarlet shop coat for tweed to meet the cattle, a breeding herd of three-year old Belted Galloways. In calf (but surprisingly agile when farmer John Smith shakes a sack of feed), the cows are turned out for as long as the weather permits to graze the lush, picturesque Holkham Estate pasture on Chalk Hill Farm. They are docile, inquisitive, dark-eyed and tousle-haired, the white 'belt' of their name running round their pregnant bellies.

Ben is no stranger to the hospitality industry, his parents having owned the Lifeboat Inn at Thornham, and having worked as head chef at The White Horse, Brancaster Staithe, and, most formatively, at the Melbourne restaurant, Ruby Ruby. "It was there that I first experienced the notion of cooking with passion, something that has never left me." But enriching though travelling was, he is now happiest here, visiting John Smith's herd, catching up with Arthur, staying connected with the area immediately around his pub. He looks back on John's field. "Coming out to see this reinforces exactly what we're trying to do at The Duck. I love it."

Seared Belted Galloway beef fillet, honey and ale-braised short rib, wild mushroom risotto

For this indulgent main course, we braise the ribs in our landlord's Elgood's Cambridge Ale but you can choose a rich malty Norfolk beer. I suggest you sauté the fillet steak from raw for ease, though we poach ours first. Start the fillet and mushrooms to coincide with beginning the risotto. (Serves 4)

Braised beef
1 large piece of beef short rib on the bone
Rapeseed oil
1 onion, roughly chopped
2 sticks celery, roughly chopped
3 carrots, roughly chopped
1 pint rich malty beer
2 bay leaves
1 sprig fresh thyme
1 tbsp Norfolk honey
2 pints beef stock, warmed
(good bouillon or home-made)

Pre-heat the oven to 150c. Seal the seasoned short rib in a very hot, oiled, frying pan until well-browned. In a very hot, oiled, casserole dish (ovenproof and lidded), caramelise the roughly-chopped vegetables before adding the rib. Deglaze the frying pan with the beer, add the bay leaves, thyme, honey and stock, then bring to a simmer. Cover and bake for 5 hours or until tender. Cool for an hour and then carefully remove from the stock. Sieve the liquor into a saucepan and boil to reduce to a glossy sauce. Cut the rib into 4 boneless pieces and cover with the sauce in a snug container. Keep warm or refrigerate.

Fillet
800g thick end of beef fillet, trimmed
Local rapeseed oil
100g unsalted butter, melted
1 tsp thyme leaves

Before starting the risotto, pre-heat your oven to 200c and put in a snug roasting tin. Brown the beef in a very hot oiled pan on all sides. Transfer to the tin and brush all over with the butter, season, and scatter with thyme leaves. Bake for approx. 20 minutes for rare (check it after 12 minutes and every few thereafter, until cooked to your liking). Remove to rest somewhere warm.

Risotto
100g unsalted butter
1 onion, finely chopped
2 sticks celery, finely chopped
2 cloves garlic, crushed
1 tsp thyme leaves
200g arborio rice
1 litre vegetable stock, simmering
200g wild mushrooms, cleaned and in bite-size pieces
Good rapeseed or extra virgin olive oil
70g Parmesan cheese, grated
White truffle oil
1 lemon, halved

In a deep, heavy, frying pan, melt 50g of the butter over a low-medium heat and sweat the onion, celery, garlic and thyme leaves together. Once they are softened but not browned, turn up to medium heat, add in the rice and stir until it is translucent and 'crackles'. Season lightly at this stage. Gradually add the stock a ladleful at a time, stirring and allowing the rice to absorb the liquid before the next. Meanwhile cook the beef fillet and rest somewhere warm. In a separate pan, fry the mushrooms in a little oil until just tender and keep warm. Depending on how you like the 'bite' of your risotto will influence the cooking time of the rice, we suggest around 15 minutes for al dente grains, avoiding it becoming 'porridgy'. When the risotto is nearly cooked, add the drained mushrooms, the remaining butter, Parmesan and a good drizzle of truffle oil. Stir in seasoning and lemon juice to taste.

To serve
Spoon out the risotto, place the hot braised beef to one side, carved fillet on the other and sauce generously.

THE DUCK INN BEN HANDLEY

Seared local woodpigeon breasts, celeriac purée and Norfolk black pudding

I love that an unwelcome pest for farmers which feasts on their fields, ends up unsurprisingly tasting so good. Here at The Duck Inn, we brine our pigeon for extra tenderness and flavour and then serve this recipe with crispy black pudding bonbons, pickled celeriac and a rich gamey jus. (Serves 4)

1 head celeriac, peeled and roughly chopped
150g unsalted butter
1 bay leaf
1 tsp celery salt
100ml boiling water
White pepper
400ml double cream
Lemon juice to taste
4 woodpigeon breasts
Rapeseed oil
150g good black pudding in 1cm dice (we use The Fruit Pig Co.'s excellent one)
More butter for frying

Cook celeriac in a large, hot, saucepan over a low-medium heat in the melted butter with the bay and celery salt, for a few minutes. Carefully pour in the water with a little salt and white pepper. Cover and gently simmer for 1 hour until soft. Add in the cream and bring to a boil. Remove and carefully blend to a purée and then sieve. Season and add lemon juice to taste, mix again before covering and keeping warm.

In a heavy sauté pan over a medium-high heat, heat up a few tablespoons of oil until hot. Place the seasoned pigeon breasts skin-side down and fry for about 2 minutes until nicely-browned, turn them over and lower the heat. Add a good knob of butter and when foaming, spoon the butter over the breasts carefully while cooking for 2 more minutes. Remove from the pan and rest somewhere warm for 5-10 minutes.

Put the pan back on a high heat and sauté the black pudding until lightly crisp and cooked through. To serve, spoon the purée onto plates. Slice the pigeon breasts in half lengthways and arrange on top. Scatter with the black pudding.

Crispy crab beignets

These beignets go down very well as an appetiser on a summer's evening, with nothing more than a spritz of fresh lemon juice and a sprinkle of sea salt. Our slightly more involved dish teams the beignets with a rich bisque soup made from the crab legs and shells, a coleslaw-style celeriac and crab remoulade, and shavings of fennel. (Serves 4)

75ml milk
40g unsalted butter
60g plain flour
1 large egg, beaten and passed through a sieve
60g flaked cooked white crabmeat
Zest of 1 lemon
1 tbsp chopped fresh dill

Start the beignet mix by heating the milk and butter to a rolling boil. Remove from the heat and beat in the plain flour with a wooden spoon. Allow to cool for five minutes then transfer into an electric food mixer with a dough hook. Start mixing the dough on a medium speed while slowly adding the egg. Mix in the crab, lemon zest and dill until well-incorporated, plus seasoning to taste. Transfer mix to a tub and refrigerate.

Using two dessert spoons, shape the mix into nice quenelles straight onto silicone baking parchment and chill again for five minutes. When ready to cook, pre-heat a deep fat fryer to 180c with oil as appropriate. Carefully place the crab quenelles into the fryer. Cook for 4-5 minutes or until golden brown and floating on the surface. Drain on absorbent kitchen paper, season and serve.

Pear tarte tatin

We like to put a little of our own twist on dishes at The Duck. With this classic French pâtisserie recipe, a crisp pastry galette of caramel and pear, it's a black pepper honeycomb for contrast and rich vanilla ice cream for indulgence. Individual tart cases look good. (Serves 4)

2 firm local pears (we use Williams)
1 litre stock syrup (equal volumes of sugar and water gently dissolved)
1 sprig rosemary
1 star anise
100ml dry white wine
150g golden caster sugar
150g unsalted butter, cold, in small cubes
Good puff pastry, ready rolled to fit
1 free range egg
Splash of milk

In a large pan, bring the stock syrup to the boil and carefully add in the rosemary, star anise and white wine. Bring back to the simmer, turn off and allow to infuse while you peel the pears. Lower the peeled pears into the syrup and cover the pan. Bring back to a simmer and cook gently over a low heat until the pears are cooked and soft. Remove the pears and leave to cool. Halve and carefully scoop out the core. Keep warm.

Pre-heat the oven to 180c. Warm your metal tart cases in the oven on a baking sheet. Heat the sugar gently without stirring over a low-medium heat in a wide frying pan. As it starts to caramelise and become syrupy, scatter in the butter and start to move the pan very carefully, swirling in the butter to mix. Use a wooden spatula to bring it together. Stir in a pinch of freshly-ground black pepper and then remove the caramel from the heat. Add a shallow layer to the bottom of each tin. Lay in a pear half. Cut a square of pastry to completely cover the top, trim the edge to a small overlap and tuck inside the tin carefully. Repeat for all four.

Whisk the egg and a little milk for an eggwash glaze and brush over the pastry. Bake until golden-brown, remove and allow to cool for 20 minutes. Invert a warm plate over each tart, and holding both parts tightly with a tea towel, very carefully turn over. Tease out the tarts from the cases and serve.

RECENT FOODIE DISCOVERIES?

I've been really inspired by the Korean-American chef, David Chang, who is the genius behind Momofuku. It's not particularly new but he has an amazing way of putting vegetables into puddings, an avocado frosting on a cake or a beetroot, lime and chocolate ganache. I do a brandy snap of chocolate and pistachio, finished with celeriac ganache – I don't mention the celeriac on the menu as it might put people off but it gives a really interesting flavour profile.

WHAT GETS YOU UP IN THE MORNING?

My iPhone!

BEST DISHES EVER EATEN?

Easy – for my birthday, Sarah took me to Dinings in Marylebone and I had the most amazing aubergine glazed with sweet miso. It didn't look anything but it was creamy, like custard or crème brûlée in texture, absolutely exceptional. If you go, get a seat at the bar!

WELL-THUMBED COOKBOOKS?

Under Pressure: Cooking Sous Vide by Thomas Keller at the French Laundry in California. I am a big fan! He is to America what the Roux brothers and Raymond Blanc are to the UK. I am also a big fan of David Everitt-Matthias at the Champignon Sauvage in Cheltenham – the way he presents his food, his knowledge, use of ingredients. I love his book, *Essence*. My former sous chef, Yusuf Lovett is now a chef there which is a great feather in our cap and a very good reason to go to Cheltenham some time soon!

SIGNATURE DISHES

Starters

Monkfish cheeks, Brancaster mussels, vanilla, chorizo, leeks, caviar

The original 'Mr H' scotch quail's egg, mustard & tarragon mayonnaise

Scallops, squid ink fettuccine, dashi, dill, keta

Mains

Poach-roast breast of guineafowl, confit leg & leek lasagne, wild mushrooms, jus noisette

Rare-roast haunch of Holkham Estate venison, ragù, saffron pappardelle, carrots

Butter-poached fillet of skrei cod, brown shrimp, dashi & caper velouté, potato beignet, sea purslane

Puddings

Sticky toffee apple pudding, textures of apple, toffee sauce

Vanilla cheesecake, berry compôte, cherry crumble crunch

Brandy snap, white chocolate parfait, pistachio, ganache

WHAT AMBITIONS DO YOU STILL HAVE?

I just want to make sure we keep improving what we have at The Duck. The first year was difficult but now we've built our confidence and every day I feel happy to be here. I hope the staff feel the same, I think they do. I don't want to expand at The Duck but who knows, down the line we might look at another venture as well. We'll see...

BEN ON HIS...

LUCKY DAY OFF?

A walk round Wells or along the beautiful north Norfolk beaches with my wife Sarah, the kids and Boomer our dog. Maybe a bite to eat at the White Horse or get nearer home and meet friends for an early supper in the garden at the Rose & Crown.

INSPIRING NORFOLK VIEW?

There's a spot at the back of Thornham called Beacon Hill. From the top you can see all the way over to Lincolnshire and as far as Holkham in the other direction. The sunsets are amazing!

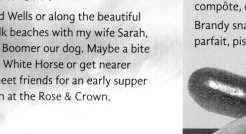

FAVOURITE TIME OF YEAR FOR FOOD?

Spring. I love it when the first spring ingredients start to come in: lamb, elderflower, lovely courgettes, the first local crab, wild garlic, morels.

A big-hearted business

Ben and Sarah Handley took over the tenancy of The Duck Inn on Valentine's Day 2013 and it's been a happy pairing. Elgood's (the Cambridgeshire brewer that owns the pub) have given the couple free rein to develop the property into a recognised dining destination.

Getting the look and feel right inside has been Sarah's domain. With help from friend Abbie Conway, the Handleys have gone for exposed flint and brick, muted shades of Farrow & Ball, bare wood floors, plenty of candles and vibrant accents of colour in soft furnishings. A corner sofa creates a relaxed bar area while the dining space with its scrubbed pine tables, each decorated with a delicate orchid, stretches through several characterful rooms. Local artists display their work throughout.

The couple, who live in nearby Snettisham with their children, Noah, Ruby and Nancy, are happy here. "My brother Sam is now on board as general manager, and Sarah is hugely influential," says Ben. "It really is a family business. Customers know that at least one of us will always be in the pub which I think is vital in a community like this."

He talks about his kitchen team as if they were family too. "Shaun [Ireson] was my KP at The White Horse; he really is my right hand man and a fount of knowledge when it come to plants and herbs. Richard, my junior sous, is fantastic, a great character and then there's Josh my chef de partie and Becky, my apprentice who runs the larder single-handed. Bee in pastry is a very enthusiastic baker and has a great sense of humour. All of them have an incredible work rate. I think the secret is that there is real harmony between our kitchen and front-of-house staff."

Two sprawling double en suite bedrooms have all the mod cons you'd expect. They're the perfect reason to linger over dinner and not worry too much about that extra glass of wine.

The Duck Inn
Burnham Road, Stanhoe,
King's Lynn PE31 8QD
W: www.duckinn.co.uk
T: 01485 518330
E: info@duckinn.co.uk

f /duck.in
🐦 @duck_inn
📷 /theduckinn_

Accolades: Waitrose *Good Food Guide* 3; Runner-up, 'Best Sunday Lunch', *Observer Food Monthly* Awards 2014 & 2015; *Michelin*; *Sawday's*

Covers: 60 inside; 80 outside

Cost: carte average £30 (bar bites from £3.50); wine from £16.50; pint from £3.60

Open: L Mon-Sat 12-2.30, D 6.30-9; Sun 12-8; closed Christmas Day

Details: daily-changing specials; sandwich menu; children's menu; bar drinks; two bedrooms; garden room; wheelchair access; parking

Fair-feathered game

Wood pigeon is a tasty mainstay of Mitch's creative Dabbling Duck menu

THE DABBLING DUCK JASON MITCHELL

Tess doesn't mind the weather tipping down from above, or the mud under-paw: the opportunity to be out with her master, picking up pigeons is too good for any Labrador to miss, even an eight-year-old who's had a lifetime of such activity. She picks her way through the undergrowth in a patch of woodland on the edge of Park Farm, coming to heel when called by the gamekeeper, her master Rob Peacock, who manages the shoot on Dominic Symington's arable farm in Wormegay near King's Lynn.

Dominic is roost-shooting pigeons, targeting the birds as they come into the trees this chill, grey late afternoon. It's as much about pest control, Dominic explains, as it is about sport – pigeons can do untold damage to the freshly-drilled crops that are his livelihood – and he will go out regularly in early spring when the birds flock in search of food to control their all too healthy population.

As much as pigeons are a curse for farmers, they are a joy for chefs. Jason Mitchell (everyone knows him as Mitch) at The Dabbling Duck, the exquisite pub on the green in Great Massingham, is no exception: he happily takes all the game on offer and given that Dominic co-owns the inn, it all makes beautiful, local sense.

"Dominic or Rob will often drop in with pheasant or partridge in season, or pigeon which they can shoot year round," says Mitch, whose career has seen him at The Gin Trap, Ringstead and The White Horse, Brancaster Staithe, when Ben Handley, now at The Duck Inn, Stanhoe, headed up the kitchen there. "I certainly never go short; we have game on our menu ninety per cent of the time I reckon!"

Fortunately, pigeon is an ingredient Mitch loves cooking. The dark, flavoursome meat is versatile, sitting as comfortably with fresh Asian spices as it does with the more conventional earthiness of juniper and crushed peppercorns. It can happily be slowly pot-roasted whole, maybe with port and dried fruit, but works just as well pan-fried quickly to retain the juices. Mitch does just this when we visit, setting the seared breasts on quenelles of creamy Binham Blue risotto. Wild mushrooms nod to autumn, as do pieces of pickled pear and dots of pear ketchup, perfectly fruity partners to the tang of the blue cheese and richness of the meat.

"We've done some really popular dishes with pigeon," he says, working and talking at the same time, bending close to the plate as he garnishes. Other chefs weave in and out, checking on bubbling stockpots, putting a crimped edge on a pie. "We do a smoked pigeon pastrami on a charcuterie board with Park Farm rabbit rillettes and rapeseed rye cracker – that's a popular starter – and a pigeon and partridge sausage roll with horseradish and beetroot coleslaw is good."

Game appears in other forms too. Pheasant breast and sausage works well with black pudding and salt-baked beetroot, and rabbit (another

critter Dominic prefers to see on a plate rather than on his fields) is often turned into savoury rillettes and served with Jersey black butter, a traditional Channel Island spiced apple preserve. Duck liver pâté is ever-popular, Mitch serving his with orange and pink peppercorn marmalade, malt loaf, chestnuts and cranberries.

"Game is a big feature of the menu," says Mitch who has recently been heading up the kitchen team of five full-time chefs (including an apprentice from the College of West Anglia in King's Lynn), having cooked at The Dabbling Duck for a loyal eight years. "And it's absolutely a favourite of mine. I love slow-cooked autumn, winter food, those deep flavours."

Elsewhere, Mitch takes the best that Norfolk's coastline offers: Brancaster mussels pop up in various guises, as do King's Lynn brown shrimps, perhaps potted as a starter or as an accompaniment to whole baked plaice. It goes without saying that fish and chips (beer-battered hake cooked in dripping) is always on, as is the handsome beef burger with Mitch's rich bacon jam and on-trend charcoal mayonnaise. Up the elegance scale is chargrilled salmon served with smooth mussel bisque and finished with sea purslane plus a scattering of aromatic dill pollen to bring out the flavour of the salmon. Combinations are classically paired, the "theatrical part"

as Mitch calls it, coming from using interesting textures and cooking styles, for example dried and ground scallop roe as a crust and seasoning for a favourite scallop dish.

The food fits with managing partner Mark Dobby's aims for The Dabbling Duck. "We are about providing good English pub food with a twist," Mark says. "Nothing pretentious, and all good value." He caters for a variety of diners: locals pop in, perhaps for a pint and sandwich, there are walkers following the Peddars' Way wanting something hearty, while the warmer months bring tourists visiting the nearby stately homes of Sandringham, Houghton and Oxburgh.

Mark is in tune with Dominic's vision too. "When we set about buying the pub, all we wanted was a boozer really, somewhere to go for a pint and a pie," says Dominic. "I couldn't bear the thought of not having one in the village, especially as there used to be seven!" He's proud of what's been achieved, glad with the direction Mark has taken the pub, but pleased that best-selling burgers and steaks are prepared conventionally. "I always say chef can express himself with what I call the 'funnies', the woodcock or the roast crown of partridge, but mustn't mess with what is most popular with our customers! I think Mitch does exactly that."

Pan-fried Park Farm woodpigeon with Binham Blue risotto and pear ketchup

With farmer owners at The Dabbling Duck, I am lucky to get wonderful game from their land which is always popular on our menus. In the picture, we have garnished the dish with candied walnuts and pickled mushrooms and a syrupy reduced game jus from the pigeon bones to drizzle around the risotto, but a rich reduction of any meat stock with red wine and balsamic works almost as well. (Serves 4)

Pear ketchup
**2 Williams pears
2 tbsp light brown sugar
2 tbsp lemon juice**

Peel, core and roughly chop the pears. Simmer in a lidded saucepan with the sugar and lemon juice until very soft. Season, then cool until warm before blending to a smooth puréed texture. Refrigerate or keep warm until required.

Poached pear
**100ml water
100g sugar
Juice of 1 lemon
1 pear**

Dissolve the sugar in the water in a heavy saucepan over a low heat and bring to a good simmer. Meanwhile peel and cut the pear lengthways into thin slices. Remove the syrup from the heat and stir in the lemon juice. Place the pear into a bowl and pour over the hot syrup. Set aside till needed.

Risotto
**1 long shallot, finely diced
1 tbsp olive oil
1 small garlic clove
1 bay leaf
1 thyme sprig
1 tsp unsalted butter**
**200g risotto rice
50ml dry white wine
450+ml good chicken or vegetable stock, simmering
Spare reduction from the game jus to make more stock if necessary
20g Binham Blue cheese, in small pieces**

In a wide heavy saucepan, soften the shallot in a splash of oil over a low-medium heat without browning.

Add in the garlic, bay leaf and thyme and then fry for I minute. Stir in the butter to melt, followed by the rice. Fry the rice mixture until it starts to dry and crackle. Pour in the wine and allow to absorb while stirring.

The pigeon will need to be started at this point while continuing with the risotto. For the next 15 minutes, add a small ladleful of hot stock to the rice, stirring while it absorbs, before adding another. Keep adding stock and allow to be absorbed, until the rice is just softened to al dente or to your liking, keeping the thick but spoonable consistency. Heat up more stock if required.

To serve
**Breasts from 2 woodpigeons
1 tsp rapeseed oil**

Using a heavy very hot sauté pan, pan-fry the pigeon breasts in a little hot oil and a knob of butter over a high heat for one minute on each side. Remove to a hot dish, season and allow to rest for a few minutes somewhere warm.

Stir the cheese into the risotto and season to taste. Plate up the dish by spooning risotto into the centre of the plates, carve a pigeon breast and place on top, dotting the pear ketchup and pear slices around the outside before serving.

98

Rabbit rillettes

Start the sultanas a day ahead. The rustic coarse pâté also needs to chill overnight for the flavours to mingle. Great as a starter with granary toast, a sweet fruity relish and pickled vegetables. Perhaps a simple green salad too for a light lunch. (Serves 4)

100g golden sultanas
1 pinch ground mace
Rich malty beer
1 rabbit, oven ready and jointed
400g skinned and diced pork belly
1 stick of celery
1 carrot
1 clove of garlic
3 bay leaves
1 pinch of mace
1 pinch mixed spice
2 sprigs of thyme
100g butter

Warm the sultanas with the mace and sufficient beer to cover. Decant to a container and cover to steep for 24 hours.

Pre-heat the oven to 200c. Place the remaining ingredients in a very deep but snug roasting dish and cover with a sealed double sheet of tin foil. Bake for 30 minutes, then turn down to 130c for the next 2 hours. Check to see if the meat is very soft and falling easily off the bone and remove. If not, continue cooking until it does so.

Transfer to a shallow dish, ensuring the meat is under the liquor. Cover and cool for an hour.

Remove and discard all the bones carefully plus the vegetables and herbs as you go. Flake the meat with two forks and fold in the strained cooking juices. Season to taste and fold in the sultanas. Pack into a container, cover and refrigerate overnight.

Bacon and beer jam

An interesting American condiment, we use this as a delicious unusual garnish on many starters such as pork and game terrines or as a contrast to add flavour and texture to meat main courses (as here with roasted partridge and root vegetables). (Serves lots)

500g good smoky Norfolk back bacon, minced
500g white onion, finely diced
2 garlic cloves, grated
2 sprigs each of rosemary and thyme, tied in muslin
75ml good dark ale, we use local Redwell
1 heaped tbsp maple syrup
1 heaped tbsp dark brown sugar
1 heaped tbsp treacle
70ml white wine vinegar

Starting on a low heat in an oiled, deep frying pan, fry the onions and bacon until dark and caramelised (turning up the heat once the fat is released). Add the remaining ingredients and cook until the liquid has almost simmered away. Season and then leave to cool. Stir again before sealing in a storage container and refrigerate.

Brancaster mussel and Norwich Pils bisque

This makes a lovely rich seafood soup, which you can make into a more substantial broth with the addition of mussel meats, flaked crabmeat or other cooked seafood plus softened sliced vegetables or greens of your choosing. The dish is pictured here with roast salmon, mussels in the shell and wilted greens using the bisque as a sauce. (Serves 4)

Rapeseed oil
500g Brancaster mussels, cleaned
500g crab shells
1 tsp dill seeds
Half bunch of fresh dill
850ml proper lager, we use Redwells Norwich Pils
650ml double cream
650ml water
250g tomato purée

To a very hot deep frying pan, add a small glug of oil and stir-fry the crab shells and mussels for 10 minutes, stirring occasionally. Add the rest of the ingredients. Keep boiling to reduce the liquid in the pan to one third of its volume. Add the cream and reduce again by half. Pass the contents through a colander into a clean saucepan, discarding the solids. Pass the sauce through muslin or a new kitchen cloth into another pan. Taste and adjust seasoning before serving.

WHO IS OR WAS YOUR MENTOR?

Ben Handley from The Duck Inn at Stanhoe, and the late Andy Bruce from The Gin Trap, Ringstead. They have both been a huge influence on my cooking, my style and my passion for food. Your own style is built from the bits you admire, absorb and handpick from others as you learn, from the way they poach an egg at breakfast or prep a squid for lunch, to how they organise orders and clean down at night.

QUICK SNACK OR MIDNIGHT FEAST?

Mature Cheddar cheese on toast with home-made apple chutney – or a bowl of Fruit'n'Fibre!

WELL-THUMBED COOKBOOKS?

David Everitt-Matthias' book, *Essence* (I'm a big fan of David's approach to foraging and how he uses the ingredients he picks); Jamie Oliver's *30 -Minute Meals*; and Dan Doherty's *Duck & Waffle: Recipes and Stories*.

FAVOURITE TIME OF YEAR FOR FOOD?

Late autumn, winter. It's the earthy aromas, rich flavours, deep colours.

COOK'S CHEAT OR CHEF'S TIP?

Always use a timer and food probe. That way you don't have to leave food cooking for that 'just in case' scenario. It will be perfect every time.

MITCH ON HIS...

DREAM DINNER?

I'd have the guys from Pitt Cue sorting the BBQ, Yotam Ottolenghi on salad and breads accompanied by a small lorry load of ice-cold beers and good wine, with Newton Faulkner playing live on a grassy hilltop in the Peak District. It would be late afternoon in the middle of summer and I'd be with everyone, friends and family, that matters to me.

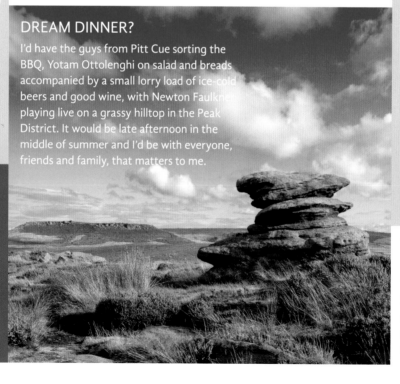

FOODIE NOSTALGIA?

Marsh samphire. It brings back one of my favourite memories of me and my dad stepping out of our door in Brancaster and walking 10 minutes down the road to the marsh, fighting our way through the reeds and jumping over dykes until we reached a good patch of samphire. We would cut what we needed, then head back home to cook it up and smother it in malt vinegar. We'd eat it with a fresh crusty white loaf and tonnes of butter!

SIGNATURE DISHES

Starters

Seared scallops, salted crispy pork belly, pickled pear, artichoke purée, sherry vinegar caramel

Park Farm woodcock rillettes, toasted brioche, hazelnut & brandy smoked butter, burnt leek salad

Salt cod croquettes, wild garlic velouté, dill pickled egg, dill pollen

Mains

Pan-seared fillet of roe deer, potato gratin, wild mushrooms, confit shoulder, stuffed cabbage, café au lait sauce

Suet-crusted maple & tarragon confit duck leg pie, candied carrot, duck reduction

Pan-roasted breast of Park Farm hen pheasant, pheasant sausage, black pudding, salt-baked beetroot, barbecued sprouting broccoli, mash, pheasant sauce

Puddings

Massingham elderflower jelly, lavender & gooseberry pannacotta, elderflower funnel cake

Treacle & pecan tart, brown bread ice cream, maple & Redwell stout syrup

Carrot cake Arctic roll, cream cheese & vanilla ice cream, carrot jam, walnut mousse

WHAT GETS YOU UP IN THE MORNING?

The thought of coming into the kitchen after ordering some never-used-before ingredient for a dish me and the lads came up with over a few beers the night before.

Ducks are a-dabbling, up tails all!*

The Dabbling Duck is packed with charm. Leather sofas, squashy with comfortable age, are the spots to choose, especially when the woodburner and candles are lit. In the three distinct dining areas, scrubbed pine tables, wooden floors and tones of (appropriately) duck-egg blue are the look; back copies of *National Geographic*, novels and countless food and beer guides fill bookshelves, walls are busy with old drawings and photographs. Specials and a sandwich menu are chalked up daily alongside the tally of toads saved by caring residents from being squashed: 157 at last count.

None of the charm will be diluted as managing partner Mark Dobby embarks on the next stage of the pub's development. Three years into his tenure (he left – not easily – his role as general manager of Titchwell Manor to take on the pub in September 2013), he is brimful of ideas: a wood-fired pizza oven in the enclosed garden, an orangery to extend one of the private dining rooms, and four new bedrooms. These will join the nine existing rooms, styled with input from co-owner Dominic Symington who was keen to recognise Great Massingham's World War Two RAF connections with photographs and memorabilia.

As if that weren't enough, Mark is also about to launch an outside catering business. Sally, Mark's wife and chef Mitch will run The Flying Duck, leaving the pub kitchen in the capable hands of latest recruit, Dale Smith, formerly head chef at The Orange Tree, Thornham.

Mark and Sally are shortly to join the partnership of local farmers that invested in The Dabbling Duck to retain it as the village pub rather than let it be turned into housing.

* 'Duck's Ditty' from *The Wind in the Willows* by Kenneth Grahame.

The Dabbling Duck
11 Abbey Road, Great Massingham
PE32 2HN
W: www.thedabblingduck.co.uk
T: 01485 520827
E: info@thedabblingduck.co.uk
🇫 /The-Dabbling-Duck
🐦 @DabblingDuckGM
📷 /dabbling_duck_pub

Accolades: CAMRA 'Norfolk Pub of the Year' 2011; Waitrose *Good Food Guide* 2; *Sawday's*; *Good Pub Guide*

Covers: 75 inside; 40 outside

Cost: carte average £25; wine from £15.95; pint £3.50

Open: all week L 12-2.30; D 6.30-9 Sun-Thurs, (9.30 Fri, Sat). Sun L 12-8

Details: children-friendly menu; high chairs; play area in enclosed beer garden; nine bedrooms, three pet-friendly (£10 per stay); large function room; occasional live music; walks from pub; parking

Spears of the realm

Nik Hare pours heart and soul into
celebrating local asparagus at The Vic,
making the most of its short, tasty season

104

Sometimes, when you watch a chef at work, you just know they're in the right job: there's a fluidity in the way they move, a calmness and serenity in their absolute focus at the pass, an instinctiveness as they create a dish.

"This is where I'm most at home, here at my stove," says Nik Hare, head chef at The Victoria – or just The Vic – an inn with rooms on the Holkham Estate. "Even when it's mad busy, this is where everything makes sense to me, where I feel good karma, in control."

It's just as well. The Vic's six-strong brigade will cope with upwards of 300 guests over a busy summer lunchtime, just as Nik, in post since 2013, is developing his new role as the estate's executive chef. He's now in charge not only of The Vic but also the Courtyard Café and wedding and function menus in the new Lady Elizabeth Wing, both in Holkham Park. "I'm honoured to have been asked," he says, modestly, "and I'm looking forward to the challenge enormously." His existing compact kitchen will be extended to provide space to develop ideas away from the pressure of service; it's not surprising his eyes light up at that prospect.

For now, though, there's a 5kg crate of asparagus to prep. The tight spears, cut that morning, are from Roger Crane at Wood Farm near Aylsham, a supplier Nik has worked with since his days as head chef at the Parson Woodforde inn, Weston Longville. Nik snaps the stems swiftly, puts the trimmed tips to one side before finely chopping most of the remaining stalk to use in a garnish or salad, keeping the tougher ends for stock. "I love working with asparagus, particularly a bit later in the season when the spears are a bit finer, the flavour sweeter," he says. "I like that it's local and still has a very defined season." It might appear as an asparagus and spinach quiche on The Vic's Favourites menu, or a classic starter of grilled spears tossed glossily in butter and served with home-made hollandaise.

Roger grows asparagus on 25 light, sandy acres, a small part of Wood Farm's big arable and potato operation. "It's very labour-intensive – we cut daily when things are in full swing – and matching supply and demand can be frustrating because the crop is so weather-dependent," Roger explains. "But you get to talk directly with your customers which I really value; it's a crop I love to grow." Graded, washed and bunched, Wood Farm asparagus is sold from a caravan in a layby near Hedingham church, direct to local restaurants and hotels, and through London wholesale markets.

"I'm so lucky to have amazing ingredients close by," Nik says, appreciatively. He talks as he curls ribbons of courgette carefully around a handful of sugar snap peas and a crosshatch pile of trimmed asparagus that has been blanched and tossed in butter. He tops the vividly-green plate with a poached and panéd hen's egg. The dish is popular on The Vic's early summer menu, and fits perfectly with the preferences of Lord and Lady Leicester, who live in Holkham Hall and are keen for The Vic's dishes to be simple, tasty, uncomplicated by 'cheffy' technique.

"Sustainability is very important to them too," Nik says, "so I try and use all the vegetable or animal – that's not difficult when I have the best beef and lamb right here!" He indicates the marshes that stretch towards the stunning Holkham National Nature Reserve and the small herd of Belted Galloway cattle that graze it.

Much of the meat on Nik's menu comes from Holkham Estate tenant farms, the family shoot or the park itself where deer roam and are culled as necessary. "Of course I take the prime cuts, but I'll have the offal, and lesser cuts too. We've had sweetbreads with crispy tripe on the menu recently and I cure Galloway silverside to make pastrami."

A black pudding scotch egg is popular, a crispy coating encasing a perfectly-seasoned sausagemeat mix: it's rich, sweet, savoury, matching the vinegary piccalilli deliciously.

"Then we've got sea vegetables from the marshes, oysters from Thornham, lobster from Wells, mussels from Brancaster," Nik continues. The estate's historic six-acre walled garden (it's currently under renovation) provides some fruit and vegetables, but Nik buys most through Barsby Produce. Sweet Chantenay carrots from the King's Lynn supplier are transformed into a sweep of deep orange purée, a base for a rack of tender, Estate-reared lamb and Roger's asparagus.

Nik is settled happily at Holkham, but after qualifying from Norwich City College, his career took him around the world. He recalls happy travels in Australia and New Zealand, and in Singapore, where he worked on a street food noodle bar. "That was a fantastic place! I learnt a deep understanding of Asian flavours and ingredients, particularly crab and lobster which I know put on the menu here whenever I can. My customers enjoy it," he says. "And that's the most important thing, that's what makes me really happy."

Asparagus spears, rack of Holkham lamb, fondant potato, carrot purée and pea shoots

With our acres of rolling pasture on the estate, we are lucky to have such delicious slow-reared parkland lamb, a great partner to sweet tender Norfolk asparagus. The fondant and purée can be made an hour ahead and easily reheated in the oven. (Serves 4)

Fondant potato
2 large potatoes, peeled
Unsalted butter
6 garlic cloves
3 sprigs thyme
250ml dry white wine

Pre-heat the oven to 180c. Slice four 1-inch high rounds from the potatoes. Then take a large cutter and cut a disc from the centre of each.

Add 2 tablespoons of butter to a hot deep ovenproof sauté pan over a high heat with 3 garlic cloves and a sprig of thyme until foaming, add in the potatoes carefully, frying for 3 minutes on each side. Pour in the wine and season the potatoes. Bake for 15-20 minutes until cooked and soft in the centre. Keep warm.

Carrot purée
8 large carrots, trimmed and chopped

Boil the carrots until tender for 10-15 minutes and drain. Add to a processor with a good knob of butter and season to taste before blending smooth. Keep warm.

Vegetables
12 baby carrots, trimmed
8 asparagus spears, trimmed

The vegetables should be cooked separately. Bring the carrots to the boil from cold, then take off the heat; cook the asparagus, cut into 2 or 3 pieces on the diagonal, in boiling water for 2 minutes. Drain both and cool immediately under the cold tap before chilling.

Lamb cutlets
2 x four bone plump racks of local lamb, French-trimmed
Local rapeseed oil
3 garlic cloves
2 sprigs thyme

Pre-heat the oven to 200c. Score the fat lightly on the back of the lamb racks. Rub with oil and season generously. Lay the racks fat-side down into a hot heavy ovenproof frying pan, add in the garlic and thyme. Seal over a high heat until browned, turn over, basting well as it caramelises on the meat side. Bake for 10-12 minutes to keep it pink or longer if preferred.

To serve
150ml good meat stock reduction or lamb jus
Small handful of pea shoots

Remove the racks once cooked to your liking to a warm plate and allow to rest for 5-10 minutes. To the lamb pan, add the stock reduction or jus and simmer for a minute or two. Strain into a clean pan.

Meanwhile put a good knob or two of butter into a hot sauté pan and toss the carrots and asparagus gently over a high heat until fully reheated.

Carve the lamb by slicing through the racks into single or double cutlets. Serve the dish by putting a bed of purée and a fondant potato onto warm plates, lay on the cutlets, garnish around with the vegetables and finish with the sauce and pea shoots.

Black pudding scotch egg

A quirky twist on this hearty classic, with the savoury richness of the pork and added peppery spice. We serve it with leaves and our piquant home-made relish for contrast. (Serves 6+)

10 large hens' eggs
150g black pudding
3 eggs
150g sausagemeat
20g flour
75g breadcrumbs plus more

Simmer the 10 large eggs for 6-7 minutes in salted boiling water before running under the cold tap to cool. Peel carefully.

Dice the black pudding and blend in a food processor with 1 of the 3 eggs into a paste before adding sausagement and mixing until smooth.

Make 10 equal portions of the mix on a clean surface and with wet hands, pick one up along

with a peeled hard-boiled egg. Encase the egg with the meat until smooth and even. Place onto a clean tray and repeat. Chill to set for 30 minutes.

Beat the 2 remaining eggs. Roll each scotch egg in flour in a soup plate, then the same with the beaten egg, and finally repeat with the breadcrumbs (ensuring each layer is evenly coated). Lay onto a tray sprinkled with more crumbs. Repeat with all the eggs and chill again for a few minutes. To serve, heat up your deep fat fryer with oil to 180c and cook for approx. 3 minutes until golden and cooked through.

Asparagus hollandaise, crisp hen's egg

With its short season, crisp field-fresh Norfolk asparagus is very popular here and pairs perfectly with eggs of all varieties. (Serves 4)

50ml white wine vinegar
50ml dry white wine
4 large hens' eggs
4 egg yolks
250g unsalted butter plus more
Polenta
Large bunch of asparagus, trimmed
Paprika for sprinkling

Boil the vinegar and wine together until reduced to a few tablespoons and cool.

Crack the eggs into simmering water and poach for 2 minutes before placing into lots of iced water. Drain and dry on a clean tea towel and set aside. Blanch the asparagus for 3 minutes in boiling water, drain and cool under the cold tap. Whisk the yolks with the vinegar reduction over a bain marie until doubled in volume. Melt 250g butter and ladle a few drops into the egg mixture while you whisk, continue adding more, gradually getting faster until all the butter is absorbed. Season the sauce to taste and keep warm.

Coat the eggs thoroughly but gently in the polenta. Heat a deep fat fryer with oil to 180c then cook the eggs for two minutes until crispy. Drain and lay onto kitchen paper before seasoning.

Quickly reheat the asparagus in a hot frying pan of foaming butter for one minute until hot. Serve with the hollandaise and eggs, sprinkled with paprika.

Apple & vanilla bavarois

A light fruity finish after a heavy main course, we serve it individually with our own honeycomb for texture and caramel flavour. (Serves 4+)

5 gelatine leaves
6 egg yolks
150g sugar
400ml milk
2 vanilla beans, pods split and seeds scraped
200g apple purée
600ml whipping cream

Cover the gelatine with cold water to soften. Whisk the eggs and sugar in a large bowl until light and fluffy. Simmer the milk and vanilla.

Slowly pour half the milk into the egg while mixing. Add in the remainder and stir to thicken slightly. Stir in the drained gelatine and then mix in the apple purée. Whip the cream to soft peaks and fold in. Pour into prepared moulds and chill to set.

MUSIC TO COOK TO?

Hip hop for motivation in the morning, maybe some 80s and 90s hits on a Sunday. It's either the radio or me singing, so the guys usually go for the radio – but it's never on during service.

UNFULFILLED DREAM JOB?

To race motorbikes! I sold my bike last year but I want to buy a Honda CBR1000 Fireblade. I toured New Zealand on a bike, I've been around them since I was a kid.

FAVOURITE LOCAL FOODIE PLACE?

I don't get to eat out that often, but the Hunny Bell in Hunworth is my local and it's a lovely relaxed place.

DREAM DINNER?

I'd be with Michelle, my partner, who is front of house supervisor at The Vic, in a hammock in the Seychelles. We'd be eating crab, lobster, oysters and it would be just the two of us.

NIK ON HIS...

SIGNATURE DISHES

Starters

Sweetbreads, shallot, bacon, crispy tripe

Lobster thermidor, bisque, lemon

Goats' cheese croquettes, tomato, fine beans

Mains

Venison sausages, champ mash, caramelised onion

Pork tenderloin, fondant potato, cabbage, bacon

Salmon en croûte, spinach, brown shrimp beurre blanc

Puddings

Crème brûlée, shortbread

Chocolate torte, berries

Pear & almond frangipane tart

IF NOT A CHEF?

An architect probably. I did a year of the course, then jacked it in to cook. I have a love-hate relationship with the chef world – the hours are so long and it's quite a selfless job, but I love it and get a buzz from it still. To find that people enjoy the end product is worth those 14-hour days! Being an architect would have been so boring in comparison.

ULTIMATE DINING DESTINATION?

It would have to be a café in Dorset or Devon that I stumble across and that does the best scones. I like places that are honest and homegrown and of their region. Also, I've never really explored the West Country, even though I've travelled a lot overseas.

WELL-THUMBED COOKBOOKS?

I don't use them! I've never cooked to a recipe; I work out the science in my head and then use my palate and my eyes. I did love Marco Pierre White's book, *White Heat*, and I have Tom Aikens' books.

FOOD HEROES?

Norfolk is full of them. Billy Ward, my lobster man, is a one-off. He lives in Holkham, fishes from Wells and drops lobsters into my kitchen within half an hour of catching them. Also Paul Graves, my butcher in Briston, and Arthur Howell in Wells who does our lambs and pigs – amazing people!

WHO HAS BEEN YOUR MENTOR?

Peter Rogers. I worked for him on and off for five years when he was head chef at Park Farm Hotel in Norwich. He's the best chef I've ever seen in a kitchen and everything I am now roots back to him. He was calm regardless of what was thrown at him – we'd easily do up to 1100 covers a day if there was a big function – and he'd work six splits a week to pay the mortgage, year in, year out. He could run his kitchen with his eyes shut. I remember thinking 'one day I want to be like you'.

LUCKY DAY OFF?

I'd be on the golf course. I play with my dad once a week, often at Bawburgh; I really value that time with him.

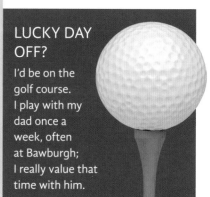

A right royal inn

The Victoria Inn – or The Vic as it's affectionately known – couldn't be more of its time if it tried. Built on the edge of Thomas Coke's Holkham Estate in 1837, the year Queen Victoria acceded to the throne, it was named in honour of the new monarch, and retains echoes of the era to this day. Coke was elevated to the peerage by the young Queen, and the Earls of Leicester live in Holkham Hall to this day.

For all The Vic's high-ceilinged rooms, antique furnishings, open fires, and displays of country pursuits paraphernalia and pictures, it is a bang up-to-date operation. Locals, coastal day-trippers visiting Holkham Hall, and weekenders are accommodated and fed with ease in 21st century comfort.

Stay over and you might find yourself sleeping in Tutsia Clump, Honk's Pit or Mouse Hill, but whichever of the estate's shooting drives your room is named after,

it'll be individually designed in luxurious country style. Even dogs, welcome in several rooms, are cosseted, loaned their own tartan bed and given a bag of treats. Downstairs, the various dining areas and fresh, bright conservatory are comfortable places to enjoy dishes from varying menus throughout the day. Afternoon tea is served in the lounge area where a fire crackles in winter.

The Vic is part of Green Tourism, a programme that champions and encourages businesses to function in an ethical, sustainable way. This chimes readily with Nik Hare's approach to minimising food wastage and his support for local producers. Elsewhere, too, steps are taken to reduce, reuse or recycle whenever possible: a biomass boiler is fuelled sustainably using woodchip from the estate, and myriad conservation projects are undertaken as a way of protecting the environment around this precious part of north Norfolk.

The Victoria Inn
Park Road, Holkham, Wells-next-the-Sea
NR23 1RG
W: www.holkham.co.uk/victoria
T: 01328 711008
E: victoria@holkham.co.uk
f   /VictoriaHolkham
🐦   @VictoriaHolkham
📷   /holkhamestate

Accolade: *Michelin*

Covers: 80 inside; about 150 outside

Cost: carte average £35

Open: all year. Breakfast 8-10; Vic's Favourites menu 11-9; main menu L 12-2.30; D 6.30-9; Bar 11-11 (Sun 12-10.30)

Details: children's menu; 20 bedrooms in The Vic and Ancient House; dogs welcome in certain rooms; small fee for use of a kennel; walks from the pub; parking

114

A sense of Norfolk 'terroir'

Fruitful harvest of estate produce and wild foods anchors The Fritton Arms' chef-director Stephen David

THE FRITTON ARMS STEPHEN DAVID

I n The Fritton Arms' kitchen, there is a quirky juxtaposition of pace and slow food: a pig's snout poking out of a barely-simmering stockpot, fiery embers fading in the wood-fired oven, a roasted haunch of venison resting, fresh bootlace pasta hanging to dry. This genteel 'still life' before service belies the pent-up energy of a busy kitchen attuned to necessary haste, practised discipline maintained until the last dishes are served. Come high days, holidays and every weekend, the cosy dining rooms and suntrap terrace of this destination country inn-hotel may buzz, lunch and dinner but the proceedings are well-versed: tables relaid, beer pumps primed, wines chilled, bedrooms swiftly turned around, all readied as if by clockwork.

Back at the stove after an impromptu tour, Somerleyton Estate chef-director Stephen David sets about jointing a pair of young harvest rabbits, fresh from the game larder. "Transforming what is an abundant pest, well-fed on our crops, and best of all, free, into something as tasty and elegant as a home-made ravioli is a joy, paired with delicious seasonal vegetables and herbs, often foraged or home-grown, always local. Today it's asparagus spears and the last of the wild St George's mushrooms" he enthuses. "We confit the saddles in goose fat before shredding into rillettes with parsley and shallots for the filling. The tender, more delicate loins we use elsewhere, perhaps seared pink in a primavera salad of peas, broad beans and mint."

Stephen's contentment as a chef at heart is clear, despite the demands of his much wider role. The Fritton Arms is just one of

several businesses he oversees on the family estate's holdings straddling the Norfolk/Suffolk border, his kitchen teams also looking after The Duke's Head pub-restaurant, the Hall's grand function venues and Private Somerleyton, catering for outside events. The welcome challenge of this huge hospitality operation was given to Stephen and his wife Rebecca, when head-hunted at the turn of 2016 by Lord and Lady Somerleyton into newly-created director roles for the estate.

To understand more about the source of his game meats, Stephen accompanied Somerleyton gamekeeper and stalker, Matt Roe on essential summer crop management, sustainably reducing the masses of gluttonous pigeons and hungry rabbits. Keeping both restaurants plentifully-supplied with furred and feathered game and venison of all sorts, a keen eye and a love of the countryside are key requirements of Matt's job, "I could never see myself sat down in an office," he says. "Dad got me into shooting and gundogs when I was seven, and I started gamekeeping at 16."

NORFOLK TABLE

The visceral realities of this necessary pest management unfolding in front of him, courtesy of the keeper's trusty rifle, brought home how fortunate Stephen was to have such earthy, well-sourced produce close to hand.

Wild foods are just part of the myriad home-grown ingredients at his fingertips, agricultural and horticultural enterprises providing much more. While the farmland is mainly in-hand arable for grain or let out to tenants, Somerleyton's rare breed parkland herds like Norfolk Horn sheep and Welsh Black cattle ensure fine estate-reared lamb and beef bolster the restaurants' menus whenever possible. "It's great for the junior apprentices to learn about butchery and proper meat, working with all manner of different cuts and joints; the likes of bavette, cheek, Jacob's Ladder and onglet call for ingenuity and skill to get the best out of them; offcuts and offal are much harder to cook properly than prime steaks and rib. I love that it gives the diners a tangible connection, seeing the beasts happily grazing on their drive through the estate, then reading our menu explanations and finally tucking in with relish, that's field-to-plate in action and food yards not miles. I just hope it doesn't turn too many vegetarian!"

The Hall's wonderful listed gardens are another welcome supply of the freshest produce. Head gardener Anna Outlaw and her eager team are restoring the kitchen plots back into full production, with trugs full of interesting unusual produce heading daily to the respective kitchen doors. Stephen is excited to be planning with Anna the best use of the kitchen garden's couple of acres for future growing years, focussing on the quirkier, tastier and more culinary crops, favouring delicacies like rainbow chard, yellow and stripy beetroots, purple borlotti beans and multi-coloured heritage tomatoes.

To understand the interaction between Somerleyton Estate's landscape, history, climate, geology and nature, the final piece in Stephen's intuitive jigsaw of what the French would call 'terroir' here comes from foraging the 5,000 acres of rolling fields, woods and lakeside for wild foods; hedgerow greens like hop shoots, sorrel and wild garlic or edible mushrooms like the St. George's, puffballs and blewits. What Stephen forays for captures the essence of the estate, its verdant lifeblood. "That these things have grown here for decades, perhaps centuries, is quite humbling," he says. "Once I am long-gone as a chef here or even after several generations of Somerleytons, this brief fruiting will still happen in the same place year in, year out, that is nature's magic. And it is symbolic of what motivates Hugh and the family in their careful stewardship of giving more back and conserving this green and pleasant land. A very special piece of local 'terroir' indeed."

Ravioli of Somerleyton rabbit rillettes, charred radicchio, St George's mushrooms, asparagus

Making pasta at home might seem daunting but it is much easier than it seems. Wild game birds or free-range local chicken are great alternatives to the rabbit filling. We serve it with a wild mushroom consommé but a herb vinaigrette works well. (Serves 4)

Rabbit confit

   1 young rabbit, loins and thighs only
   Few rosemary sprigs
   2 bay leaves
   2 garlic cloves, peeled and flattened
   2 tbsp coarse sea salt
   1 carrot, onion, leek, celery stalk – roughly chopped
   Parsley stalks
   Good Norfolk rapeseed oil

Lay the rabbit, rosemary, bay and garlic into a plastic lidded container and rub in the salt. Cover and chill for 6 hours. Pre-heat oven to 130c. Clean off the meat and rinse the herbs and garlic. Place into a snug roasting tin with the root vegetables and parsley. Pour over rapeseed oil to the top of meat and cover tin with loose foil. Cook until the rabbit is tender (approx. 3-4 hours). Remove and cool the rabbit joints, covering with the strained oil before chilling.

Pasta

   250g of 00 durum wheat flour
   1 whole egg and 4 yolks
   1 tbsp good rapeseed oil
   1 tbsp cold water

Pulse the flour, egg, 4 yolks, a little salt and oil in a processor for a few short bursts. Then add the cold water and quickly pulse in bursts until it starts to come together as a dough. Tip out onto a clean surface and knead for 4 or 5 minutes. Wrap in clingfilm and refrigerate for 30 minutes.

Ravioli

   Rabbit (as above)
   1 long shallot, peeled and finely chopped
   Small handful of parsley leaves, shredded
   2 egg yolks
   Semolina flour

Reserve the oil and remove bones, skin and gristle from rabbit meat before shredding well. Then fold in the shallot, parsley and seasoning, plus a little oil to moisten. Set aside.

Using a floured pasta roller, run the dough through twice on every setting down to the second narrowest. Lay out a long strip of pasta on a clingfilmed surface. Starting 5cm in, place a heaped tablespoon of the filling approx 10cm apart in the centre of the pasta, only using half of its length. Whisk up the yolks and brush over the pasta on the filling side. Fold back the other unused half back over the top. Carefully seal together and then using an 8cm round cutter, gently cut out the ravioli. Firm edges and lay out individually in a tray of semolina. Refrigerate if needed.

To serve

   2 heads radicchio, quartered
   Good rapeseed oil
   6 asparagus spears, cut in two
   Handful of St George's mushrooms, halved

Brush the radicchio with oil and sear on a hot griddle until charred. Meanwhile cook the asparagus until al dente while sautéing the mushrooms with a little oil and seasoning in a hot frying pan. Season all three and keep warm.

Cook one ravioli in a very large pan of salted simmering water for three minutes to check timing. If perfectly cooked, repeat with the remaining pasta or adjust time accordingly. Drain and dress with more oil. Serve, garnished with the vegetables.

Wild sorrel and pea soup

A real fresh green taste of springtime, this can be finished with fresh oysters, lobster meat or smoked fish or keep it veggie as here with spinach and ricotta gnocchi and charred asparagus. You can use regular garden sorrel or other zingy greens too. (Serves 4)

Good rapeseed oil
Unsalted butter
1 medium leek, finely sliced
1 medium potato, peeled and cubed
500ml good chicken stock
500ml breakfast milk
300g wild buckler sorrel leaves, stalks trimmed
100g petit pois, defrosted

Melt a knob of butter in a lidded frying pan over a gentle heat. Add a glug of oil and the leeks. Cook, lightly-seasoned, until soft, strir often. Add the potato and stock, simmering until soft, before adding the milk and bringing to a boil. Add the sorrel and peas, simmer for a few minutes covered. Purée carefully with a handblender and adjust seasoning before serving.

Cromer crab and pickled radish salad, lemon and anchovy purée

This is the easiest freshest-tasting seafood starter or light lunch. We serve it with crispy capers and a green peppercorn crumb for texture. Use the brown crab meat for crab soufflés or rich bisque. (Serves 4)

100ml rice vinegar
100g caster sugar
1 tsp sea salt
Large handful radishes, cleaned
1 cucumber
2 medium dressed crabs, white meat only
Lemon halves
50g anchovy fillets, drained
Lemon juice
Rapeseed oil
Red onion, finely sliced
Handful baby greens

First make a pickling syrup by dissolving vinegar, sugar and salt. Finely slice the radishes, preferably on a mandolin carefully. Submerge into the hot syrup and leave to marinate for an hour. Halve the trimmed cucumber lengthwise, deseed but leave skin on. Finely slice into 10-15cm long strips, discarding those with too much peel. Gently fold the crabmeat with lemon juice and seasoning to taste, keeping it chunky. Blend anchovies with a squeeze of lemon juice and oil to taste, into a smooth thick purée.

Plate with cucumber slices wrapped around the crab, dotted with drained radish and the anchovy purée and scattered with red onion and baby greens.

Wood-fired flatbread

This is so easy. It makes a richer Indian-style bread and can be griddled on a chargrill or barbecue, failing that just in a dry frying pan. You can brush them with a garlic herb butter too. Here served pizza-style with heritage beetroot, goats' curd, caramelised onion purée and estate herbs. (Serves 4+)

350g local self-raising flour
1 tsp baking powder
350ml organic natural yoghurt
Pinch of sea salt

Mix up all the ingredients in a bowl or pulsed in a processor until just coming together. Tip onto a clean board and briefly need into a dough. Chill for 5 minutes.

Cut into four pieces and each into 3 balls. Roll out to a few millimetres thick, perhaps 10cm diameter, well-floured on each side. You can make fewer balls and roll them wider.

Heat up your griddle pan or wood-fired oven until hot, wipe bars with oiled kitchen paper. Place dough pieces on the bars or pan and cook for a minute or two on each side, until well-marked and puffy, turning with tongs. Keep warm and repeat.

WELL-THUMBED COOKBOOKS?

Not a cookbook exactly, but I like *Kitchen Confidential* by Anthony Bourdain. It's a look behind the scenes at a chef's life in New York and what inspired him.

CHEF'S TIP?

Microwave limes for a few seconds, then roll them in the palms of your hands for maximum juice.

MEMORABLE DISH?

Monkfish ravioli with a perfectly cooked quail's egg at the Manoir aux Quat'Saisons. And dessert at Restaurant Gordon Ramsay: the acetate paper had been left on the chocolate mousse we were all sharing. The waiter went white when he saw what had happened. There followed a smash in the kitchen!

FAVOURITE PLACE TO EAT?

Darsham Nurseries café: it's inspired food with a lot of middle eastern influence, unplayed with. The lightness and freshness of the ingredients, the care with which they are cooked and the standard to which they are served makes it special.

QUICK SNACK?

Poached eggs, blackened tomatoes, sourdough toast and marmite.

A 'TAKE FIVE' RECIPE?

Deben oysters, batter, soy, chilli and rice wine. Deep fry the oysters in batter and combine other ingredients as a dipping sauce.

RECENT DISCOVERY?

Wild food on the Somerleyton Estate. It was Mark Hix who first discovered ceps in the woodland here when he was out shooting. Of course, no keen forager gives away the secret of exactly where!

STEPHEN ON HIS...

A DISH THAT TAKES YOU BACK SOMEWHERE?

Diving in Cape Town for oysters with a couple of local guys. We could only bring 12 ashore so we shucked a few more and ate them while treading water, and then had the rest on the beach with some Castle beer.

LUCKY DAY OFF?

A simple lunch at home with Bec and the kids, Madeline and Sebastian. We'd have a simple but really good roast chicken, some great salads, smoked salmon, breads and olives and oil.

AMBITIONS?

Everything's about the estate now for me: to have a successful pub, hotel and associated businesses, to inspire the chefs on board to have the same ethos as Hugh and me, so that using local food is the natural thing to do.

SIGNATURE DISHES

Starters

Superfood salad: ptium couscous, broccoli, chilli, marinated feta, toasted almonds, pomegranate yoghurt

Charred, marinated halloumi, puy lentils, flat leaf parsley, wood fired beetroots, Somerleyton shallot & honey dressing

Asparagus wrapped in locally smoked bacon, Norfolk Medlar brûlée

Mains

Slow-braised pork belly, crushed Jersey Royals, braised & fresh baby gem, petits pois à la française, poached apple, Aspall's gel

Wood-fired hake, warm salad of chorizo, cherry tomato, butter bean, chilli

Cromer crab, pickled salad, lemon & anchovy purée, avocado, cucumber, green peppercorns

Puddings

Dark chocolate brownie, honeycomb, chocolate ice cream, mocha sauce

Raspberry pannacotta, strawberry & raspberry sorbet, spring berries, coulis

Vanilla-baked cheesecake, apple & rhubarb compôte, salted caramel ice cream

ULTIMATE DINING DESTINATION?

The French Laundry in Napa Valley, California, because of its consistently high end, world-class food and field to plate ethos. I haven't been there yet.

Lakeside escape

Stretching across the southern Broads, Somerleyton Estate straddles a pair of villages and two counties, Fritton to the north is in Norfolk, while Somerleyton, home to the Hall and Gardens, sits south over the border in Suffolk.

The huge Fritton Lake is an iconic vista in the Estate's lush landscapes, a historic decoy, once used for trapping wild duck, which now thrive in its deep waters as do the pike. The latter artfully illustrate the swinging pub sign for The Fritton Arms, which sits on its banks. Down a hidden lane off the looping Beccles to Gorleston road, guests wend their way past the thatched 12th century village church to what was the old rectory, with its ochre-yellow walls and parkland setting, now home to this relaxed country inn-hotel. The welcome informality and jovial team add to the feel of 'home-from-home' and the signature laid-back dining and drinking vibe. A familiar, almost 'lived-in' indulgence comes from squishy delightfully-shabby sofas, mismatching chairs and distressed mirrors, but combined in style with proper napkins, luxury touches and fine china.

More relaxed boutique than country house, The Fritton's boho-chicness has been inspired by the likes of the Holkham Vic, The Gunton Arms and further afield, Soho Farmhouse; Hugh and Lara, Lord and Lady Somerleyton, shared a similar vision for here, creating a cosseting bolthole, a sense of refuge away from the humdrum of everyday life. The nine comfy bedrooms upstairs are being joined by three hidden cottages while, for those preferring to sleep under canvas, there's a new campsite nearby. And for those who never want to leave, buying one of the luxury woodland retreats dotted around the lake makes The Fritton Arms their 'local', a lucky escape indeed.

The Fritton Arms
Church Lane, Fritton NR31 9HA
W: www.frittonarms.co.uk
T: 01493 484008
E: info@frittonarms.co.uk
f /The Fritton Arms
🐦 @FrittonArms
📷 /frittonarms

Accolades: Waitrose *Good Food Guide*; *Sawday's*

Covers: 70 outside, 50 inside

Cost: carte average £27; pint from £3.90

Open: Mon-Sat 12-11; Sun 12-10.30; L 12-2.30; D 6.30-9; Sun 12-6

Details: outside dining on terrace; nine en suite bedrooms; three cottages; camping (no electric hook-up; tents only); wheelchair access downstairs; dogs welcome in bar and rooms; bikes and boats for hire

Gruff love

Leigh Taylor embraces the fresh flavour of
Fielding Cottage goats' cheese with enthusiasm
and creativity at this welcoming village pub

THE KING'S HEAD LEIGH TAYLOR

One day, back in 2009, Sam Steggles arrived home with ten goats. "Our son was three months old and I think my wife thought I'd gone mad!" he recalls. "I come from a farming background, love working with livestock and we had been trying to find a different route, something we could add value to. At the time, nobody was rearing goats commercially round here and I saw an opportunity."

And so Fielding Cottage was born. In a few busy years, this family business based in Honingham, just outside Norwich, has grown to become an efficient supplier of the freshest goats' cheese, meat and milk to local pubs, restaurants and delicatessens, as well as the general public through farmers' markets and the tiny, bunting-bedecked Goat Shed shop that stands next to the dairy. Milk is processed two or three times a week depending on the

season. "Goats' milk is known to be particularly digestible so it's great for people with allergies, and the meat is the most widely-eaten in the world," says Sam. "We are slowly catching on in this country!"

In the Fielding Cottage dairy, a purpose-built, high-tech space (capable of pasteurising 1,000 litres of milk an hour) oblong blocks of brie-style Wensum White are ranged on a slab. They'll be turned and salted daily for seven days by chief cheesemaker, Emma Tabrett, before being wrapped in wax paper and chilled on racks, alongside eight-week matured Mardler with its yellow wax coat, soft fresh roundels of feta-like Ellingham ("they're made on a Monday, wrapped on the Thursday, then sold" Emma explains), and tubs of the freshest curd cheese intended for spreading or stuffing.

Back in the kitchen at The King's Head, Bawburgh, head chef Leigh Taylor uses Ellingham goats' cheese to make a sausage-shaped mousse that he slices into pucks, panés with ground almonds and pan-fries. "We serve this warm as a starter. It ends up a bit like a mozzarella stick and it went down really well on our Valentine's Day menu this year." He watches the pan carefully as he talks, turning the cheese as the buttery, nutty crumb turns golden. Three spears of grilled asparagus and some fresh watercress add vivid green to the plate, while a black olive tuile gives crunch and a swirl of gazpacho dressing adds punchy taste.

"We've worked with Fielding Cottage for several years now. We were the first to try their Wensum White – Sam just popped in, wanting our feedback – and I've been using it ever since." It might appear as a simple red onion and goats' cheese filo tart, or a Wensum White bruschetta with a minted bean salad and lemon dressing.

Leigh loves that the cheese is made barely five miles from the pub and that a small family business manages the operation – but above all that it tastes delicious. "We have goat meat on every so often, but it's the cheese that's really popular," he says, gesturing enthusiastically and smiling readily. "The freshness of the milk keeps the flavour mild, not too goaty, which fits our customers' tastes." He uses the curd for a chocolate cheesecake and at Sam's suggestion that he should give it a go, a goats' cheese ice cream has become popular too.

"I like to keep things simple – so many chefs overcomplicate things – and if you have great ingredients you really don't need to do much with them. We do make an effort with presentation though. I like it when people say 'wow' because they weren't expecting a plate like that to come out of a pub kitchen!"

There is a firm commitment to locally and home-grown produce throughout The King's Head menu, an ethos that the Wimmer family has embraced ever since they bought the pub 33 years ago. Leigh talks daily to suppliers, named on the menus as VIPs (very important producers). These include the likes of Downham Market-based Accent Fresh, Wayland Eggs, Norfolk Quail, The Cheese Truckle, and Wood Farm in Marsham where Richard Crane specialises in strawberries and asparagus, and home-grown produce from Pam's Garden (Pam being Anton Wimmer's mother).

Leigh came to The King's Head in 2011. "I did my NVQs on day release while working at St Giles' House in Norwich. Once qualified, I travelled in Australia for a year with my (now) wife and while there

I did some agency work – I helped cater for 1,500 people at the FIFA Congress dinner, an amazing experience," he explained.

Since becoming head chef, Leigh is enjoying running a hard-working team that includes Jake Armes, Geoff Smith, Amber Burchinshaw and Denise Smith who has worked at the pub for no fewer than 30 years. "It's a great place to work," says Leigh "I like having the flexibility of a specials board to try out dishes – it means we can be adventurous without risking too much – but I would love to have my own pub one day. When that happens, it would not be too different from The King's Head."

Chargrilled asparagus, almond-crusted Ellingham goats' cheese, gazpacho dressing, black olive tuile

This is a great dish for early summer, using our favourite Fielding Cottage goats' cheeses, their soft curded feta-style Ellingham is ideal for this. It eats brilliantly with crisp local asparagus, the spears charred on the grill for a contrasting edge to the flavour. I also make a heritage tomato and basil salad to give more texture and zing to the dish. It is best to fry the cheese croûtes and chargrill the asparagus at the same time so bring in some help. (Serves 4+)

Goats' cheese

Half red onion, peeled and finely diced
Unsalted butter
250g goats' cheese
50ml cream
5 chive leaves, finely chopped

Add a knob of butter to a hot pan on a low-medium heat and gently soften the red onion without colouring. Allow to cool. In a food processor, blend the cheese with the cream. Decant to a bowl and fold in the onion and chives. Lay out a long double layer of clingfilm onto the kitchen worktop, tip mix on to it and shape into a long sausage. Wrap up tightly and reshape. Chill overnight.

Gazpacho dressing

Quarter cucumber, peeled, seeded and diced
1 green pepper, seeded and diced
250g ripe tomatoes, seeded and diced
1 tsp salt
Half clove garlic
1 spring onion, trimmed
20g stale bread
1 tbsp white wine vinegar
50ml virgin olive oil

Combine the first three ingredients in a bowl with salt and leave for at least 1 hour. Strain and blend the liquid with the remaining ingredients in a blender. Sieve and season to taste. Refrigerate until needed.

Tuile biscuits

100g black olive paste
40g flour
40g ground almonds
80g butter
70g egg white
60g glucose syrup

Process all the ingredients together, blending well for at least 1 minute. Chill and rest in a bowl for 30 minutes. Pre-heat the oven to 160c. Using part of a clean ice cream tub lid, remove any edges and then cut a triangle shape out of the centre for a template. Lay lid onto parchment on a baking tray and smear a thin layer of mix over the template, lift it up and repeat in separate places on the parchment. Bake for 8-10 minutes. Remove from the oven and allow to cool before carefully peeling off to a rack to dry. Repeat until all are baked.

Cheese croûtes

240g ground almonds
200g white breadcrumbs
Unsalted butter
Rapeseed oil

Mix together the ground almonds and breadcrumbs. Cut the set cheese into 15mm slices and coat well with the nutty crumbs, pushing them in firmly. Transfer to a board, removing any excess crumbs. In a wide sauté pan, heat up a thin layer of butter and oil over a medium heat. Carefully lay in the cheese croûtes and fry on both sides until golden brown. Drain off to kitchen paper and keep warm.

To serve

16 spears asparagus

Pre-heat your chargrill pan. Blanch asparagus for 3 minutes in salted boiling water. Drain well and then chargrill immediately, colouring on both sides using tongs. Remove and season well.

Onto warm plates, place the asparagus, goats' cheese croûtes and a drizzle of the gazpacho dressing with a tuile to one side.

128

Cucumber crab rolls, avocado mousse, basil mayonnaise, lambs lettuce

This is a lovely fresh seafood starter, good with simple flatbread. Ideally use a mandolin with care for slicing the cucumber. (Serves 4)

2 dressed crabs
2 tbsp crème fraîche
2 limes zest and juice
Half a red chilli, deseeded
Small handful coriander leaves
1 tbsp basil purée
50g mayonnaise
2 avocados
100g cream cheese
Half a cucumber
Small handful lambs lettuce

Combine the crabmeat, crème fraîche, zest and juice of 1 lime together and then mix in the finely-chopped chilli and shredded coriander. Season to taste and refrigerate. Blend the basil and mayonnaise before seasoning and chilling.

Halve and stone the avocados, blend flesh with remaining zest and juice before mixing with the cream cheese and seasoning to taste. Chill for two hours. Very finely slice the cucumber lengthways, discarding the first peel-heavy slices and the centre seeded ones.

Place a wide ring onto a bed of cucumber slices on the first plate, half fill with avocado, top up with crab. Remove ring and wrap around some cucumber slices. Garnish with basil mayo and lambs lettuce. Repeat with three more plates.

Roasted rump of Norfolk lamb, tagine sauce and spiced couscous

We serve this with a tomato chutney and apricot purée for colour. (Serves 4)

2 onions, finely chopped
1 stick celery, finely chopped
1 tsp cayenne
2 tsp smoked paprika
2 tsp ground ginger
1 tbsp turmeric
1 tsp ground cinnamon
10 ripe tomatoes, roughly chopped
4 lamb rump portions
Rapeseed oil
150ml good chicken stock
50g raisins
1 tbsp tagine paste
100g cous cous (giant preferably)

Soften the onions, celery and spices over a medium heat in a covered frying pan, stirring occasionally. Mix in the tomatoes, cover and simmer well, stirring occasionally, until reaching a sauce consistency. Sieve and keep warm.

Pre-heat the oven to 200c. Brown the seasoned rumps well on all sides in a hot oiled pan and then roast for around 15 minutes. Simmer the stock, add the raisins, paste and cous cous, stir, turn down to a simmer, cover and leave on the lowest heat until fully absorbed. Remove the lamb to rest for a few minutes before carving and serve with the sauce and fluffed-up cous cous.

Strawberry bavarois

This is a perfect summertime dessert. Ours comes with poached strawberries, a yoghurt jelly and amaretti biscuits for crunch. (Serves 4)

4½ gelatine leaves
200g milk
800ml double cream
200g sugar
200g egg yolks
375g strawberry purée
1 punnet of strawberries

Soak the gelatine in cold water. Heat the milk and 300g of cream in a pan until steaming. Beat the sugar and yolks together and whisk in the hot cream mixture. Return to a low heat and stir the custard mixture well with a spatula to stop it catching. When it coats the back of a spoon, remove from the heat and mix in the gelatine and purée. Cool and refrigerate until cold.

Whip up the remaining cream and fold into the custard. Line moulds or glasses with the de-hulled and sliced strawberries and pour in the mix. Set in the fridge overnight.

UNFULFILLED DREAM JOB?

Wait for it...to be a vicar! I got it in my head when I was younger that vicars only work one day a week and I thought that sounded perfect. Look at me now – it couldn't be more different!

ULTIMATE DINING DESTINATIONS?

The Hand and Flowers in Marlow which I visited as a birthday surprise! I'd describe it as homely and the food as exquisite. Another place that is special to me is the Boudin Bakery, the home of sourdough in San Francisco, which I visited while on honeymoon.

WELL-THUMBED COOKBOOKS

Larousse Gastronomique is my most precious book! When I left Norwich City College I read it cover-to-cover over the course of six months, I was so enthusiastic to take what I'd learnt at college to the next level. And of course, you never stop learning as a chef!

FOOD NOSTALGIA

My grandmother Doreen, her butterfly buns – which always rose perfectly – and had the sweetest cream filling ever! All made with the eggs from the chickens in the garden.

WHAT IS YOUR BIGGEST EXTRAVAGANCE AS A CHEF?

Knives! Like most chefs I have an obsession with knives, I have a whole toolbox of them, though I only use about five regularly of course.

WHERE ARE YOU HAPPIEST?

It never fails to give me the buzz, when I'm being bombarded by checks on a Saturday night and everything is running smoothly. However, I do love to chill out and relax with family and friends!

LUCKY DAY OFF

I'd go for a long walk on the beach with my wife Stephanie. I'd love to take a Labrador with us, but Steph's not keen to have a dog, yet..!

LEIGH ON HIS...

CHEF'S TIP?

Buy an avocado hard then when you want to use it, wrap it in tin foil and pop it in the oven at 100c for 10 minutes. It'll come out perfectly ripe and ready to use!

SECRET MIDNIGHT FEAST?

I have two favourites depending on my mood: either something quick, like an omelette, or filling my plate with various cheeses, lashings of home-made red onion chutney and a variety of crisp crackers.

SIGNATURE DISHES

Starters

Braised pork belly, pan-seared scallops, spiced cauliflower & raisin purée

Tempura king prawns, sushi rice cake, vegetable noodles, ginger and soy dressing, baby coriander

Chargrilled pigeon breast, braised leg nugget, apple & pickled walnut salad, game chips

Mains

Norfolk pork: pan-fried fillet, braised belly, home-made black pudding, mashed potato, sautéed spring cabbage, apple sauce

Pan-fried chicken breast, mixed beans & pancetta, rosti potato, minted pea purée, dressed watercress

Roast salmon fillet, grilled asparagus, warm salad of courgette, spring onion & radish, crab cake, lemon hollandaise

Puddings

Salted peanut butter tart, milk chocolate & banana ganache, rum jelly, raspberry sorbet

White chocolate & passionfruit mousse, vanilla meringue, pineapple & mango compôte, crème fraîche sorbet

Custard pannacotta, poached rhubarb, stem ginger ice cream, shortbread crumb

WHAT GETS YOU UP IN THE MORNING?

The difference and uniqueness that each day will bring! I love rising to the challenge of achieving the high standards I always set myself and for the customers to enjoy every morsel of food created.

A Wimmer way

The Wimmer family has been serving up generous hospitality at The King's Head for a remarkable 33 years. The warren of rooms, inglenook fireplaces, beams and cosy corners in this village freehouse just outside Norwich gives the pub a 'something for everyone' feel: dogs are welcome, there's space for bigger groups, and food can be served in the squashy sofa area just as easily as the rustic bar or restaurant.

It's now possible to stay overnight too, thanks to a sympathetic conversion of the first floor that has created six luxurious ensuite bedrooms. Many of the rooms overlook the river Yare that runs through Bawburgh, and all have quirky elements: original beams and trusses, lath plastered walls and curious 17th century details such as an exposed patch of wattle and daub or a carving in the wood. Neutral shades of taupe and duck-egg blue complement the ancient structure, while traditionally hand-stitched beds, striking mirrors and very much 21st century furnishings mean the rooms are contemporary too. Each is named: the Langtry and Keppel after two of King Edward VII's mistresses (he is the King in question here), the stunning Walstan suite after the 11th century patron saint of farm landlords, who is said to have been born in Bawburgh, and the Tilney after William Tilney who built the pub in 1602.

Anton Wimmer, whose Dutch wife Tet, guided the look in conjunction with local interior designer and friend Tami Collins, is determined that The King's Head should remain a pub, not a hotel, however. "I want it to be an inn in the true sense of the word, a place that makes visitors welcome, provides good food and drink and a place to stay." In time, he would like to open a small village shop on site, to reinforce the place of The King's Head in this rural community.

The King's Head
Harts Lane, Bawburgh, Norwich NR9 3LS
W: www.kingsheadbawburgh.co.uk
T: 01603 744977
E: hello@kingsheadbawburgh.co.uk
f /kingshead.bawburgh.1
🐦 @BawburghKingsHd
📷 /kingsheadbawburgh

Accolades: Two AA Rosettes; 4 AA Gold Stars (accommodation); *Good Pub Guide*; *Sawday's*

Covers: 58 inside; 40 outside

Cost: carte average £30; set menu £17 (two courses), £25 (three courses); wine from £16.50; pint £3.50

Open: all week L 12-2 (Sun 12-2.30, 12-4.30 in winter); D 5.30-9. Closed D 1 Jan

Details: private dining and bespoke menus possible; child portions available; 6 boutique en suite bedrooms; dogs welcome in top bar area; wifi throughout; TV and board games in the bar; parking

Blazing saddles

The roaring Elk Room fire, where prime –
and lesser – cuts of meat sear and spit is central
to The Gunton Arms' unique style

floor is as much a part of the operation as the spectacle of the Elk Room fire and Stuart Tattersall's fiercely local, seasonal food.

It's kind of obvious that venison should be centre-stage. "We are blessed with a steady supply [the pub is on the Gunton Estate deer park]," says Stuart. "I take the whole carcass, squander nothing." You would expect nothing less from this Mark Hix-trained chef who headed up the kitchen when Hix opened his acclaimed Oyster & Chop House in 2008. "But it's daunting," he admits, thoughtful for a moment. "It's important to do these magnificent beasts justice."

The man bringing in the carcasses is James Ellis, the Estate's gamekeeper of 25 years (he even has a bedroom in The Gunton Arms named after him) who manages the herd of red and fallow deer that roam the 1,000 acres. A lifelong deer farmer, he culls as necessary in winter, breaking down carcasses in the on-site butchery, hanging meat until it's needed. It's a relationship that Stuart cherishes: there can't be many chefs who have such ready access to venison and work with such an expert stalker as James.

The kitchen team of eight chefs, between them covering three services a day with up to ninety guests on busy evenings, are well-trained not to waste. "It's easy to use the loin, fillet, haunch, but what about the shin, the neck, the innards, the off-cuts? That's the challenge," Stuart says. "I'm privileged to get offal still warm from slaughter; most chefs would be envious of that." Kidneys will often be devilled on toast, and bones of course go into a stock. Other cuts might go into a giant venison sausage roll for the bar menu (generous slices are cut to order); he might make a slow-braised tagine with the shin and shoulder.

"I shy away from the term 'signature dish' but I suppose the venison mixed grill has become that," Stuart says. "You get loin chop, sausage, a sliver of offal – heart, liver or kidney – and a faggot from the shoulder meat. It's served with rowan berry jelly."

He works with chef Glen Wardle to put the dish together at the Elk Room fire. It's a roaring, licking beast of a fire, orange tongues wrapping themselves hungrily round logs gathered from the estate. A platter of slippery, squeaky-fresh offal, fat sausages and well-hung chops are ready to cook in the appropriate order, each piece sizzled to just-cooked pinkness. The elements, well-seasoned, are arranged simply on a wooden board.

The Gunton Arms is not just a story of meat, however. Wild sea bass, line-caught by Cromer Pier fishermen and served with seashore vegetables and King's Lynn brown shrimps, is popular; ditto herb-baked Manx queen scallops with wild garlic butter, and Cromer crab,

A t the risk of sounding sexist, The Gunton Arms is a place for manly food, masculine, muscular, meaty food that is deep and rich and flavoursome, food that might put hairs on your chest and make you grunt with pleasure. It seems fitting that a vast pair of 10,000-year old elk antlers should hang over the fireplace in the double-height main dining room, and that they should have belonged to an animal that left them – after an Ice Age brawl? – in a peat bog somewhere in Ireland. The uncompromising art fits too; the collection is that of the pub's owner and renowned art dealer, Ivor Braka.

But the Gunton Arms is also an ordinary pub. It's a place where the clack of pool balls, the low-level hum of a big screen showing the midweek football match, and the scrape of bar stools on the wood an obvious inclusion as The Gunton Arms is just five miles from that stretch of coast. "There's a sweetness from Cromer's chalky seabed that makes them special. We get our crab and lobster from Martin Newland who sells what he catches each day." The brown meat is mixed with a dash of mayonnaise, Tabasco and lemon juice, and finished with flakes of white meat; it's served on toasted sourdough. "We've put a few more fish dishes on recently, and we do vegetarian and children's menus, so we do cater for everyone!"

The simple menu changes twice daily to reflect what's been brought in that morning. "It does include fish fingers because we are a pub," says Stuart, uncompromisingly. "And I keep it quite short so that the kitchen can deliver consistently." It's an approach he learnt during his time with Hix. "I realised that there doesn't have to be a mystique about cooking. As long as your ingredients are good and you prepare them simply you can't go wrong. People yearn for honesty and simplicity." You're unlikely to see dibs and dabs of anything on a Gunton Arms plate; this is no place for smears or foams or tweezered greenery. "I'm really not into finicky cooking."

Will anything change? Beyond the exciting prospect of re-opening The Suffield Arms next to Gunton train station, and opening four new rooms in the coach house, Stuart is happy right where he is. "There is genuine affection for this pub, locals share in our pride. The challenge is to deliver every day; we can't let people down."

Gunton fallow deer dumplings with wild rowanberry jelly

Cooking over an open log fire gets lots of attention at The Gunton Arms but it is far more than just culinary theatre, giving a distinct flavour and texture to the great steaks and other meats, we griddle and roast over the embers.

Venison steaks and chops work very well flash-grilled on a searingly-hot griddle, cooked fast, caramelised outside and rare and juicy within. I urge you to give pink-cooked venison cuts a try, even if you usually eat your meat more cooked. It easily can come out overdone, that's never a pleasure.

This dumpling dish makes a hearty starter or light main course but usually appears as part of our venison mixed grill, always a popular choice on our Elk Room restaurant menu, served alongside the kidney, liver, sausage and cutlet, giving a combination of savoury gamey flavours and rich textures.

As a main course by itself, the dumplings eat well with creamy mashed potato, wilted greens and sweet-sour red cabbage. (Serves 4)

Rowanberry jelly
  500g rowan berries, stalks removed
  500g crab apples or Bramley apples, chopped
  6 thyme sprigs
  600ml hot water
  Jam sugar
  Juice of half a lemon

Simmer all ingredients together until soft. Strain overnight through a muslin cloth, suspended above a bowl to slowly drip through. Do not be tempted to squeeze it.

The next morning, measure the juice into a preserving pan and for every 600ml of juice, add 450 g of jam sugar. Mix together well and bring to a simmer, stirring until the sugar is dissolved. Boil rapidly until the setting point is reached on a jam thermometer (about 9-10 minutes usually). Take off the heat and skim the top for impurities. Pour into sterilised containers, seal and leave to set.

Fallow deer dumpling
  500g venison meat, minced
  250g pork belly, minced
  100g venison liver, minced
  200ml good red wine
  3 juniper berries, crushed
  Good pinch thyme leaves, chopped
  6 shallots, finely diced
  2 garlic cloves, peeled and crushed
  Unsalted butter
  225g fresh white breadcrumbs
  Caul fat crépinette

Marinate all the meat in red wine, juniper and thyme for 24 hours. Pre-heat the oven to 200c.

Drain the meat well (make use of the liquor for a rich wine gravy or a stew). Cook the shallots and garlic slowly in butter until soft and then leave to cool. Mix into the meats with the breadcrumbs and season well. Roll into golf balls and wrap snugly in crépinette, trimmed to fit. Place into a shallow oiled roasting tray and bake for 10 minutes to set. Remove and using a slotted spoon, transfer to a hot frying pan or griddle. Brown on all sides until cooked through. Serve with the jelly.

Cromer crab on toast

A lovely high tea dish or light lunch and a great way to celebrate the rich simplicity of wonderful Norfolk crab. To season crab, I prefer white peppercorns, not black. (Serves 4)

300-350g brown crabmeat, cooked
Tabasco sauce (optional)
2-3 tbsp good quality mayonnaise
4 slices good brown bread
Unsalted butter, softened
150-200g white crabmeat, cooked
1 lemon, cut into wedges

Break up the brown crab meat in a bowl using a fork, season and mix in mayonnaise to taste with a dash of Tabasco to spice it up. Toast the bread on both sides and butter liberally. Spoon the brown crab mix onto the toast and scatter over flaked white crabmeat. Grind over some more pepper and serve with a lemon wedge.

Sea buckthorn berry posset

Tangy, fruity buckthorn has a unique flavour and once tasted is never forgotten. Credit for creating this delicious, refreshing dessert is due to an old chef colleague, Jesse Dunford Wood, now of Parlour, Kensal Green in London. (Serves 4)

450ml double cream
Zest of half an orange
125g caster sugar
30ml lemon juice
30ml sea buckthorn juice
1½ gelatine leaves
50ml water
50ml stock syrup
15ml sea buckthorn juice

Put the cream and zest on to boil. In a bowl, whisk up the sugar, lemon juice and 30ml buckthorn juice. Stir in the simmering cream and then after a few minutes, pass through a sieve into a jug. Fill suitable ramekins, leaving some space at the top for a small jelly layer. Cool and chill to set.

Soak the gelatine leaves to soften. Simmer 15ml water and stock syrup. Whisk in the drained gelatine. Stir in the 15ml buckthorn juice, sieve into a jug, allow to cool before pouring on top of the ramekins. Chill to set.

Venison kofta kebab

Instead of the more traditional lamb, we use venison shoulder or scrag end of neck. It has a good balance of fat for succulence and lots of flavour, holding up well to the spices and the chargrilling. Soaking the skewers helps to stop them burning. We serve these with a red onion salad and creamy coriander yoghurt on the side. (Serves 4)

500g minced venison
2 tbsp chopped fresh coriander
2 tsp turmeric
2 tsp chilli powder
4 tsp ground cumin
2 tsp ground coriander
2 garlic cloves, finely chopped

Place all the ingredients in a large bowl and mix up well, before placing in the fridge overnight.

Before cooking, soak wooden skewers in water for a few hours.

Divide the kofta mix into even balls then thread one or two on to each of your skewers. Oil your hands and shape the balls into even sausages along the skewers. Flatten slightly.

Heat up your griddle, chargrill pan or barbecue to smoking hot, oil the bars and then cook the kebabs for a few minutes on each side. Ensure they are cooked through but not dried out.

WELL-THUMBED COOKBOOKS?

Roast Chicken and Other Stories by Simon Hopkinson. It's an honest book written by a very knowledgeable cook. I also love my copy of *Lulu's Provençal Table* by Richard Olney with a foreword by Alice Waters [renowned chef-patron of Chez Panisse, Berkeley, California] which Ivor gave me as a gift when we opened. The recipes and the approach to food it conjures up are very in tune with what we do.

FOOD HEROES?

People forget or maybe are not aware of what Delia Smith has given to the world of food. She's definitely a food hero.

ULTIMATE DINING DESTINATION?

I'd love to go to Thomas Keller's French Laundry in the Napa Valley, a place I've dreamt of visiting. It must be amazing to cook in California, with the climate and the wealth of produce and wine on the doorstep.

STUART ON HIS...

SIGNATURE DISHES

Starters

Norfolk free-range rose veal pastrami on rye, pickles

Wood Farm asparagus & feta salad

Gunton-smoked Loch Duart salmon, Irish soda bread

Mains

Rib of beef to share, goose fat roast potatoes, béarnaise sauce

Tagine of red deer, couscous, flatbread

Whole grilled Cromer lobster, chips, wild garlic butter

Puddings

Gunton honey cheesecake, ginger ice cream

Aylsham rhubarb & almond tart, custard

Amadei chocolate & hazelnut mousse

IF NOT A CHEF WHAT WOULD YOU HAVE BEEN?

A music journalist for NME. I love good live music, indie or punk-inspired mainly. When I lived in London I'd pick up NME, see who was playing, get a ticket from somewhere and head there on my own or with friends.

FAVOURITE LOCAL FOODIE PLACE?

I love Wiveton Hall Café. It's the perfect, unfussy place for lunch, tucked away in an idyllic spot. I like the blackboard menu, the fact that they grow a lot of what they serve such as asparagus, soft fruit and vegetables.

WHAT AMBITIONS DO YOU STILL HAVE?

To open a fish restaurant somewhere on the Norfolk coast. I have to keep it a bit quiet – if I tell Ivor, he'll say 'do it' and actually I've got plenty to keep me busy here at the moment!

MUSIC TO COOK TO?

The first person in the kitchen in the morning gets to choose the radio station, though we don't have it on during service. If I'm choosing, it will be Northern Soul, ACDC or any radio station playing 60s music – that shows my age, doesn't it?!

FOODIE NOSTALGIA?

Black pudding reminds me of Lancashire, where I'm from. We buy a spicy, crumbly Cumbrian one for the pub, which we put on a rabbit salad or on the breakfast menu as part of a full English.

LUCKY DAY OFF?

I'd head for Mundesley beach with Simone, Alice and Nell our gorgeous sable coloured cocker spaniel!

An artful business

There aren't many pubs where you'll find an original Gilbert and George hanging on a back corridor wall by the gents, a Damien Hirst in the ladies' loo or a trio of pink neon signs by Tracey Emin above a doorway.

But The Gunton Arms is different. This unique pub-bar-restaurant-hotel is packed with pieces from the intriguing, provocative collection of its art dealer owner, Ivor Braka. It was he who spearheaded the pub's renovation, opening to acclaim in 2011 and recruiting directors Simone Baker and Stuart Tattersall (the couple are from celebrated chef Mark Hix's stable) to run the operation.

"Ivor believes passionately that pubs should be at the heart of rural communities, a place for locals to socialise, especially as churchgoing is in decline," says Stuart. "It was very tempting to turn the bar into more tables, but it's right that we've got a darts team instead."

The look throughout is determinedly 'undone', a place where sofas envelop, rugs are a bit threadbare (but very beautiful), leather chairs are creased from years of bottoms. "We want guests to feel like they are coming into a friend's country house, and for locals to feel as welcome as weekenders," Simone explains. "Our bar is thriving, we're not just giving lip-service to it."

The eight comfortable bedrooms have no TV or tea/coffee facilities – the better to encourage conviviality in public spaces – but will soon be joined by four new suites in an adjacent coach house.

The team is also renovating the long-closed Suffield Arms. Bought by Ivor in 2015, the nearby pub will offer small plates of Spanish- and North African-inspired food in an informal, no bookings, setting. "I'll oversee the kitchen," says Stuart, looking forward to the challenge. "I hope it'll be the sort of relaxed place I will want to eat at on my days off!"

The Gunton Arms
Cromer Road, Thorpe Market,
Norwich NR11 8TZ
W: www.theguntonarms.co.uk
T: 01263 832010
E: office@theguntonarms.co.uk
f /TheGuntonArms
🐦 @TheGuntonArms
📷 /chefglengunton

Accolades: *Michelin* Bib Gourmand; Waitrose *Good Food Guide* 3; *Michelin* 'Pub of the Year'
2013; Best New Entry, *Good Food Guide* 2013; Top 20, Budweiser Budvar 'Top 50 Gastropubs Awards' (and highest new entry in 2013)

Covers: 75 inside; 100 outside

Cost: carte average £35; wine from £20; pint from £3.40

Open: year round (closed Christmas Day) L 12-3; D 6-10; bar food all day; sandwich menu until 5; no open fire cooking in Elk Room Sun

Details: children's menu; vegetarian menu; eight bedrooms; four new suites in converted coach house; dogs welcome (£10/night); bar with pool table, darts, television; wheelchair access; parking

Gone crabbing

The bounty of the North Sea is the anchor
for Will Jackson's appealing seaside menu

THE GLOBE INN WILL JACKSON

I f there were ever an award for 'itchy-footed chef of the year', Bradford-born Will Jackson would be a strong contender. Free-spirited, stove-hopping adventures have taken him to deepest Wales, across his native Yorkshire, and into Terry Laybourne's renowned north east kitchens; they've seen him slotting behind stoves in dining pubs and rosetted restaurants with ease, hungrily absorbing culinary experience along the way.

Thankfully, the feverish activity has calmed down in East Anglia. "I was exec chef for Marco [Pierre White] for three years – he called me 'Yorkshire boy' till he learnt my name – looking after the Norfolk pubs he used to own [The Chequers and Lifeboat Inn in Thornham and The Wayford Bridge Inn, Stalham]. It was a great opportunity, but I'm happy here now in Wells, I feel settled. I have wonderful bosses who are involved and interested in the food I'm cooking."

Will's appreciative employers are Antonia and Stephen Bournes who bought the then Adnams-managed Globe Inn in Wells-next-the-Sea from the Holkham Estate back in 2013. They transformed it into a fresh-faced small hotel, winning the accolade of Best Independent Hotel in the Visit Norfolk Tourism Awards just two years after taking on the property, and appointing Will to lead a six-strong kitchen brigade in October 2015. They like their head chef's grounding in classical French cooking, and his ability to turn out seasonal, modern brasserie food that tastes as good as it looks.

Will talks bent over the pass, building a dish of dressed crab with heritage tomatoes ("the flavour, the colours are so much more interesting"). The tomatoes are tossed with chives, tarragon and spring onions and set on a pool of horseradish mayonnaise, golden-yellow with Hillfarm Oils' cold-pressed rapeseed oil. The crab, brought up from the quay that morning by Wells fisherman Andrew Frary, makes a generous centrepiece. "We'll get through 30 a day easily in the summer," says Will, barely looking up as he finishes the dish with toasted almonds and a flutter of purple and green micro basil from Nurtured in Norfolk. "There. A lovely light lunch. I might finish it with samphire in season to give a salty edge, but to me that's perfect."

Minutes' away, on Wells' picturesque working quay, Andrew Frary welcomes us on board *Arandora Star II*. She's a tough-nut of a boat, capable of taking Andrew and his brother Martin 12 miles out into the North Sea to lift their crab and lobster pots, some 200 at a time in summer. Their work is dictated by the tides, their days at sea long. "We go out on a high tide and come in 12 hours later," explains Andrew whose family has fished for crabs, lobster, whelks and mussels since his grandfather set up the business in the mid-1930s. "We were the first to crab commercially round here. We used to sell live crabs to Nottingham when local people weren't interested, but now most go to local restaurants and to Billingsgate." The Frary's shellfish stall, set up on Wells quay by Andrew's father in 1957, is something of a local legend and such is the demand that the family now employs five full-time 'dressers', capable of processing 150 crabs a day. "The crabs are purged in fresh water overnight to get rid of grit. The next day they are cooked, dressed and delivered to the market, to chefs like Will or sold on our stall," Andrew explains.

Will doesn't need to venture far for other suppliers either. Briston butcher, H V Graves delivers meat for dishes such as braised blade of beef with dauphinoise potatoes, red cabbage and celeriac purée, or chargrilled pork loin steak with mustard mash; Direct Seafoods in Colchester supplies wet fish; King's Lynn-based Barsby Produce and the Potato Warehouse near Fakenham supply fresh fruit and vegetables.

Glossy kiln-smoked Scottish salmon comes from Cley Smokehouse, a few miles along the coast. Will pan-fries the fish to crisp the skin, and serves it with a peppery combination of Norfolk Peer potatoes, wild garlic and pieces of Marsh Pig fennel salami. Roast fennel and a swirl of fennel purée finish the dish sweetly. "If you have beautiful ingredients like these, there's no need to do anything more complicated, is there?"

If he is not instilling in his team a love of fresh, straightforward food, Will is drilling into them the importance of preparation. "We can easily do 120 covers on a Saturday and Sunday lunch, I reckon up to 220 in the height of summer, so we have to have a menu that works at speed! And if your mise [preparation] isn't right then you'll have a tough service however simple the dishes are." Luckily, his young team appears to be on song – Bogdan Lung from Romania, is extremely diligent and hard-working, Will says, while Gary Douglas, kitchen porter for a loyal 11 years is "amazing, he never bats an eyelid at hard work".

A pudding of prettily-pink rhubarb and ginger is ready in moments, thanks to the team's meticulous prep, tiny meringue blobs folded gently into chantilly cream and spoonfuls of sweet-sour ginger-poached rhubarb. A crunchy scattering of aromatic basil sugar finishes the bowl. "That's the sort of food I like," he says. "Fresh, simple, seasonal."

Dressed Wells crab with horseradish mayonnaise, marinated heritage tomatoes, little gem and herbs

We are so lucky to have the iconic Norfolk brown crabs landed a short walk down the hill in the harbour by our good friend and supplier, fisherman Andrew Frary; he and his family worked the first ever commercial fishing boat in Wells. This is one of our most popular menu choices. The males contain more white flaky crabmeat so I tend to use them for colourful salads and for fishcakes, the flavoursome brown meat of the females is better for soups. (Serves 4)

Dressing a crab

It is easy if fiddly to boil and crack a crab for the table followed by dressing it out but it's perhaps not for the squeamish and it can get a little messy. The good news is your good local independent fishmonger can sort you out easily. But if you are up for a fishy challenge, there are some great online culinary guides about how to sedate, humanely despatch and boil your crustacean to get the best out of it before removing the meat and returning it to the halfshell as dressed crab. Contrary to popular belief, there is nothing actually poisonous inside, just bits you really don't want to eat. So if you are short of time or not that confident, get a recommendation and pop along to a local trusted fisherman or fishmonger and ask them to furnish you with a crab or two, suitably dressed for dinner. And please note, like all seafood, if it smells fishy, it isn't fresh, so avoid it and look elsewhere.

We prepare our crabs by boiling them with roughly-chopped carrot, celery, leek and garlic, fresh bay leaves, lots of parsley stalks, sprigs of thyme and rosemary, a good glug of white wine and water.

Horseradish mayonnaise

10g horseradish root, freshly grated
1 tbsp Aspalls white wine vinegar
1 tbsp English mustard
Pinch of salt
45g (pasteurised) egg yolk
500ml Norfolk rapeseed oil
2 tbsp warm water
Lemon juice

Whisk together the horseradish, vinegar, mustard, salt and egg yolk until fluffy. Continue to whisk slowly while starting to drizzle in half of the oil. Then whisk in a tablespoon of the warm water. Continue to whisk in the remaining oil as a drizzle, followed by the final spoonful of water. To finish, mix in lemon juice and seasoning to taste.

Salad dressing

1 tbsp Colmans English mustard
1 tbsp Aspalls white wine vinegar
4 tbsp water
120ml Norfolk rapeseed oil
1 shallot, diced

Whisk all the ingredients together in a bowl. Season to taste and chill.

Marinated tomatoes

2 large handfuls colourful tomatoes
Small handful of soft herbs, eg tarragon, chives, basil
I bunch spring onions, finely sliced

Slice your tomatoes, halving if needed first. Fold together with the herbs and spring onions, plus seasoning to taste. Chill to marinate for at least 1 hour.

To serve

8 large leaves of Little Gem lettuce
4 dressed crabs
100g whole toasted almonds, seasoned
Micro herbs (optional)

On one side of each chilled plates, place two lettuce leaves, topped with a crab. On the other side, spread out 3 tablespoons of the horseradish mayonnaise with the back of a spoon as a base for the tomatoes, laid out artfully. Spoon 1 tablespoon of the dressing over the tomatoes, before sprinkling with the almonds (and micro herbs, if used).

150

Ham hock, pickled beetroot, celeriac remoulade

Norfolk has fabulous field-reared pork and smokehouses scent the coast, so great smoked ham is a given. I like to use the under-rated cured hocks from Graves, our Briston butchers. A simple shallot and mustard vinaigrette is an easy salad dressing and micro herbs are optional. (Serves 4)

3 beetroot – 1 each of red, yellow and rainbow
Good rapeseed oil
4 garlic cloves, sliced
Rosemary and thyme sprig
200ml Aspalls white wine vinegar
200g sugar
Quarter of a celeriac
1 tbsp wholegrain mustard
1 cooked smoked ham hock, meat in chunks
Rocket leaves
Salad dressing

Pre-heat the oven to 180c. Foil wrap the beets with a drizzle of oil, garlic, herbs and seasoning in a loose parcel. Bake for 2 hours until tender. Remove and set aside until just warm. Peel the beets. Dissolve the vinegar and sugar together. Dice half of the yellow and rainbow beets and slice the other half for contrast. Grate the red beetroot and the celeriac together, mixing in the mustard and a little syrup to loosen the slaw.

To assemble
On four plates, place a centre of the celeriac mix, dot around the pickled beets, ham chunks and dressed rocket leaves.

Gingered rhubarb mess with basil sugar

A seasonal change to the berry classic, this pud always goes down well. Folded together like a sundae, it makes a lovely family dessert. We preserve our own root ginger batons in syrup but diced stem ginger is just fine. (Serves 4)

Rhubarb purée
1kg rhubarb, chopped
500g sugar
100ml water
Split vanilla pod and scraped seeds

Simmer all together in a heavy lidded pan until tender. Cool, discard pod and blend pan contents to a purée.

Vanilla cream
50g icing sugar
Seeds of a scraped vanilla pod
500ml double cream

Whip up all the ingredients in a bowl to soft peaks. Chill.

Basil sugar
Equal weights of basil and caster sugar blended together in a processor before storing in an airtight container.

To serve
Jar stem ginger, balls finely diced and folded in the syrup
2 large handfuls of mini meringues
100g good custard sauce

Place the sweetened vanilla cream in a bowl, lightly swirl in most of the rhubarb and ginger before folding in the meringues. Serve in wide sundae glasses, on plates or in a communal bowl, garnish with the rest of the purée and ginger, plus the custard sauce before scattering with the basil sugar.

Kiln-smoked salmon, wild garlic potatoes and fennel salami

Hot-smoked salmon is a lovely alternative to the classic cold-smoked salmon we know so well; it has a quite different cooked texture but the same delicious wood-smoke flavour. We love Jackie's Marsh Pig Norfolk pork charcuterie and her fennel salami is a real favourite. At The Globe, this dish comes with fennel top purée, the hearts roasted, plus our own zesty lemon curd. (Serves 4)

20 new or baby potatoes (we prefer Norfolk Peer)
Bay leaves
Mint sprigs
100g Marsh Pig fennel salami, diced
1 bunch of spring onions, finely chopped
200g wild garlic leaves, cut in lengths
4 portions of kiln-roasted hot-smoked salmon fillets
Rapeseed oil
Unsalted butter
Lemon half

Pre-heat the oven to 180c. Simmer the potatoes with a few bay leaves and mint sprigs,

plus sea salt to taste, until just tender, not soft. Drain and allow to cool for 15 minutes. Cut into 1cm pieces while still warm and set aside.

To finish, you need to cook the salami and salmon at the same time.

In a hot deep sauté pan, heat up a knob of butter and rapeseed oil over a low-medium heat, gently fry the salami and spring onions until lightly browned. Add the warm potatoes and wild garlic, folding in gently, before cooking through until hot, adding more oil if needed.

Meanwhile for the salmon, heat up an oiled frying pan and place it skin-side down over a medium heat. When the skin is crispy, turn the fish over and after a few minutes, add a knob of butter and a spritz of lemon, then baste and turn heat off.

To serve, place the salami and potato mixture on the warm plates, topping with the salmon.

DREAM DINNER?

It's got to be the Fat Duck in Bray. I'd take Claire of course. I went there a couple of years ago; the food is incredible but the service is out of this world. It cost £250 just for the food but it was worth every penny. I loved the 'not so full English breakfast' which was actually a dessert, a crème anglaise inside an egg shell – it was very theatrical.

CHILDHOOD AMBITIONS?

All I wanted to do was be a snooker player! I had a cue aged 10, was always playing while my parents were having a drink in the pub, and even beating people in their 20s or 30s. I once got to play in the snooker hall in Morecambe where Alex Higgins played. Then at about 14 or 15 football took over and I lost interest in snooker though I'll still play a bit if I go up north.

INSPIRING NORFOLK VIEW?

Wells quayside. From where I live I can just see the quay and it's a beautiful sight to wake up to in the morning.

WILL ON HIS...

SIGNATURE DISHES

Starters

Blue cheese pannacotta, garlic tuile, walnuts, grapes

Potted Cley salmon, crème fraîche, crisp focaccia

Crispy belly of pork, black pudding, spiced apple purée, home-made crackling 'Quaver'

Mains

Pan-fried fillet of hake, clams, mushroom gnocchi, butternut squash purée, braised Little Gem

Venison burger, smoky bacon, Mrs Temple's Binham Blue, tomato chutney, chunky chips

Pan-fried stone bass, new potatoes, chorizo, spinach, crayfish butter

Puddings

Lemon tart, raspberry sorbet

Sticky toffee pudding, butterscotch sauce, clotted cream

Rich dark chocolate mousse, oranges, pistachio ice cream

FAVOURITE CULINARY MOMENT?

Definitely the day we college students cooked for Albert Roux. I shook Albert Roux's hand aged 18 – amazing! What an icon of cooking.

WELL-THUMBED COOKBOOKS?

I love Philip Howard's cookbooks from The Square, both his sweet and savoury ones. I've eaten there once and it was a very memorable meal.

COOKS CHEATS OR CHEF'S TIPS?

When braising meat or making confit, wait till the meat is cool enough to handle before picking it. You've just got to be patient and let it cool in the liquor so that it stays moist.

UNFULFILLED DREAM JOB?

When I was at Lancaster and Morecambe College I went round with a copy of Marco Pierre White's *White Heat* cookery book and decided then that I wanted to work for him – and I did. That's the last time I remember dreaming about a job.

FOODIE NOSTALGIA?

Fish and chips! It just takes me back to holidays with my parents by the sea in Yorkshire and Morecambe Bay.

FAVOURITE TIME OF YEAR FOR FOOD?

Spring! Everything is new and fresh and exciting – the wild garlic, asparagus, English radishes, outdoor cabbage. It's a great time to be cooking!

A sprinkling of stardust

Tucked away from Wells' seasonal bustle in a charming grassy square is The Globe Inn, its blue façade and celestial, starry symbol standing out among the neighbouring, more conventionally elegant, Georgian buildings.

Since buying the property, Antonia and Stephen Bournes (formally of the award-winning Southwold Pier, The Crown Hotel, Southwold and Snape Maltings) have transformed it into a fresh, unpretentious, family-friendly small hotel. Head chef Will Jackson's food is served on bare tables, decorated this spring day with pots of dainty bulbs and sunny daffodils. Comfortable window seats have views over the courtyard or square; paint colours are muted and there's plenty of exposed brickwork, some of it hung with bold original work by well-established artists.

Holly Pagani at Salt Interiors put her skills with colour to work, particularly in the seven en suite bedrooms where a single wall of strikingly-patterned wallpaper anchors a scheme. "We wanted a maritime feel, but to avoid clichés," says Antonia. So, while there is plenty of blue and white, there are also nods to Morocco with the bathroom tiles and to Georgian flamboyance with the stunning Imperial Pheasant wallpaper in Room One.

Back downstairs, a new Orangery extends the main dining space; above it a spacious residents' terrace with delightful views over Wells' red-tiled rooftops can be hired for private parties. A walkway will eventually connect the terrace to 11 new rooms in the adjacent coach house.

Charity and community-based work is important to the Bournes. "We've worked very hard, but we've been lucky too so it's right that we give something back," says Stephen. He and Antonia support the Norfolk Wildlife Trust, and also organise a winter programme of talks by fascinating, notable people, titled 'The Talk of Wells', to raise funds for charities such as the RNLI and the Wells Harbour Maritime Trust.

The Globe Inn

The Buttlands,
Wells-next-the-Sea NR23 1EU
W: www.theglobeatwells.co.uk
T: 01328 710206
E: hello@theglobeatwells.co.uk

- 🄵 /theglobeinnwells
- 🐦 @theglobewells
- 📷 /theglobeatwells

Accolades: Winner, 'Best Independent Hotel', *EDP* VisitNorfolk Tourism Awards 2015; Platinum Award, 'Loo of the Year Awards' 2015; *Sawday's*; *Best Loved Hotels*

Covers: 115 inside, 135 outside

Cost: carte average £29; wine from £16; pint from £3.70

Open: all week L 12-2.30, Sat & Sun 12-3; D 6-9

Details: Children's menu; seven en suite bedrooms; sunny courtyard; residents' roof terrace; dogs welcome in certain rooms; a newly-renovated four-bedroomed self-catering house, Spicer's, on the Buttlands

KINDREDS, WYMONDHAM
MARK DIXON

Give a chef a fish...

Gleaming sea bass, fresh from the
Lowestoft day boats, is an ingredient
Mark Dixon puts on his Kindreds' menu
whenever the season allows

Wightman who goes out about six miles from shore to find sea bass, one of five types of fish he catches by long-lining with bait.

"Wild sea bass is so versatile, and the fish I get from Steve is so fresh you could even do a cured ceviche with it," Mark says. "It even stands up to a red wine sauce – in winter we do a fantastic dish with parsnip purée, shallots, girolles and a red wine and veal reduction.

"I cook cod all-year-round, a real favourite with me and the diners, and I love mackerel and turbot. You don't see that one on many menus these days because it's expensive, but I want to serve something our guests definitely wouldn't cook at home. They expect a bit more now, and that's good, it keeps us on our toes!" Steve is optimistic about fishing stocks: "Skate and cod stocks are turning the corner, I think," he says. "I wouldn't be averse to my two young sons going into fishing, as quotas seem to have done the trick rebalancing things."

Although he gets to the market whenever he can, Mark receives a daily delivery of fish, changing his menu on the spot if needs be to reflect the catch. "Fishing is definitely a hard job and must be awful in the winter. I wouldn't do it! Really, we have the easy bit: all the quality produce just comes into the kitchen and we just turn it into a delicious plate of food. With ingredients like this, that's not hard!"

It goes without saying that Mark always cooks with the seasons. Early summer samphire and brown shrimps complement sea bass perfectly, the vivid green of the sea vegetable contrasting strikingly with golden saffron potatoes. He serves it with a silky chive beurre blanc, fresh pea shoots and tiny flowers to garnish.

Mark was born in Great Yarmouth. He started out as an apprentice chef at the town's family-run Imperial Hotel, where he quickly felt he could learn more in a day than in two months on day release from the town's college. "I got a bit bored at college," he says, "and they kicked me out. Things have a habit of coming full circle though, don't they - now I give lessons there!"

Eight of his fourteen years at the Imperial were spent learning classical cooking skills under the then head chef Stephen Duffield and Roger Mobbs, owner of the hotel. The other six he spent as head chef before stepping out on his own in 2013 to open his first restaurant at The King's Arms in Fleggburgh on the Norfolk Broads. Kindreds came to fruition a couple of years later.

Mark's style is calm, precise, technical, accurate. Everything in the kitchen – where four chefs weave seamlessly around each other in

Mark Dixon's new restaurant may be inland, but the Norfolk coast is never far from his mind – or his menu. Kindreds, which opened earlier this year in the centre of Wymondham, reflects the richness of the North Sea's bounty. "Fish is always a big seller," Mark says. "Plenty of people don't realise just how lucky we are in Norfolk and what we can get from this coastline. I try and get to Lowestoft every so often, to refresh my memory, be among the hustle and bustle of the fish market, be inspired anew by the fish that's being caught."

It's May, and wild sea bass is coming into season, the fish plump, silver-sparkling and glossy. Mark has been buying his fish from Lowestoft merchant William Masterson and Sons for the past fifteen years, where four generations of the family in turn have bid for the local fishermen's catch. Compared with the heyday of herring fishing off the east coast, today there's a very small fleet of just fifteen or twenty boats. One of them is *Georgie Girl*, skippered by Steve

the limited space – is measured down to the gram, the millilitre and the second. Everything is made from scratch, from bread to sorbets to ice cream; nothing is bought on the cheap, which means that nothing can afford to be wasted.

"Taste is definitely the most important element of everything we do," he says. "There's no point in food being on a plate if it doesn't taste of anything." There's plenty of chef skill on show too, though: a vanilla pannacotta of the softest texture and just the right amount of wobble, seems, almost magically, to hold together on the plate. "It's about taking everything to the absolute limit," Mark says, pleased with the end result.

"With my dad being a farmer, I appreciate all the time and effort that goes into producing food. People respect food and animals around here, and loads of people have allotments. In the summer everything's on the doorstep, especially in Fleggburgh. There, locals bring surplus produce to swap at the pub so there's a really convivial, community atmosphere which I love. Here in Wymondham I've been using the town's Friday market for bits and pieces – I'm not used to having shops at hand so it's exciting for me! – and again I manage to find plenty of fantastic ingredients that have been grown within a very few miles of my restaurant."

Wild sea bass, saffron potatoes, brown shrimps, samphire and chive beurre blanc

A delicious elegant but earthy expression of Norfolk's coast and sea on a plate. You can replace the chives with shredded wild sorrel or fennel tops for a different herby edge. (Serves 4)

Beurre blanc

250ml dry white wine
250ml fish stock
250ml double cream
120g salted butter, diced and well chilled
Handful of chopped chives

Boil down the wine and stock until just two tablespoons' volume remains. Whisk in the double cream, bring back to a simmer over a high heat and whisk in the butter, melting in one or two cubes at a time before the next, finally folding in the chives and keeping warm.

Saffron potatoes

12 new potatoes
600ml good chicken stock
Pinch saffron strands

Top, tail, and thickly trim the potatoes into curved cylinder shapes. Simmer in the chicken stock with saffron and seasoning. When tender after 10-15 minutes, drain and set aside somewhere warm.

To serve

Unsalted butter
Good rapeseed oil
200g samphire, trimmed
Four 120g sea bass fillets
100g peeled brown shrimps
Handful pea shoots

Blanch the samphire in boiling water until al dente, drain and put under cold running tap.

Heat up a heavy frying pan on a hot heat, add a knob of butter and a drizzle of oil. Once foaming place in the bass skin-side down, turn down heat to medium and cook until golden brown, (avoid touching it for first 5 minutes then check every 2 thereafter). Turn over, add in the potatoes and cook for a further 5 minutes, pull the pan off the heat and rest, while preparing the other garnishes.

Melt a knob of butter in another frying pan over a hot heat, add in the samphire and the shrimps, stirring well occasionally until piping hot.

To serve, spoon the hot sauce in the middle of warmed deep plates, add a bed of samphire and shrimps, plus three potatoes around the side and place on bass skin-side up, finishing with the pea shoots.

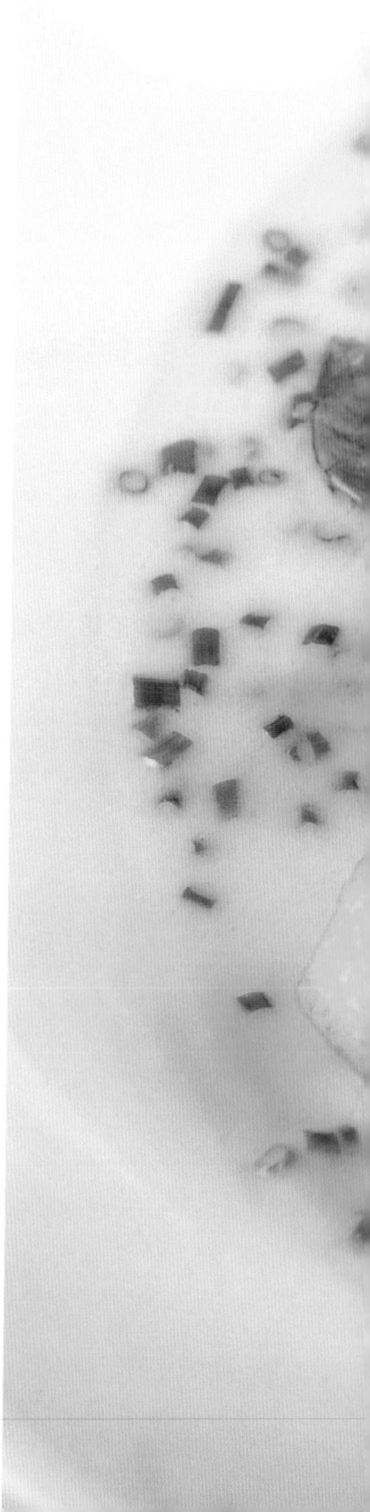

Grilled asparagus, ham and pheasant egg

A rich seasonal asparagus dish that combines texture, flavour and simplicity. Hens' eggs are a good alternative. (Serves 4)

4 slices Serrano ham
Good rapeseed oil
2 bunches Norfolk asparagus, trimmed
4 pheasant eggs
Pea shoots or watercress
Handful Parmesan shavings
Modena balsamic vinegar

Pre-heat the oven to 200c. Bake the ham on a baking sheet for 8-10 minutes or until crispy and golden, then set aside. Oil and season the asparagus and griddle in a hot oiled chargrill pan over a high heat, turning as it colours, cooking until tender. Heat up a frying pan with a shallow layer of oil over a medium heat, fry the eggs until the whites set but the yolks are still runny. Season to taste.

Place the asparagus on the plate, with an egg on top, scatter the pea-shoots or watercress around, and finish with crispy ham, Parmesan shavings and a drizzle of balsamic.

Norfolk 'strawberries & cream'

We serve this dish of set vanilla cream pannacotta and strawberry jelly alongside zesty lime sorbet and brown sugar meringue. (Serves 4)

7 gelatine leaves
240ml double cream
60ml whole milk
40g caster sugar
1 vanilla bean, seeds and scraped pod
200g caster sugar
500g strawberries, dehulled and chopped

Soak 2 of the gelatine leaves in cold water. Dissolve the next 4 ingredients together in a heavy pan and bring to a simmer, remove and whisk in the strained gelatine. Sieve and pour into clingfilmed moulds. Chill in the fridge for at least 6 hours.

Soak the remaining gelatine leaves in cold water. Simmer the caster sugar and strawberries with 600ml of water in a heavy pan while stirring, then turn heat to low for 10 minutes. Remove and infuse for a further 10 minutes, straining through a sieve without mashing and leave to drain for 5 minutes. Stir in the gelatine, sieve into a jug and pour into a clingfilmed plastic tray. Leave to set for a minimum of 12 hours. Cut into cubes and serve with the turned-out creams.

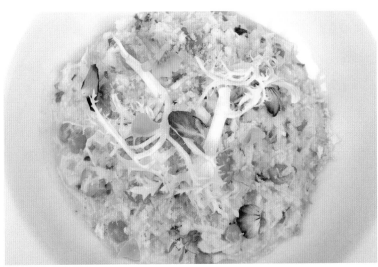

Cromer crab, green herb & pea risotto

*A colourful favourite, the fresh herb flavours contrast the crabmeat.
I finish it with crisp breadcrumbs and Parmesan. (Serves 4)*

Good rapeseed oil
Unsalted butter
3 shallots, finely chopped
280g arborio rice
120ml dry white wine
**900ml good chicken stock,
simmering**
**300g peas, podded or
defrosted**
1 lemon, zest and juice
50g Parmesan, finely grated
Meat from 2 dressed crabs
Chopped tarragon and chives

Heat up 1 tbsp of oil and a
knob of melted butter in a hot
heavy saucepan over a low heat
and soften the shallots for 5
minutes. Turn up to medium
and add the rice, frying until
'crackling'. Add the wine and stir
until absorbed. Repeat with the
stock, a ladleful at a time, letting
it absorb before the next goes
in. If the stock runs out before
the rice has softened, add a little
boiling water. Once al dente,
fold in the peas and cook for 2
more minutes, then take off the
heat, stir in a knob of butter,
zest, juice, Parmesan, crabmeat
and a small handful of the herbs.
Cover and serve after 5 minutes,
scattered with more herbs.

161

INSPIRING NORFOLK VIEW?

I love walking my dog, Mollie, down Sea Palling beach in winter. (I say dog, I mean pug!)

CHILDHOOD AMBITIONS?

I always wanted to be a chef, or become a farmer. My dad was a big meat and veg man and growing up we were never allowed to eat bad food!

FAVOURITE TIME OF YEAR TO COOK?

Spring and summer are certainly the easiest times of year to cook. I look forward to crabs, strawberries, spring lamb, all from Norfolk. It's best to keep everything simple; there's a lot more labour in winter dishes.

WHO IS OR WAS YOUR MENTOR?

Stephen Duffield, my then head chef at the Imperial Hotel, Great Yarmouth, definitely set me up for life. He taught me to always worry about flavour before all else.

BEST DISH EVER EATEN?

Last year to celebrate our first anniversary of opening The King's Arms in Fleggburgh, I took all our team as a thank you to Restaurant Gordon Ramsay in London for their tasting menu, amazing food and service. When they found out we were all in hospitality, we were treated superbly.

MARK ON HIS...

LUCKY DAY OFF?

I love a trip up to north Norfolk to walk along Holkham beach and have some fresh Cromer crab. You can't beat local crabmeat, no matter where you go in the country it's the best – and it's on our doorstep, how lucky is that!

AMBITIONS

If you had asked me this question a few years ago, it would have been to own my own restaurant. Now I have two, it is just to ensure all the customers and staff are happy, no better feeling than finishing a fully-booked service with happy diners and enjoying a beer afterwards.

ULTIMATE DINING DESTINATION?

I would love to travel to Asia just walk around the markets eating street food and enjoying seafood dishes around the amazing coastline there. I love all those spicy flavours, ginger, lemongrass, coconut and chillies.

SIGNATURE DISHES

Starters

Pan-seared king scallops, crispy pig's head, baby watercress, Granny Smith, caper, crème fraîche

Salad or rare-roast fillet of aged Norfolk beef, Cropwell Bishop Stilton, toasted hazelnuts, black truffle vinaigrette, baby herbs

Salt-baked golden & red beetroot tart, crispy Gurney's Gold beignet, truffled goats' cheese, raspberry, pickled shallots

Mains

Grilled fillet of North Sea cod, crispy fish goujons, parmentier potatoes, bronze fennel, baby gem, garden peas, warm tartare sauce

Pan-roasted rump of spring lamb, confit lamb belly, Norfolk asparagus, garden pea purée, fondant potato, broad beans, rosemary jus

Belly & fillet of pork, fondant potato, apple purée, black pudding, kohlrabi, sprouting broccoli, lovage, rich thyme jus

Puddings

Iced peanut butter parfait, malted milk chocolate mousse, bruléed banana, honeycomb, dark chocolate brownie

Dark chocolate and caramel delice, blood orange sorbet, almond tuile and chocolate crumb

Passion fruit brûlée, salted caramel macaroon, raspberry sorbet

QUICK SNACK OR MIDNIGHT FEAST?

I love a late night Thai curry, or cheese on toast with all the left-over smelly cheese.

Kith and Kindreds

Kindreds Restaurant is named after Mark's grandmother who passed away towards the end of 2015, and to whom he was very close. Step inside through the low doorway to find a comfortable cosy seating area with large leather sofas and a wood burning stove on one side and white linen-covered tables set for dining on the other. Beyond, more tables are tucked away in beamed alcoves, while a bright, modern bar area contrasts with the traditional feel elsewhere.

Relaxed fine dining is at the heart of this 480-year-old former pub in the centre of Wymondham. Bridewell Street drops away behind the Market Cross that marks the middle of this historic town, and the restaurant – the former Queen's Head – is set right on the pavement. Just a few miles from Norwich, Kindreds is ideally located for an evening out of the city, but, Mark says, is far enough from his other pub-restaurant, The King's Arms at Fleggburgh, not to compete

with himself! Great tasting seasonal, local produce, is the focus. There are daily set lunch offers, a full à la carte, and seasonal tasting menus, plus a large wine list, draught ales, and a selection of cocktails, mocktails and spirits, including twenty-five gins alone.

If running Kindreds and The King's Arms doesn't keep him busy enough, Mark was recently invited to become one of the founding UK chef members of JRE Jeunes Restaurateurs, a European network of top chefs, with Norwich-trained chef Tom Aikens as its UK ambassador. As well as being given international billing for his work at home, it also puts him in demand cooking for events abroad, such as Milan Fashion Week. Mark is the first to acknowledge that his eager hard-working teams in both restaurants are part of his success and he has confidence in head chef Reece Eden, previously long-standing sous chef at The Ingham Swan, who heads up the Kindreds' kitchen in his absence.

Kindreds Restaurant
2 Bridewell Street, Wymondham NR18 0AR
W: www.kindredsrestaurant.com
T: 01953 601872
E: kindredsrestaurant@hotmail.com
🅵 /Kindreds_Dining
🐦 @kindredsrestaurant
📷 kindreds_restaurant

Accolades: Winner, 'Chef of the Year' *EDP* Norfolk Food and Drink Awards 2013 (and Highly-Comm. in 2014); *AA Restaurant Guide*

Covers: 70

Cost: carte average £33; wine from £19; pint from £3.40

Open: Wed-Sat L 12-2; D 6-9; Sun 12-4

Details: private parties; bar drinks; free parking within 2 minutes' walk.

Mark also owns The Kings Arms, Main Road, Fleggburgh near Caister-on-Sea NR29 3AG www.kingsarmsfleggburgh.com 01493 368333

A pilgrimage to feed the soul

A different kind of earthly calling
fills Neil Rutland's kitchen
with natural provender

THE NORFOLK RIDDLE NEIL RUTLAND

"The call of the wild keeps you fit and it's a whole lot cheaper than my greengrocer!" commented Neil Rutland, chef-proprietor of The Norfolk Riddle as we walked tirelessly and dug deeply on our hunt for alexanders' roots deep in the rich soil of a local farmer's hedgerow up behind his bucolic home village of Walsingham. Neil's regular forays in pursuit of wild food and native ingredients are as much a pilgrimage, his to Mother Nature, as the tens of thousands of Christians and Hindus, who visit the famous shrines down the road every year.

As a "simple Norfolk chef", Neil's self-effacing description of himself might run as a mantra at the heart of his laid-back welcoming restaurant, but the lack of pretension and simplicity belie the effort and intent behind his passion for good food and the many years of experience in some of the county's best kitchens, like the well-known Hoste in Burnham Market, The King's Head at Great Bircham and most recently heading up Heacham Manor.

Neil's zeal to find great local ingredients and his energy to showcase them pushes him each day, not just finding the best suppliers on his doorstep but taking on a more personal challenge, getting out there after the tastiest wild foods in all weathers, picking, cutting, digging

(with owners' permission) to sustainably harvest the rich bounty of hedgerow, woodland and meadow.

Today found Neil and new-found friend, Norwich-based foraging enthusiast, Jon Tyler of Wild for Woods – who educates the public in bushcraft on walks for the likes of the Forestry Commission and heritage bodies – out searching for new-season hedgerow greens, not hard in these verdant parts after a week or two of springtime sunshine and showers. "This really is a prolific time of year, tender shoots sprouting up all over in this warm weather. We should find some of the different native garlic, perhaps some chickweed and hop shoots, and of course lots of alexanders" Jon ventured as we headed up the hill, leaving The Riddle in the background. Jon explained it is hard to miss alexanders, or horse parsley as it is also known, the statuesque thick stems towering to five feet high with lush bright green foliage and yellow umbrella flowerheads; it certainly makes its presence felt in early summer, especially near the coast and is perhaps Norfolk's most iconic wild plant.

"Few people know how delicious the whole alexanders plant can be, it is a veritable menu of tastes and textures," Jon explained to Neil, who was soaking up his foraging wisdom about each and every

plant they came across on their edible amble. "Right, alexanders are members of the carrot family, you can smell and taste the similarity," as they nibbled some young leaves, "but you have to be careful, closely-related and easily-confused in appearance are both cow parsley, also called wild chervil, pleasant to eat as a punchy herb garnish but not half as tasty, and more importantly, the deadly hemlock, which you really don't want to get muddled with, Socrates wasn't very philosophical after eating it! I would encourage people to make more use of alexanders as it is very prolific; harvesting in moderation won't do any harm to it as a species".

Foraging guru and chef were soon in a secretive huddle, discussing what they might cook up, Neil clearly inspired with the alexanders. "So I'm thinking deep-frying crisps from the starchy roots, making a pickle from the tender peeled stems in a spiced sugar-vinegar syrup and for crunch, a crisp tempura fritter of the young unopened flower buds, matching all that up with a rich pork terrine. That whole herbal-vegetal character and those savoury, bitter flavours will cut through its meatiness, a real contrast of lovely textures too."

After picking armfuls of long fleshy stems and a few dirty tap roots, carefully teased out from down deep, they carried on with their foray through the peaceful Norfolk countryside, only a few minutes' distance from the restaurant but a world away from the hubbub of tourists descending on Walsingham.

"How could you not want to be out here, the sun on your back, looking at that beautiful sight, a wood full of three-cornered garlic in bloom, and smell that scent…" mused Neil as we wandered back. In fact, Jon had soon uncovered three types of native garlic, all joining the now-laden faithful trug. "These look nothing like the cloves in the shops, it's all about the leaves with very different delicate flavours, great for salads and pesto," commented Jon, as he plucked a few leaves of fleshy sorrel-like wild garlic, mustardy hedgerow garlic leaves and bluebell-looking three-cornered garlic.

Back in The Riddle's kitchen came the hard work. "Working with wild foods is all about time and labour, it might be free but it does have a cost in chefs' wages, though it is great value and above all, tasty produce," said Neil. Acting as Neil's new-found and enthusiastic apprentice chef, Jon was clearly impressed by the transformation of the alexanders and other greens from dirty trug to an elegant plateful. "This just shows how delicious and interesting wild foods are, there is a natural larder out there for all to sustainably harvest so long as it's carefully identified – one man's weeds are clearly a chef's delicacy!"

Ham hock and garlic terrine, alexanders pickle, root crisps and tempura, hedgerow herbs

An earthy elegant expression of our landscape around the restaurant, how can 'weeds' taste this good? The bitter herby flavour of the alexanders is a great foil to the rich local rare breed pork. (Serves 4+).

Pork terrine

3 ham hocks, cooked and shredded
150ml of ham hock stock
4-5 sprigs of wild garlic, shredded
1 tsp Dijon-style mustard
1 tsp cider vinegar

Start the terrine by boiling the stock to two-thirds. Line a small loaf tin with two layers of clingfilm. Place the shredded ham, garlic, mustard and vinegar in large bowl with the warm stock. Mix well and season to taste (watch out for the ham's saltiness). Level the mixture in the tin, cover the surface with double clingfilm, press down with a board and heavy tins before refrigerating overnight.

Sweet alexanders pickle

250g young thick alexanders stems
1 banana shallot, finely diced
Pinch coriander seeds
Pinch fennel seeds
Pinch pink peppercorns
1 rosemary sprig
Rapeseed oil
50g soft brown sugar
1tsp cider vinegar
2 bay leaves
Alexanders flowers

Pull off the shiny outer layer from the alexanders stems with a knife, then thinly remove the inner fibrous layer with a potato peeler, leaving you with pale green celery-textured cylinders. Cut them into half cm rings.

In a heavy deep pan, gently fry off the shallot, coriander and fennel seeds, peppercorns and rosemary with a little rapeseed oil. Add the alexanders stems to this mix and continue cooking for a minute or so until they have softened and turned slightly opaque. Then add the brown sugar, cider vinegar and bay leaves and cook down slowly until the sugar has melted fully. Allow to cool naturally and store overnight in the fridge.

To serve

75g plain flour
50g cornflour
25g baking powder
150ml soda water or good lager
4-6 tight alexanders flower buds, trimmed of leaves
12 wild chervil sprigs
12 ground elder sprigs
2 alexanders roots, washed and peeled thinly

Pre-heat your fryer to a hot setting. Mix up a tempura batter by adding the flour, cornflour and baking powder in a large bowl, pour in the soda water and whisk well. Set aside and stir occasionally as it expands. Wash the flowers, chervil and elder in a light brine and dry well shaking in a tea towel or salad spinner.

Gently deep-fry the alexanders root until golden and keep warm. Dip alexanders flowers in tempura then deep fry until golden. Drain as before and keep warm.

Turn out the terrine and cut into 2cm wide slices. Place onto plates with the pickle to one side, top with tempura flowers, sprinkling crisps and the greens around.

168

Cheesy polenta and mushroom tart

This works well with any edible fungi you can safely forage or the less savage wild mushrooms sold in good greengrocers. Feel free to use other seasonal greens too. (Serves 4)

800ml cold water
50g unsalted butter
200g polenta
100g firm Norfolk cheese, grated
Rapeseed oil
100g shiitake mushrooms, sliced
40g rainbow chard, shredded
50g Parmesan cheese, grated
100g purple sprouting broccoli
Handful of baby rocket leaves and pea shoots
Balsamic vinegar

Boil water and butter together in a large saucepan before whisking in the polenta and bring back to a simmer. Cook according to the packet instructions and then stir in the cheese, seasoning to taste. Pour out the polenta into a clingfilmed roasting tray, smooth top, cool and refrigerate until fully cold. Slice into approx 5cm x 8cm pieces. To serve, bake polenta in a pre-heated 190c oven for around 10 mins.

Meanwhile, take a deep frying pan, heat up a little oil and sauté the mushrooms with the chard over a hot heat, seasoning to taste. At the same time, blanch the broccoli until al dente and drain, before keeping warm.

Plate up the polenta and top with the mushroom mixture and the broccoli, sprinkle with Parmesan, garnish with the salad leaves and drizzle with balsamic vinegar.

Cherries and raspberries jubilee

A pretty summer fruit dessert, light on the carbs but great for those with a sweet tooth. (Serves 4+)

16 cherries
50g caster sugar
100ml water
250ml double cream
75g icing sugar
Seeds from a vanilla pod or 1tsp good extract
16 raspberries
4 dark chocolate twirls or grated chocolate
Baby or shredded mint leaves

De-stone the cherries and put them in a deep heavy pan with the caster sugar and water and bring to a good simmer.

Remove the cherries and continue boiling the liquor until reduced to a syrup.

Whip the cream with the icing sugar and vanilla to stiff peaks.

To serve, spoon cream neatly onto plates with the cherries and raspberries, garnish with chocolate and mint plus a trickle of the cherry syrup.

Norfolk dressed crab with pickled fennel, pink grapefruit and pine nuts

This makes a deliciously light and fragrant summer lunch dish, the fresh citrussy flavours bringing out the sweetness of the crab. (Serves 4)

100ml white wine
50ml water
50ml white wine vinegar
50g caster sugar
Two garlic cloves, crushed
Few thyme sprigs
Bay leaf
1 bulb of fennel, thinly shredded
2 handfuls bitter salad leaves
2 pink grapefruits in de-pithed segments
100g toasted pine nuts
4 dressed crabs

Boil up the wine, water, vinegar, caster sugar, garlic, thyme and bay together and pour over the fennel in a large bowl before clingfilming and leaving to cool.

To serve, fold together the leaves, grapefruit, fennel strips and pine nuts with some of the fennel liquor as a dressing. Plate up and top with the crab.

BEST DISHES EVER EATEN?

Years ago, the much-missed Paul Whittome took all us kitchen boys from The Hoste Arms to El Bulli, then named the World's Best Restaurant and we enjoyed a 23 course tasting menu, just awesome.

INSPIRING NORFOLK VIEW?

Come on, all of it inspires, especially Holkham beach and the pine woods at Wells.

SIGNATURE DISHES

Starters

Seared king scallops, pork belly confit, pea shoots, crackling, apple sauce

Crisp-crumbed goats' cheese & lavender mousse, assiette of beetroot

Roast pigeon breast, rosemary brioche, balsamic strawberries, black pepper ice cream

Mains

Steamed fillet of black bream in a mussel, leek & asparagus broth with saffron oil

Roast venison loin with braised red cabbage, pommes anna, chilli chocolate jus

Sea trout, asparagus, tri-cornered garlic, crushed jersey royals, dried cherry tomatoes

Puddings

Honey-roasted parsnip crème brûlée, rosemary shortbread

Pecan & treacle tart with home-made clotted cream

Pineapple & mincemeat tart tatin, rum & raisin ice cream

LUCKY DAY OFF?

Start with a round of golf with friends from Heacham, home to Tina and the boys, down the park for footy, back for fish & chips from The Riddle, beer, sleep, good times...

FAVOURITE TIME OF YEAR FOR FOOD?

Every season is special, probably winter, can't beat shepherd's pie and a pint by the fire, probably followed by a little nap.

COOK'S CHEATS OR CHEF'S TIPS?

Refrigerate pastry cases and tartlets before baking, line them with parchment and fill with copper coins, they transfer heat much better than baking beans.

NEIL ON HIS...

FAVOURITE CULINARY MOMENT?

One night at The Hoste after dinner, the chefs were moaning about having to stay late to do room service and got roped in to serving it, but we were all suddenly happy to find out we were looking after *All Saints*, the rather gorgeous girl group in the charts at the time, who got back late from filming a music video.

WELL-THUMBED COOKBOOKS?

Has to be Nan's old collection of family recipes – ginger cake, casseroles, game dishes, rabbit pie – farmer's wife cooking at its best! Also Philip Howard's *The Cookbook* from his restaurant, The Square in London and *On The Menu* by James Mackenzie from The Pipe & Glass in East Yorks.

WHAT AMBITIONS DO YOU STILL HAVE?

Just to make our little restaurant the best it can be, really enjoying this new journey, how could I not enjoy cooking in Norfolk?

QUICK SNACK OR MIDNIGHT FEAST?

Bacon butty – plain sliced white, Arthur's crispy smoked bacon, tomato ketchup, Moongazer ale from Hindringham on the side!

CHILDHOOD AMBITIONS?

To be a professional footballer, I played for Norfolk under 15s but a badly-dislocated knee killed that idea off. Discovered cooking at home with Nan, loved baking cakes so had to reconsider my career options and became a chef by accident.

A chef for all seasons

Taking on this converted, listed red brick shop at the end of 2015, Neil and his partner Tina were thrilled to get their hands on The Norfolk Riddle, already established as a village restaurant with an attached fish & chip shop. In fact, they grew up on the outskirts of Walsingham, the family farm being just nearby in Great Snoring.

Neil knew this building well as it was then the local butcher's, where he would bring wild rabbits his grandfather had caught in the fields and also buy the meat for dinner with his nan. That family nostalgia runs deep and the Rutland family are completely threaded through the business, Tina running front-of-house looking after the diners and their two boys eager helpers at their young age. Neil's mother Rita as one of the co-owners is an eager supporter of their hard work, and guests from her Vine Park Cottage farmhouse B & B are regular visitors.

Living above the business with his family, there is evident delight for Neil that the local farming estate is their landlord and from where he sources much of his game and farmed produce in season, its famed farm shop being just opposite the restaurant. In fact it was the Walsingham Farms Partnership who created the Riddle and ran it for its first eight years, born out of the former shop of celebrated Wells-based butcher Arthur Howell, who now supplies Neil.

The evident symbiosis and sense of community around here ripples as wholesomely as the food. Local is the not-so-new black in foodie circles but rarely delivers as robustly as this; meat journeys a few miles, fish and greengrocery from King's Lynn, beer and cider brewed not far away and if it isn't native to Norfolk, then it is sourced via the county's best suppliers.

And wherever possible, Neil goes out to his own personal chef's larder, the great outdoors and finds what's tasty and free. His pilgrimage to showcase what has been foraged and to do something different, earthy and elegant on the plate in equal measure, does rather make The Norfolk Riddle stand out amongst its plethora of restaurant peers in this fortunate well-furnished part of north Norfolk.

173

The Norfolk Riddle
2 Wells Road, Walsingham NR22 6DJ
W: www. norfolkriddle.co.uk
T: 01328 821903
E: Info@norfolkriddle.co.uk
 /NorfolkRiddle
 @norfolkriddle
 thenorfolkriddle

Accolades: *Square Meal*; *Harden's*

Covers: 40 inside, 30 outside

Cost: carte average £30; Sun L £20; wine from £15

Open: Tue - Sun L 12-2, Tue - Sat D 6.30-9; fish & chip shop Tue - Sat 12-8, Sun 12-4

Details: children's menu; wheelchair access; parties welcome; fish & chip shop; parking

174

Food that chimes

The Wiveton Bell's Simon Haynes shares
a love of Norfolk's rich coastal larder
with Cley Smokehouse owner,
fisherman Glen Weston

THE WIVETON BELL SIMON HAYNES

The restorative, healing power of the sea has long been celebrated. "There is nothing I like better than being out on my boat at four in the morning, it's all I thought about while I was recuperating."

"My best times are spent wandering the coastline picking sea vegetables."

The first speaker is Glen Weston, owner (with his wife, Andrea) of Cley Smokehouse and the third generation of Westons to have run fishing boats from Cley and Blakeney; the second is Simon Haynes, the newest recruit to The Bell. The Leicestershire-born chef came on board in spring 2016 from Titchwell Manor, and is now the man carrying the foodie ambitions of this village pub on his shoulders.

Glen's days at sea nearly ended when he was diagnosed with a serious illness, but one life-saving operation and various treatments later, the energetic fisherman is back where he belongs. He has also discovered just how highly he is regarded as a producer of smoked kippers, prawns, undyed haddock and salmon, not to mention home-made pâtés, dressed crab, lobster and meats from Norfolk's acclaimed Marsh

Pig Charcuterie. "When I started, I thought of myself as a fisherman carrying on a family tradition, but I now understand that here you are surrounded by people who respect what you do, who want to buy your food."

It's a respect for local produce that Simon recognises. "I have only been here a short while, but Cley Smokehouse is the real deal. There are three generations of fishermen in the family, so Glen and the guys really know their stuff. You can buy smoked fish from any number of big suppliers but why would you when you have such experience right here?" Glen shows the young chef the smoking process; here it's all done over oak. "The thing about mackerel," he explains, "is that its flavour profile is unique. Salmon and trout taste similar; white fish tastes quite similar, but mackerel is distinctive. I also love the fact that it is sustainable and from this coastline."

The chef's and the producer's enthusiasm for local produce is matched by Sandy Butcher and Berni Moritt, owners of The Bell since 2007 and devout in their pursuit of a menu that reflects locality and the seasons. "He won't even put lamb on the menu because there are no sheep in the immediate area," says Sandy, indicating her partner,

NORFOLK TABLE

Berni, with a cheeky thrust of the thumb. "But we are surrounded by the best pork in the country, in season we have an abundance of game, and we are two miles from the sea!" Berni counters. Despite the teasing, Sandy nods in agreement.

Simon's arrival has heralded a change in direction for the pub. "We have a reputation for serving good food, but we need to make the next step," says Sandy. "Our dining will not be all things to all people, we will have a smaller menu – six mains, six starters and a daily special – but it will always be the best. It might just be fish and chips, but it will be the best fish and chips."

In their search for a chef, Sandy and Berni looked for exceptional cooking and, just as importantly, an appreciation of Norfolk cuisine. "I asked all the candidates the same introductory question," says Sandy. "What produce is local to Norfolk and when is it in season?" The lack of knowledge from some of the – mainly London – hopefuls appalled her.

Simon shone, however. He won a Gordon Ramsay Scholarship (the scheme is now defunct) aged 17 and worked in various AA Rosetted restaurants, before spending a year in Australia. "I learnt a lot about molecular gastronomy there and use some of the techniques now – they can give you quality, consistency and control. I always knew I wanted to be a chef, which is odd because my parents are musicians, not interested in food really, and yet I haven't got a musical bone in my body!"

Since his arrival, he has been busy redesigning the menu and planning a new kitchen, not to mention feeding record numbers coming through the door. "We certainly threw him in the deep end," Sandy laughs. "I just thought we should leave him to it, let him settle in!"

As he works Glen's mackerel into a beautiful roulade and delicately places pickled apple discs onto the plate, Simon is the picture of concentration. Around him the kitchen staff prepare, busily, for lunchtime service, but Simon is in his own oasis of calm. "My style?" he says, looking up from the plate. "I suppose it's about getting the very best from seasonal, fresh local produce. Using superb fish like Glen's is amazing, and I love Brancaster mussels, Cromer crabs – in fact most of the shellfish you get round here – but I also love gathering sea vegetables from the marshes, things like sea purslane, sea beet, samphire, sea aster, all of them beautiful ingredients. I think that using ingredients like these really brings the menu up to the next level."

Sandy flits past in her customary whirl of activity. She gives a wink. The Wiveton Bell vision seems to be in good hands.

Smoked mackerel pâté, Granny Smith apple, sourdough wafers, mustard leaves

Great smoked fish such as the mackerel fillets from Cley Smokehouse need little help with their wonderful flavour but for a more restaurant-style dish, here is a favourite recipe for a pressed pâté, married with the sweetness of apple in three different textures plus peppery leaves and a little bread crunch. Ideally to make the pâté, the pickled apple and the ketchup the day before. (Serves 6)

Mackerel pâté
Small handful flat leaf parsley
4 smoked mackerel fillets
125g unsalted butter, melted
1 lemon, zest and juice

Finely shred the parsley. Remove the skin and bones from the fillets and break up into flakes into a large bowl. Mix in the butter, parsley, zest and juice before seasoning to taste. Roll out a large double-layered sheet of clingfilm on a clean surface. Tip out the pâté, shape into a rough sausage shape before covering and wrapping up into a cylinder. Roll evenly and tie one end of the clingfilm sausage, give it a final shaping and knot the other end before refrigerating. Allow to set for at least 6 hours.

Apple 'ketchup'
2 large Granny Smith apples
300ml apple juice
50g caster sugar
Cider vinegar

Peel, core and finely slice the apples. Place in a heavy pan with the apple juice and sugar, cover and cook on a low heat until the apple is tender and starts to break down. Remove the pan from the heat and decant to a blender. Purée until very smooth and pass through a fine sieve. Season the purée with a little salt and vinegar to taste. Cool and refrigerate, where it will thicken.

Pickled apple
200ml cider vinegar
200ml water
200g caster sugar
2g salt
2 large Granny Smith apples

Place the first 4 ingredients into a pan and bring to a simmer, stirring occasionally to dissolve the sugar. Remove from the heat. Peel, core and cut the apples into your desired shape, I like balls cut with a melon baller but cubes may be easier. Add the apples to the liquor, cool and cover before leaving to pickle overnight in the fridge.

Sourdough wafers
1 sourdough loaf
Good rapeseed or olive oil

Pre-heat the oven to 160c. With a sharp bread knife, cut the loaf into very thin slices and place on baking trays. Brush with oil, season and bake for about 10 minutes until crisp and lightly golden.

To serve
2 large Granny Smith apples
Large handful mustard leaves
Good rapeseed or olive oil

30 minutes before serving, cut the pâté into portions and allow to warm out on the side. Place it onto plates. Drain and dry the pickled apples on a clean tea towel. Place a few of these and blobs of the ketchup around the pâté. With a corer, take the centres out of the apples and very finely slice into rings carefully with a knife or mandolin. These can be used as garnish or cut further into fine matchsticks. Take the sourdough wafers, snap into two and garnish around the apple. Lightly dress the leaves with oil and scatter around to finish.

Smoked ham terrine

We use one smoked and one unsmoked hock for this to give a lighter flavour but adapt to suit what you enjoy and what your local butcher can provide. Ours is pictured with a piccalilli purée and honey-soused vegetables. (Serves 4+)

2 ham hocks
1 carrot, chopped
2 celery sticks, chopped
1 leek, chopped
4 sprigs thyme
5 black peppercorns
1 bay leaf
1 shallot, finely chopped
1 tsp wholegrain mustard
Handful of parsley leaves, shredded
1 tsp very tiny capers

Place the ham hocks into a large pan, covered with water. Bring to a simmer for a few minutes. Strain and set the hocks aside to cool. Return to the pan and cover in water, adding the carrot, celery, leek, thyme, peppercorns and bay leaf. Bring to the boil and simmer until tender, approx. 3-4 hours.

Remove the hocks with tongs and allow to cool while boiling down the cooking liquor. Once reduced by half, set aside and cool. Remove the meat from the bones. Mix the shallot, mustard, parsley and capers through the meat. Add enough liquor to moisten the meat and place in a suitable terrine or mould, double-lined with clingfilm. Lay another double film layer on top, plus a board and heavy weights. Chill for at least 3 hours to set.

Plaice cooked on the bone with King's Lynn brown shrimp butter

At The Bell, we serve this dish with simple coastal vegetables such as sea beet, purslane and aster, blanched al dente in equal quantities of butter and water, plus some simple new potatoes. Samphire works well too. (Serves 4)

4 whole small plaice, gutted and skinned
2 lemons, halved
Unsalted butter
50g brown shrimps, shelled
50g very tiny capers

Pre-heat the oven to 200c. Line a roasting tray with greaseproof paper and lay on the plaice. Squeeze over some lemon juice and place a few small knobs of butter on each, plus generous seasoning to taste.

Bake for 8-10 minutes until just cooked at their thickest part. Meanwhile make the shrimp butter, by heating 100g of butter over a high heat, stirring until it foams, squeeze in juice of half a lemon and fold in the shrimps and capers. Heat through and serve with the fish once it is cooked and just flaking.

Peach melba, vanilla ice cream, raspberries, crisp meringue

Escoffier's classic recipe is a popular one with our diners, invented at The Savoy in honour of Australian soprano, Dame Nellie Melba. (Serves 6+)

2 large free range egg whites
100g caster sugar
1 litre hot water
300g caster sugar
1 vanilla pod, seeds scraped
4-6 peaches, halved and stoned
40g plain flour
35g ground almonds
35g unsalted butter, chilled
35g caster sugar
Good vanilla ice cream
Fresh raspberries

The day before, pre-heat the oven to 70c. Whisk the whites to firm peaks, gradually adding 100g sugar until a stiff meringue. Spread onto a parchment-lined baking tray and bake, door ajar, overnight or completely dried.

Dissolve and simmer the 300g sugar, vanilla seeds, pod and water together. Add the peaches and gently poach until tender and the skins loosen. Cool and chill in the syrup.

Pre-heat the oven to 160c. Rub together the flour, almonds and butter to rough crumbs and fold in the sugar. Bake the crumble in a shallow roasting tin, stirring around regularly until golden, about 30 minutes.

Place crumble in centre of plates, top with a peach half, an ice cream quenelle, raspberries and broken meringue.

DREAM DINNER?

Christmas Day with the family, my wife Hayley hosting and me doing all the cooking. Happiest times are always at home!

CHILDHOOD AMBITIONS?

I always wanted to be a chef, right from an early age. I have no idea why. I used to like watching the cookery programmes on television – Gordon Ramsay's *Boiling Point* was a favourite. I think back then the chefs were almost like an underground group. They were becoming cool, it was almost subversive in a strange way.

RECENTLY DISCOVERED TECHNIQUE?

Baking white chocolate in the oven was quite a revelation! Stick it in the oven at 150c, first it goes all lumpy and then it goes smooth again. The sugar caramelises and becomes like a Caramac bar.

BIGGEST EXTRAVAGANCE AS A CHEF?

This is one I haven't realised yet, I'd love to have a set of knives called The Blades of the Gods. They come from Bali and cost a small fortune!

COOK'S CHEAT OR TIP?

To pick sea buckthorn, which can be squishy and fiddly, I take a pair of clippers and cut off sprigs, which I freeze whole and then scrape off the frozen berries with a fork. It's prickly stuff though, so another tip is 'wear gloves'!

SIMON ON HIS...

ULTIMATE DINING DESTINATION?

Later this year I want to go to Sweden's top restaurant Faviken in the middle of nowhere. It is in the San Pellegrino *World's 50 Best Restaurants* list, regularly in the top 10. Just about everything is grown, foraged or produced there. Everything is harvested and preserved in the summer months, to be served in the winter.

FAVOURITE LOCAL FOODIE PLACE?

Thursday in Fakenham is market day and I always stop at Christie's Cheese. He makes his own pâtés and cheeses. My favourite place to eat is Titchwell Manor, although I enjoy anywhere along that stretch of coast. It is the same with going out for a drink – it is about the views as much as anything.

MUSIC TO COOK TO?

I love classic rock, stuff from the Rolling Stones, The Who, Led Zeppelin. There is a great place in Holt, The Vinyl Vault, where I buy 'proper records', which I love, I've got quite a collection!

SIGNATURE DISHES

Starters

Cured sea trout 'gin and tonic', preserved lemon, cucumber, borage

Confit pork belly scrumpet, baked apple purée, candied walnuts, mustard frills

Heritage tomato salad, Fielding Cottage goats' curd, wild fennel

Mains

Fillet of wild bass, confit tomato, caramelised onion & anchovy tart, lemon balm

Roast rack of suckling pig, crispy bubble & squeak, baked apple purée, crackling

Hay-baked cauliflower, cauliflower cheese purée, savoury hazelnut streusel, dressed cauliflower leaves

Puddings

Strawberries and cream arctic roll, shortbread crumb, clotted cream ice cream

Brown sugar baked Norfolk apple, crumble biscuit, salt caramel, crumble ice cream

Chocolate and ale cake, candied peanuts, malt ice cream

QUICK SNACK OR MIDNIGHT FEAST?

It's a bit odd but because I finish so late, I don't feel like eating. To relax, I like to take a cold beer with me into the shower after work.

FOODIE NOSTALIGA?

The smell of roast chicken immediately takes me back to Sunday dinner. I think it is the gravy – made from the fat of the chicken.

It takes all sorts

It should be mandatory for pubs to have small tubs of Liquorice Allsorts scattered around the tables. The sweets, a throwback to the seventies, immediately send out a message that this is a pub that doesn't stand on ceremony; instead, it's a place where locals and visitors alike can relax over a drink and plate of tapas in the bar, or enjoy a three-course foodie treat.

"We are religious about keeping some tables free for people who just want a drink," says Berni. "It is important that we are a pub for the local community as much as the visitors. We are not about fine dining, just fine food and drink."

Wiveton is an idyllic village, only one mile inland from the bustling coastal village of Blakeney, with a village green and magnificent local church, surrounded by wood-lined green fields. It is also a place steeped in local history. "Two centuries ago, Wiveton used to be a port," says Berni Moritt, who owns The Bell with his partner Sandy Butcher. He indicates a picture on the wall, dating back to the 18th century, showing large boats docked at the quay, with the church in the background. As we chat about the pub's past, two women come through the door. An animated conversation later, Berni returns. "Her great grandfather was the publican here at the turn of the 20th century," he says. "She is tracing her roots."

Today, The Bell is a charming, award-winning pub, with six stylish, comfortable rooms – three in the pub, three in adjacent flint cottages. The pub itself is rustic chic in look: think pale shades of Farrow and Ball, exposed timber beams and a natural, mainly wood-rich interior. It's a place that fits effortlessly into its coastal location, a draw for the many tourists, walkers, locals and dogs that enjoy this tranquil corner of Norfolk.

The Wiveton Bell
Blakeney Road, Wiveton, Holt NR25 7TL
W: www.wivetonbell.co.uk
T: 01263 740101
E: wivetonbell@me.com
f /Wivetonbell
🐦 @wivetonbell
📷 /chef_big_si

Accolades: AA One Rosette; AA Four Gold Stars (accommodation); Inspector's Favourite, *Michelin Eating Out in Pubs Guide* 2016; Reader's Restaurant – East of England, *Good Food Guide* 2011; 'Best Use of Norfolk Produce', Aylsham Show *Food & Drink Awards* 2013; '50 Best Gastropubs' list 2013, *The Independent*; *Sawday's*; *Hardens*; *Inn Places*

Covers: 70, plus large garden eating area

Cost: carte average £27; wine from £15.95; pint from £3.80

Open: All year (closed Christmas Day). L 12-2.15; D 6-9; Sun all day food, noon - 8.15

Details: food served in dining room or bar; tables reserved for drinking; alfresco dining; six luxury double rooms with breakfast hamper from Blakeney Deli and complimentary bottle of prosecco on arrival; wheelchair access; well-behaved dogs welcome; parking a short walk away

Glory days

Mark Sayers elevates the humble spud,
lavishing care and creativity on an ingredient
too often seen as an 'optional extra'.

THE SARACEN'S HEAD MARK SAYERS

Step inside The Saracen's Head and you'll soon discover that you are sharing in a daily celebration of Norfolk produce. A map of 'Our Local Larder' in the entrance hall of this rural inn shows the sheer variety of ingredients grown, caught, gathered on the doorstep. Eels caught at Heacham and smoked at Brancaster jostle for place with cheese from Wighton and Little Barningham, flour from Letheringsett and shiitake mushrooms from Little London.

"It's what we're all about here," says head chef Mark Sayers, "it's what we do, use everything we can that's in season and close-by."

The local catch dictates what fish is on the day's menu: it might be sea bass or mackerel caught in the waters off Mundesley, crabs and lobsters landed at Overstrand or fresh mussels from Brancaster. Meat is supplied by traditional butcher, Crawford White of G F White in nearby Aylsham, and fruit and vegetables come from farms, gardens, orchards and hedgerows on the doorstep.

"There's a fruit farm nearby that grows five varieties of plum," says Mark, "so we'll serve a terrine with plum chutney, pork with roast plums, a plum and almond tart. Rhubarb is another great local ingredient: when it's plentiful, I might make a rhubarb and apple chutney, bake salmon with rhubarb, white wine, parsley and cream – the tartness of the rhubarb cuts through the oiliness of the salmon – or a rhubarb and apple crumble. That is Saracen's, basically."

Even potatoes are sourced with care, Mark buying from Tony Bambridge who grows 16 varieties in the sandy loam soils of Wood Farm in Marsham, a few miles south of The Saracen's Head.

"The humble potato is an extraordinary and remarkable vegetable," says Tony. "Compared with other crops, it comes on a long journey before reaching the dinner table: from sprout to mini-tuber, pre-basic seed takes six to nine years of successive planting, harvesting and storing to develop. Only then is it ready to harvest."

Tony delivers potatoes to Mark himself. It's a good opportunity to "imbibe some ale" and catch up with locals, many of whom are farmers or suppliers of other produce to the inn. Tony's wife, Emily, supplies beef from her herd of Lincoln Red cattle, grazed on water meadows at nearby Blickling. Their horseradish also appears on The Saracen's Head menu (now only grown on a small scale for artisan condiment manufacturers, they used to cultivate it in large quantities for Colman's).

NORFOLK TABLE

In the tiny kitchen, where at most two can work at once, Mark is preparing dauphinoise potatoes, enhanced with subtly-flavoured wild garlic gathered from the local woods by neighbour – and keen forager – Mary Wilcox.

Mark builds up and seasons layers of sliced potatoes, onions and shredded wild garlic before pouring in double cream, fresh from Pointens Dairy in nearby Stody and baking it to a golden, bubbling unctuousness. A favourite from Mark's classical English and French training, the dish is a great partner for white and red meats.

"Potatoes may be a staple food but there's far more to them than that: they are an integral part of a dish. So we might have Pink Fir Apple for a summer salad, Charlotte boiled and sautéed with a sprinkling of sea salt with Tony's beef, and Desirée for a smooth and tasty mash with herb-crusted local cod or braised pork belly in winter. As we use them all the time, it's important to have different varieties and to use them in a variety of ways."

At home it's Mark's wife, Fiona, who does the cooking. A homely fish pie might be packed with cod, smoked haddock, salmon and prawns from the local fishmonger, and of course, locally grown potatoes. "In winter, mashed potato is one of those wonderful comfort foods," says Mark, "and new potatoes straight from the garden with fresh mint, a barbecue and a glass of rosé is an essential taste of summer, isn't it!"

Mark grew up in Blakeney, the son of a fisherman who went on to become a watercolour artist and whose book, *Once Upon a Tide*, documents and illustrates the creeks, inlets and salt marshes that formed Mark's early landscape. Mark's was a childhood of swimming, mackerel fishing, sailing and living in the Norfolk countryside; and as an adult becoming a chef gave him a way to travel and see more of the world. He completed an apprenticeship at Gasches in Weybourne – then the finest restaurant in Norfolk, he says – and took off, working in London, Scotland, Australia and America before finally returning to Norfolk in order, he says, to give his son, Jake, a childhood like his own. While Mark and Fiona now live just two fields from The Saracen's Head, Jake is now 22 and working in New Zealand.

"Although we're in the middle of nowhere, it's busy here as the food is so good and there's a great atmosphere. In a bigger kitchen my work would be more organisational, but I love cooking, using great products from really enthusiastic local producers. What more can I ask for?"

Roast cannon of Wolterton lamb, wild garlic dauphinoise potatoes, crushed peas and mint, madeira jus

A delicious and popular dish of simple flavours and textures to showcase great Norfolk potatoes and local lamb reared on the nearby estate parkland. Prepare the potatoes, the peas and the sauce at the same time before cooking the lamb. You can either keep them warm, covered somewhere hot or allow them to cool and refrigerate ahead of time, before reheating. (Serves 4)

Potato dauphinoise
2 large potatoes (we use Maris Piper)
2 tbsp wild garlic leaves, chopped
400ml double cream

188

Pre-heat the oven to 170c. Peel and slice the potatoes very thinly, layer in an ovenproof dish, adding garlic and seasoning in between. Warm the cream and pour all over the top surface. Bake for 170c until tender and golden. Score through with a knife into portions.

Madeira sauce
1 onion, chopped
Good rapeseed oil
1 bay leaf
1 garlic clove
100ml rich Madeira
300ml lamb stock
300ml chicken stock

Cook the onion, bay leaf and garlic in a hot sauté pan with a drizzle of oil over a low-medium heat, stirring until softened and lightly golden. Remove from the hob, add the madeira, return to a medium heat and bring to a simmer. Add the two stocks, allow to boil well and reduce by two-thirds. Remove from heat before sieving and keep warm.

Pea purée
300g peas or petits pois, shelled or defrosted
Three large mint sprigs, leaves only

Blanch the peas with the mint in boiling water until tender. Drain and carefully blend in a food processor until a thick purée. Add some butter if particularly stodgy.

To serve
600g lamb loin in four portions
1 tbsp thyme and rosemary, chopped

Pre-heat the oven to 200c. Ensure the potato, peas and sauce will be piping hot by reheating as required. Meanwhile lightly oil and season the lamb before rolling in the herbs. Take a very hot ovenproof sauté pan, add a drizzle of oil, seal the lamb on each side and then bake for 10 minutes. Remove to somewhere warm and allow to rest for 5 minutes. Carve the lamb and plate up with the potatoes, peas and sauce.

Potato and asparagus terrine

This very flexible starter is made the day before for easy entertaining. Best served warm with simple dressed leaves. (Serves 6+)

**4-8 large waxy potatoes,
6-8 fat asparagus spears
250g local brie cheese
White truffle oil (optional)
Unsalted butter, melted**

Pre heat your oven to 180C. With a mandolin or very sharp knife, carefully slice the peeled potatoes very thinly, followed by the asparagus lengthways. Cut the brie into thin slices.

Grease a terrine mould or loaf tin liberally with melted butter. Place two layers of potato in the bottom and brush with melted butter and season lightly, adding a few drops of truffle oil (if used). Next add a layer of asparagus, then a layer of brie. Repeat as before, layering and

seasoning until the mould is full or all used up, ensuring you finish with potato at the top. Brush with butter and cover well with loose foil.

Bake for approx 45-60 minutes until a thin knife passes through the centre easily. Remove from the oven and allow to cool, before transferring into the fridge. Press down with a clingfilmed board to fit and a heavy weight on top and then chill overnight.

Carefully cut into slices, 1cm wide if eaten cold or 2cm thick to reheat it, pan-fried gently on each side in a little hot oil until heated through in the centre.

Grilled sea trout, broad bean, baby tomato, basil compôte, fennel oil

Farmed rainbow or wild brown trout also works well or even salmon fillets. Start cooking the fish at the same time as the compôte. Don't overcook the fish, it just needs to start flaking at its thickest. (Serves 4)

**100ml olive oil
150g fennel
300g broad beans
4 portions of sea trout fillet
Unsalted butter
1 tbsp shallot, finely chopped
Rapeseed oil
200g ripe baby tomatoes
2 tbsp basil leaves, shredded**

Liquidise the fennel with the olive oil and set aside. Blanch the broad beans in boiling water until just tender, drain and cool under a cold running tap.

Pre-heat the grill. Place trout fillets on an oiled baking tray, season each and add a small knob of butter on top before

grilling for 5-6 minutes until just cooked through and browning.

Meanwhile for the compôte, add the shallots and a little rapeseed oil into a hot lidded deep sauté pan and soften over a low heat, stirring regularly. Next add in tomatoes and the beans, cooking for a few minutes until the tomatoes start to collapse.Fold through basil and remove from heat. Leave to sit covered for a few minutes. Spoon the compôte in the middle of warm plates, placing the trout on top and drizzle the fennel oil around.

Lemon tart

This simple classic is delicious paired with local soft fruits such as pink rhubarb or berries. Bake the pastry as you make the filling. (Serves 6+)

250g plain flour
125g unsalted butter, cubed
90g caster sugar
1 egg
7 whole eggs
2 egg yolks
400g caster sugar
5 lemons, juice only
250ml double cream

In a food processor, pulse the flour and butter into breadcrumbs. Add the sugar, egg and 1 tablespoon of cold water and just bring together into a dough. Remove and wrap in clingfilm, before refrigerating for 30 minutes.

Pre-heat the oven to 175c. Roll out the pastry and line an approx. 23cm tart tin. Blind-bake with parchment and baking beans for 12-15 minutes. Remove the parchment and beans carefully, reduce temperature to 160c and continue to bake until lightly golden and crisp, about 10 minutes. Then turn your oven down to 120c.

As the pastry bakes, in a food mixer, make the filling by whisking the whole eggs and yolks with the sugar until incorporated, followed by the lemon juice and then the cream. Mix until well-combined.

Pour the filling into the hot pastry case and bake for 30 minutes or until just set. Remove and serve at room temperature.

BEST DISH EVER EATEN?

Fish soup and a seafood platter at a beach restaurant at Collioure near Perpignan with Fiona and my young son, Jake. For six or seven years we used to stay at a friend's house a bit inland from Collioure which is a lovely little village with a harbour – I used to look forward to that trip so much!

WELL-THUMBED COOKBOOK?

Anything by Tom Kerridge. You can feel his passion, and he's in the Slow Food movement too. Paul Gayler's *Sauce* book, and his *A Passion for Cheese* are both brilliant too. They're chefs' chefs.

A 'TAKE FIVE' RECIPE?

Linguine, Cromer crab, fresh chilli, lemon, flat parsley. Chop some parsley and deseeded chilli, then zest and juice the lemon. Mix in the crab, cooked pasta, some olive oil and seasoning. Simple and delicious!

SIGNATURE DISHES

Starters

Pigeon & pork terrine, toasted sourdough, rhubarb & apple chutney

Warm pea, mint, ricotta cake, baby tomato, basil compôte

Cromer crab, pink grapefruit salad, Norfolk Dapple crisps

Mains

Roast rabbit saddle, carrot mousse, fondant potato, tarragon jus

Grilled wild sea bass, marsh samphire, lemon butter sauce

Slow roast belly pork, mashed potato, apple fritter and calvados jus.

Puddings

Lavender flower pannacotta, blueberry compôte and vanilla biscuit

Local raspberry & white chocolate cheesecake

Almond and lemon polenta cake, roast plums, cinnamon ice cream

MARK ON HIS...

IF NOT A CHEF, WHAT WOULD YOU HAVE BEEN?

I was going to be a professional footballer. I played for Norfolk, and was scouted for some trials as a teenager, but by the time I left school I was a bit too small. As a goalkeeper that was a bit of problem! I went on to grow to 6'1"... maybe I should have tried to get trialled again... maybe it was a bit of a dream. I play five- or six-a-side football on a Tuesday night, which is a fun way to keep fit.

ULTIMATE DINING DESTINATION?

The French Laundry in the Napa Valley, California. Thomas Keller's way of cooking is fantastic, and he grows so much of his own stuff. I'd love to go there!

INSPIRING NORFOLK VIEW?

From Blakeney, looking along the coast towards Wells' East Hills. I spent so much time round there playing, swimming, fishing, and later earning money: in winter we'd dig for lugworms for the fishermen, and in summer harvest samphire to sell to restaurants. That was my father instilling the values of hard work in us!

FOODIE NOSTALGIA?

My father had a boat at Stiffkey Freshers and we'd often go out fishing as a family, especially during the summer. We had some bricks and an old grate hidden in the gorse bushes on the side of the creek, and we'd come back, swim and then barbecue mackerel. There were only about six boats then, and we'd often be there on our own. There must be 36 now, and another 20 small sailing dinghies. North Norfolk has changed a lot from the '70s!

MUSIC WHILE YOU WORK?

BBC Radio 6 Music is on here all day and night. If you had to sum me up, my three passions are food, football and music. We might turn the music down a bit during service, but it's on all the time. I love it.

FAVOURITE TIME OF YEAR FOR FOOD?

I like every month. I love it when we start catching sea bass off the coast, lobster, then using all the salads and fresh tomatoes and courgettes through the summer, and then on to game, autumn fruits and winter vegetables.

A touch of Tuscany

The Saracen's Head was built as an inn on the Wolterton Estate for the Walpole family in 1806. George Stanley Repton, a pupil of John Nash, designed it in the Palladian style with perfectly symmetrical frontage and arched doorway, and followed the layout of a Tuscan farmstead, with house and barns set around a beautiful courtyard garden.

"It's unique and rustic," says Norfolk-born Tim Elwes, who took on The Saracen's Head in 2010 with his wife, Janie, having spent 12 years running a hotel in the French Alps. "Maybe one of the Walpoles had been on a 'grand tour' and wanted a Tuscan farmhouse. It may not be typical of Norfolk, but the building actually looks very at home in the surrounding countryside."

"Neither does the inn fit into a neat foodie category. It's difficult to pigeon-hole. We like to say to customers, look on the blackboard in the bar and you should know you're in Norfolk and exactly what month it is," Tim adds.

Despite being off the beaten track between Erpingham and Wolterton, walkers, cyclists, locals and visitors find their way, stopping for a pint of Woodforde's Wherry or one of the local micro-brews. Tim nearly always has Wherry on tap, it's brewed using Tony Bainbridge's malting barley. The original Woodforde's brewery was at the nearby Erpingham Arms.

Food is served in the radicchio-red parlour and the bar (both cosy with an open fire or wood-burning stove in cooler months) and come summer in the courtyard garden too. Wine is supplied by Adnams: "That works well," says Tim. "It means that customers can easily go away and buy another bottle of what they enjoyed with their meal here."

There are six recently-renovated bedrooms with views across the Norfolk countryside and out to the coast. Plans are afoot to develop the pretty red brick farm buildings around the courtyard into further accommodation.

The Saracen's Head
Wall Road, Wolterton,
Near Erpingham NR11 7LZ
W: www.saracenshead-norfolk.co.uk
T: 01263 768909
E: info@saracenshead-norfolk.co.uk
  /Saracens-Head-Norfolk
  @TheSaracensHead
  /SaracensHeadNorfolk

Accolades: winner 'Best Use of Norfolk Produce' & 'Overall Champion', 'Norfolk Hero Food & Drink Awards' 2014; Winner, 'Best Sporting Pub' – East of England, Countryside Alliance and *Country Life* Awards 2015; Four Star Inn, *VisitEngland*; *Sawday's*; *Good Pub Guide; Good Hotel Guide*

Covers: 40 inside; 25 outside in summer

Cost: carte average £31

Open: all week Apr-Oct L 12-2, D 6.30-8.30; summer L 12-2.30, D 6.30-9. Closed Sun eve, Mon Nov-Mar

Details: children's menu; 6 ensuite bedrooms; dogs welcome in back bar and with owners in bedrooms

In pastures green

Phil Milner may have travelled widely,
but his quest for wonderful local cheese leads
him just a few quiet miles down the road

194

SHUCK'S AT THE YURT PHIL MILNER

The sound of rain pelting down on canvas is a nostalgic one, the sort that takes you back, rosily-tinted, to 'summer' holidays in a field. The reality of frayed tempers and dreary-damp sandwiches blurs with time, fixing instead one of drowsily-warm, good times. Fast forward to June 2016. Rain is pelting down on canvas, but this time onto an oh-so-cool yurt at Drove Orchards, Thornham. A woodburner in the middle keeps the space cosy, there's a gentle hum of music and chatter. Customers pop in for coffee and cake, linger over lunch, or stay for dinner when candles and firelight gently illuminate the space. It's the stuff that (good) memories are made of.

"Cool, isn't it," Phil Milner says, happy to be settling in at his new workplace, Shuck's at the Yurt. It's a place that nails the zeitgeist, a relaxed, welcoming spot to enjoy tasty, fresh, food.

Manchester-born Phil has been cooking round these parts for twenty years, including at The Rose & Crown, Snettisham and The Orange Tree, Thornham. He's known for his dexterity with spices, a skill honed during travels in Asia and Australasia in 2000 that translates onto the Shuck's menu in the form of a Nepalese curry with coconut rice, beetroot and apple koshimbir, a tom yum broth with smoked eel, compressed watermelon and slow-cooked octopus, or a katsu chicken burger with kimchi. "I love Japanese flavours, miso broths, plenty of

lime and chilli – I really like healthy, punchy flavours." He reels off more favourite ingredients: yuzu, tonka beans, espelette pepper, buckwheat and quinoa.

A rump of hogget ("it's more flavoursome than lamb") is lifted with warm Moroccan flavours. He serves the meat, pink and butter-tender, with his take on zaalouk, a mix of smoky aubergine, peppers, red onion and chilli. It's a dish he and sous chef Jack Forman – the pair have worked together for nigh on ten years – came up with during one of their brainstorming cook-offs. "We have knockout, crazy, creative sessions," Phil says. "We build dishes round three core elements, have just two ingredients in the pans and finish dishes on the pass. It's important to have a menu that the two of us can manage."

Sometimes, one of those elements is Mrs Temple's Binham Blue cheese. "I've been using it for years," Phil says, crumbling pieces of the creamy blue-veined cheese into a light choux mix to make beignets. They spit in the fryer, emerging fluffy and golden-crisp, flecked green with basil. He arranges them alongside slices of pear, poached in Drove Orchards cider and a spoonful of 'boozy blackcurrants', steeped in Shuck's rum. The fruit is a sweet-sour foil to the richness of the beignets, while candied walnuts give texture.

Phil will happily cook with all of Mrs Temple's cheeses. He's keen to use the Melton mozzarella-style cheese and is already familiar with soft Copys Cloud and award-winning rind-washed Gurney's Gold. "I particularly like Binham Blue though. It's tasty, versatile, I might mix some into a leaf salad or stir it into a dressing. I really admire what Catherine and Stephen [Temple] have achieved. They've got cheesemaking down to a Mrs T!"

The cheeses are made a few winding miles inland, in the highly-specced dairy – once a cowshed – at Copys Green Farm, Wighton. It's a busy place, white-coated and hairnetted cheesemakers moving deftly among the racks of fresh-made cheeses. "At the moment we're revving up production of Binham Blue," Catherine explains. "It's our biggest summer seller but we can't stockpile it. Harder cheeses like Walsingham, a mature cheese ideal for a ploughman's and Wells Alpine last longer so we make those in the autumn and store them."

We walk briskly down the lane to meet some of the 100 or so pedigree Brown Swiss cows that make up the Temples' herd and live on the 500-acre family farm. Attractive shades of café au lait, mushroom and deeper cocoa-brown, they amble towards us through the lush water meadow grass, nuzzle, nudge, observe with their liquid-brown eyes. Catherine is clearly fond of them. "You're going all curly-haired

in the rain, aren't you," she murmurs affectionately, scratching one animal's forehead. Brown Swiss are easy to manage and thrive on grass though their feed is supplemented at times by farm-grown silage and protein-rich field beans and lucerne. "They look so healthy don't they, they look as if they absolutely enjoy life!" Catherine says. "They really put their heads down and mow the grass, and make milk with a high kappacaesin protein content, perfect for cheesemaking."

The Temples have won recognition for their environmental approach to farming. An anaerobic digester (AD) plant utilises all farm and dairy waste to produce methane gas which fuels a generator. "We are a carbon-neutral business," says Catherine whose husband is an agricultural engineer. "The AD plant keeps the dairy in hot water and electricity, we heat the cottages over the road, and sell any excess to the Grid. Oh, and it even warms the cows' water so that they can put all their energy into making milk!"

Binham Blue beignets, cider and saffron-poached pear, Waldorf salad and boozy blackcurrants

We serve this as a dish for 'afters', being part-dessert and part-cheese savoury, but it could also make a starter or light lunch if you have a sweet tooth. To make the syrup for the pears, dissolve equal quantities of caster sugar and water, before mixing with Drove Orchards cider and saffron. Macerate the blackcurrants in good rum, sprinkled with sugar to taste, for 48 hours ahead of time. (Serves 4)

Poached pears
570ml good dry cider
140ml sugar syrup
1 sachet saffron
2 firm pears, peeled, cored and halved

Simmer the cider, sugar syrup and saffron together, add the pears and gently cook for 15-20 minutes until just tender in the centre. Remove into a snug container, cover with the syrup and cool before chilling.

Cheese beignets
125ml full-fat milk
125ml water
100g unsalted butter
Pinch of salt
Pinch of sugar
50g Binham Blue cheese
150g plain flour
5 whole eggs
Small bunch of chives, chopped
50g Binham Blue cheese, crumbled into cm pieces

Add the first five ingredients into a wide saucepan and bring to a boil over a medium heat. Once melted together, whisk in the flour and beat with a flat-edge spatula while cooking. When it leaves the pan clean and is a single mass of shiny paste, remove to cool. Add to a food mixer and gently beat in the eggs one at a time. Fold in the chives and cheese and mix again. Transfer to a container.

Pre-heat a deep fat fryer with oil to 180c. Taking two dessertspoons, shape the mix into quenelles and fry until golden, for approx. 4-5 minutes. Drain and store between kitchen paper, keeping them warm as the remainder are cooked in turn.

Candied walnuts
75g caster sugar
75g water
50g walnuts

Simmer the sugar and water together in a small pan until it turns into a golden caramel. Add the walnuts and gently stir around until all are covered. Carefully lay apart on baking parchment to cool.

Blue cheese mayonnaise
50g Binham Blue cheese
50g mayonnaise

Mix the cheese and mayonnaise in a blender until smooth.

To serve
1 apple, cubed
2 celery sticks, stems finely sliced into moons plus leaves
8 black grapes, sliced into discs
Macerated blackcurrants
Binham Blue cheese, crumbled for garnish

Serve the beignets on top of the poached pear halves, garnished with the walnuts, mayonnaise, apple cubes, sliced celery and leaves, grapes and blackcurrants, finishing with more crumbled cheese.

198

Wild sea bass, peas, broad beans, wild garlic, marsh herbs

We serve this with a rich lobster cream, you can make a fair substitute with 3 parts tinned lobster bisque and 1 part double cream, reduced to a sauce texture. Foraged marsh herbs add a salty tang. (Serves 4)

150g fresh peas, podded and blanched
150g fresh broad beans, blanched and skinned
Small bunch of dill, chopped
Few leaves of wild garlic (optional)
Lemon halves
600-800g wild seabass, pin-boned and scaled
Local rapeseed oil
50g salted butter
Handful marsh herbs (optional)

Place the peas and beans into a bowl and fold in the dill and wild garlic. Squeeze over some lemon juice and seasoning to taste. Cut the bass into four tidy portions. Oil and season the fish before placing, skin-side down into a hot non-stick frying pan over a high heat and cook for 2-3 minutes. Turn the fillet over, add a knob of butter and squeeze of lemon juice to the pan, use a spoon to baste the top of the fish and cook for 1-2 minutes until flaking. To serve, place the fillets on a bed of the peas and beans, garnish with marsh herbs if used.

Roast hogget rump, lamb shoulder, haricot beans and basil

A rich but punchy early summer main course pictured here with zaalouk, a fine spiced Moroccan aubergine ratatouille. We braise the shoulder, studded with garlic and rosemary, along with celery, carrot, onion, bay leaves, fresh thyme and good stock, covered for 3-4 hours in a 180c oven. (Serves 4)

1 small lamb shoulder, slow-cooked and cooled
Small bunch of mint, chopped
1 hogget rump
Small bunch of basil, leaves only
50ml olive oil
200g tin haricot beans, rinsed
Wild fennel tops

Shred the shoulder meat well into a bowl, seasoning to taste, and mix in the mint. Shape meat on double clingfilm sheets into long sausages and roll up tightly. Knot the ends and refrigerate overnight. Pre-heat the oven to 180c. Oil and season the rump.

In a hot non-stick frying pan over a high heat, seal skin-side down until browned on all sides. Bake for 10 minutes, remove and leave to rest somewhere hot for 5-10 minutes.

Meanwhile cut the shoulder rolls into 3cm barrels. Remove the clingfilm and fry on both sides in the hot pan over a high heat until golden and crispy. Purée the basil and oil together in a blender. Warm the beans in the basil oil.

Serve the shoulder and carved rump, garnished with the beans and fennel.

Orange sponge, Drove Orchards rhubarb

We serve this as a grander dessert alongside lemongrass pannacotta, a rhubarb ripple-honeycomb ice cream, orange zest and poached rhubarb. (Serves 6)

120g butter
120g caster sugar
120g eggs, beaten
with 15ml milk
135g self-raising flour
2 oranges, zest and juice
6 sticks of rhubarb,
roughly-chopped
1 orange zest, only
1 thumb of stem ginger,
peeled and finely chopped
Caster sugar
1 tbsp water

Pre-heat the oven to 170c. For the cake, cream the butter and 120g sugar in a mixer until light and fluffy, before adding in the egg mixture slowly. Fold in the flour and zest of 2 oranges. Line a loaf tin and scrape in the mixture and bake for 45 minutes. Meanwhile measure the volume of the orange juice and boil with an equal volume of sugar, in a heavy saucepan, stirring and reducing to a syrup. Once baked and a skewer comes out clean from the centre, remove the cake. As it cools, prick the surface and sides with the skewer and brush generously all over with the syrup.

For the purée, simmer the rhubarb until tender with the remaining orange zest, ginger, sugar to taste and water. Remove, cool and blend smooth. Serve the cake, broken into inch-sized pieces, on top of the rhubarb purée.

WHERE ARE YOU HAPPIEST?

I love this place, especially when Beth and the kids come down at the weekends. They love playing round Drove Orchards and Gracie even helps out a bit. But I always look forward to our October holiday too. We generally go to Gran Canaria and have great food. Oh and guaranteed sunshine!

WELL-THUMBED COOKBOOKS?

Anything by Gary Rhodes! I'll flick through every so often to refresh ideas – I like that old-school cooking, simple food, great taste. I love the flavours in Yotam Ottolenghi's recipes, and Louisiana chef Shaun Brock's books – *Heritage* in particular – for his healthy beans and pulses recipes.

MUSIC TO COOK TO?

Generally my choice in the kitchen! If we're busy and need a boost, it'll be Rage Against the Machine or Prodigy; if we need to chill after service maybe Gomez.

RECENT FOODIE DISCOVERIES?

More 'clean' foods like buckwheat, a great gluten-free option from the rhubarb family, which can be used hot or cold in a variety of dishes.

PHIL ON HIS...

WHO IS OR WAS YOUR MENTOR?

A chap called Mike Holloway was head chef when my parents had The Golden Lion Hotel in Hunstanton. He got me into cooking aged 14 and used to tell me my prawn cocktail was better than the ones the experienced chefs were making – that made me want to carry on!

UNFULFILLED AMBITIONS?

I wanted to be a TV or movie actor! I was going to go to drama school then somehow ended up in this business! Not sure how that happened...

LUCKY DAY OFF?

I'd hire a boat on the Broads with my wife Beth and our kids Gracie who's 12, and Reuben, 8. We'll go from Wroxham to Stalham, have a picnic and a nice glass of wine and generally chill.

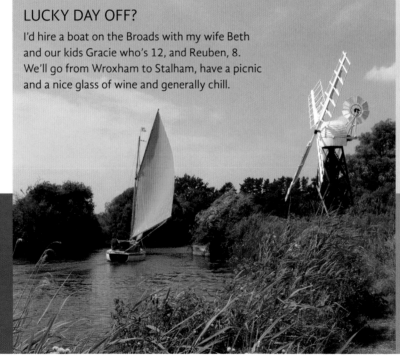

SIGNATURE DISHES

Starters

Chicken and egg: chicken & mushroom terrine, organic cider vinegar-pickled egg, textures of sweetcorn

Sack of spuds: Norfolk Peer salt-baked potatoes, wild garlic aioli, red mojo sauce

Black treacle & beetroot-cured organic sea trout, pear cider jelly, meat radish, summer kale

Mains

Shuck's fish stew: fennel, chilli, chickpeas, tomato, giant garlic king prawn, crusty bread

Blythburgh pork belly, Mrs Temple's reblochon tartiflette, salted caramel apple sauce, crackling

Ghurka curry: tandoori buttermilk chicken on the bone, toasted coconut rice, beetroot & apple koshimbir, poppadum

Puddings

Sticky toffee pudding: date purée, caramelised banana, butterscotch sauce, vanilla ice cream

Shuck's jar: Sharrington strawberries, tonka bean & elderflower cheesecake, ginger crumb

Death by chocolate: chocolate brownie, chocolate delice, salted caramel ice cream, chocolate soil

FAVOURITE LOCAL FOODIE PLACES?

We love Market Bistro in King's Lynn, eat there when we can, and you can't beat The White Horse at Brancaster Staithe for a tranquil setting with amazing views.

202

Good dog

Loyal black dog, or sinister, snarling hound...? For Phil and Beth Milner, Black Shuck – the ghostly dog that supposedly roams the Norfolk coast – is the former, a kindly spirit, and a symbol the couple have happily adopted for their new restaurant, Shuck's at the Yurt in Thornham.

The couple saw beyond initial drawbacks – the six-ring electric hob had only one functioning burner – to see a place with immense potential. "We sorted the kitchen, put the bar in and Beth has done the whole shabby-chic look brilliantly," says Phil. Tables are ranged round the central woodburner; comfy leather sofas are covered in throws and colourful cushions, a garland of flowers is wound round the internal frame.

The Milners are already planning a second kitchen to serve rustic pizzas and want to extend the outside space to include a firepit, perfect for slow-cooking lamb kleftiko or marinated Drove vegetables. Phil would also love an open-air cinema with a converted old Cadillac offering the best seat in the house.

He'd also like to take the Shuck's concept to the orchards, just a step away. "We had a wonderful experience a few years ago at Jimbaran Bay in Bali. It was a simple beach bar where they cooked the day's catch on an open fire. You'd just pick up a plastic chair and table, push it into the sand and eat with the sound of the waves and this amazing view. It would be so cool to do that here among the beautiful setting of the orchards – on nice days!"

Shuck's is located at Drove Orchards, an appealing collection of retail and foodie outlets adjacent to 40 acres of soft fruit and apple trees (there's pick-your-own in season) and a kitchen garden. It goes without saying that Phil is excited to have that on his doorstep.

Shuck's at the Yurt
Drove Orchards, Thornham PE36 6LS
W: www.shucksattheyurt.co.uk
T: 01485 525889
E: contact@shucksattheyurt.com

f /shucks

🐦 @shucksattheyurt

📷 /shucksattheyurt

Covers: 65-70 inside; 60+ outside

Cost: carte average £25; wine from £16.50; pint from £4.75

Open: all day, daily 10-9; B from 8.30 (Sat-Sun). Hours extended in summer months

Details: private parties possible; children's menu, toys and highchairs; Drove Orchards shops and pick-your-own in season; glamping; wheelchair accessible; dogs welcome; parking

The stuff of dreams

Warmly-spiced, deeply-flavourful Marsh Pig
charcuterie adds a tasty dimension to the Roots
menu and the food of talented head chef,
Gareth Crimmins

Three acres given over to wildflower meadows, beehives, an outdoor pizza oven, an amazingly-organised allotment and a recently-built gin palace were enough to send chef Gareth Crimmins and his boss Claire Yaxley into paroxysms of delight. But it was when they entered the charcuterie workshop that Gareth seriously looked as if he was about to weep.

"You are living the life I dream of," was all Claire could say as she took in the giant, gleaming mixing bowls full of spices, the boxes of salami ready for market and the stacks of meat at various stages of the curing process. Her chef in the meantime was gazing at the maturation chamber where the salamis were hanging, the meat gathering the white layer that signifies the curing process is reaching completion.

This may have been the first time that Jackie Kennedy, the owner and producer behind Marsh Pig charcuterie, and Gareth, head chef at Roots of Norwich, had met, but there was an instant chemistry between them, due to a mutual love and understanding of great produce.

"All the meat we use is free-range," says Jackie, repeating the mantra that has underpinned her ethos at Marsh Pig since she first decided to go into charcuterie production four years ago. "Too many people claim their produce is free-range but what they mean is that the animals spent some of their lives outdoors, eating natural food. We source our meat from truly free-range farmers, their animals haven't ever seen the inside of a shed."

Gareth and Claire nod in agreement. Claire, who returned to Roots as sole owner in May 2016 comes from a farming background: for many years she owned hundreds of chickens and sold the eggs and meat. "I have brought a farmer's philosophy to Roots," she says. "I wanted to open somewhere that really shouts about Norfolk and the county's producers."

Just as the relationship between Jackie and Gareth is new, so too is the relationship between Gareth and Claire. "He is passionate, enthusiastic, hungry for success," Claire says. "I sometimes have to rein his creativity in a little! I want Roots to serve uncomplicated, delicious food, that's beautifully presented and sourced locally wherever possible."

For Gareth, this is also a return trip. He had been head chef at Roots under the previous owners but had left before Claire returned. Such was his love of the restaurant and its ethos that once he heard Claire was back, he asked to be considered for his old position. Claire had no doubts: Gareth's first appointment was the Radisson Blu Cardiff, before moving to Marlow to work with acclaimed chef Adam Simmonds at Danesfield House hotel. A position at Barnham Broom Hotel and Golf Club brought him to Norfolk and just a few months later he joined Roots as head chef, working for Claire and her previous partner in the restaurant's earlier incarnation.

In the workshop, Gareth is busy investigating the charcuterie further. He tries a piece of chilli beef jerky, then cuts a piece of chorizo, smelling the spices released with obvious appreciation. "This is such great charcuterie. You could put a whole selection of cured meats in front of me and I would always pick Marsh Pig." Jackie, herself a Cordon Bleu-trained chef, explains the chorizo is oak-smoked to a traditional recipe and is Gareth's starring ingredient for his showcase chicken dish. It is one of the latest additions to the Marsh Pig range. "We changed our chorizo recipe slightly to reflect the feedback we had received from chefs," Jackie explains. "They said they wanted a little less heat and a little more fat. What we have produced is perfect for chefs to cook with but can still be eaten as part of a charcuterie board."

As Jackie and Gareth chat about food production, the conversation reflects their personalities. An ebullient character, Jackie will joke about everything except food – at that point it becomes deadly serious. Gareth has the same approach: he chats lightly about moving house, the baby that he and his girlfriend are expecting at any time, the trials of catching a rural bus, but when talk turns to matters foodie, there is no doubting his ambition to join the culinary elite.

Later, back in the kitchen, Gareth's precise, classical training is evident as he immerses himself in preparing his signature dish. He cuts the charcuterie into equal squares ready to be flash-fried before sitting the pieces on the chicken; later he makes minute adjustments to the presentation, totally focused as he places a fragile egg yolk precisely on the plate. Happy with the dish, he reflects again on the ingredients he's used. "My favourite of Jackie's products is the bresaola, but the spices in these chorizos, they just add so much to the dish. The set-up at Marsh Pig is brilliant and their charcuterie is like nothing I have ever tasted. It's people like Jackie who really get what food is about."

Pan-fried chicken thighs, Marsh Pig chorizo, wild mushrooms, spinach, confit egg yolk

A simple sauté of free range chicken in a creamy rich reduction, made more indulgent with a slow-poached egg yolk, contrasts with the spice and texture of the cured paprika sausage. Confiting an egg at home is not realistic, a fair substitute would be poaching the eggs but removing two-thirds of the white before adding to the swirling water. Have the eggs ready to coincide with the other elements before serving (Serves 4)

Chicken thighs
8 boned chicken thighs, skin-on
1 garlic clove
1 thyme sprig
Unsalted butter

Generously sprinkle salt on the meat-side of the chicken and leave to cure for 1 hour in the fridge. Rinse off and lay out tucked inside a clean tea towel to dry.

In a hot heavy sauté pan, heat 1 tablespoon of butter until foaming over a high heat, add the garlic and thyme, then the seasoned thighs skin-side down, cooking for 4 minutes or until golden-brown. Turn over and continue cooking for a further few minutes until cooked-through, basting the skin to crisp up.

Chorizo cream
Local rapeseed oil
1 large onion, finely-sliced
1 garlic clove, crushed
200g chorizo, peeled and cut into 1cm cubes
500g dark chicken stock
500g double cream

In a hot heavy sauté pan, add a drizzle of oil over a high heat and fry the onions, garlic and chorizo until the sausage is browned and starting to char slightly. Add the stock and scrape to deglaze the pan, allowing to reduce in volume by half. Add the cream and continue to reduce to a sauce, which coats the back of a spoon well. Strain through a fine sieve into a jug and season to taste. Keep warm.

Garnishes
100g chorizo, peeled and cut into 1cm dice
300g wild mushrooms, cleaned and in bite-size pieces
100g baby spinach leaves, washed

Fry the chorizo in a hot heavy sauté pan with a thin layer of oil over a low-medium heat until the oil turns deep red. Turn up to hot and add the mushrooms, frying them while stirring for a few minutes. Turn off the heat, stir in the spinach along with seasoning to taste. Allow to wilt, covered for a few minutes, tossing around with tongs occasionally.

To serve
Prepare 4 cooked egg yolks, poached or confit, and keep warm while you finish the dish.

To serve, trim the chicken into neat pieces and place into hot bowls, scattered with the garnishes, a yolk on top and the sauce spooned around.

Dill and Norfolk gin-cured salmon

A delicious alternative to classic smoked salmon, we serve this with pickled and charred cucumbers, a dill mayonnaise and a rose powder for colour and perfume. (Serves 4)

350g thick salmon fillet, skinless
25g sugar
25g table salt
3 juniper berries, crushed
50ml Norfolk gin
1 bunch of dill
Local Dijon-style mustard

Prepare the curing mix by mixing sugar, salt, juniper berries and gin together. Finely chop up half of the dill and fold through the mix. Take a snug container to fit the salmon, add a third of the mix then lay in the fish before pouring in the remainder. Cover securely and chill to cure for at least 12 hours. Once the salmon has firmed up, remove from the cure and rinse in cold water before drying well. Slice into 4 even portions and brush one side with Dijon mustard. Finely chop the remaining dill and lay on a plate, firmly pressing the fish, mustard-side down, to create a herb crust.

Norfolk oxtail bonbons

One of our most popular main courses with a gingered carrot purée, pak choi, mooli radish, cashews and Asian pickles. (Serves 4+)

1kg Norfolk oxtail on the bone, trimmed into chunks
50g hoisin sauce
1 thumb-size piece of root ginger, peeled and sliced
2 garlic cloves, peeled and crushed
1 tbsp Chinese five spice
Good beef stock
1tsp red wine vinegar
25g pickled chillies, chopped
10g coriander leaves, shredded
5g sesame seeds, toasted
Plain flour
3 beaten eggs
White breadcrumbs

Pre-heat the oven to 130c. Brown the oxtail in a hot frying pan all-over. Transfer to a snug deep roasting tin with the hoisin, ginger, garlic and five spice plus sufficient stock to cover. Seal with double tin foil and bake for 4-5 hours until flaking off the bone. Remove and allow to cool. Pour the liquor into a saucepan and reduce to a thick sauce. Flake up, removing any bones, fat or skin. Mix in the vinegar, chilli, coriander and sesame seeds. Press into a 1 inch layer in a clingfilmed container, cover and refrigerate until set. Cut into inch cubes and toss separately in flour, egg and breadcrumbs, coating well and transferring to a tray. Heat up deep fat fryer with oil at 180c. Fry a few cubes gently until crisp and golden-brown. Drain and keep warm wrapped loosely in kitchen paper, repeating until all the cubes are cooked.

Vanilla pannacotta

Delicate in flavour but creamy-rich to complement different textures of local raspberries, served alongside a cream soda granita. (Serves 4)

50ml whole milk
30g sugar
1 vanilla bean, scraped pod and seeds
2 gelatine leaves, soaked in cold water
200ml double cream

Bring the milk, sugar and vanilla to a simmer, stirring regularly. Remove from the heat and whisk in the drained gelatine before folding into the cream. Sieve into a jug and pour into 4 small lightly-oiled ramekins. Leave to set overnight in the fridge. To serve, dip the moulds briefly into very hot water and invert carefully onto chilled plates.

BEST DISH EVER EATEN?

Tom Sellers 'bread with beef dripping candles' at Restaurant Story near London's Tower Bridge with my girlfriend, seriously the best meal ever. The atmosphere was great, we were made to feel really special and Tom's cooking is just so intelligent – it is really inspirational.

WELL-THUMBED COOKBOOKS?

Stephen Terry's *Inspired...By*, and *Letters to a Young Chef* by Daniel Boulud. Stephen's book inspired me because it shows a clear respect for the ingredients. Daniel's book taught me how to stay calm and manage myself as a chef. I also love *Sex, Drugs and Sausage Rolls* by Graham Garrett.

LUCKY DAY OFF?

A day shopping for clothes and the odd random piece of cookery equipment with my girlfriend, followed by a film on the sofa with popcorn. I love Batman films, particularly the early ones with Adam West. And the popcorn always has to be sweet!

GARETH ON HIS...

FAVOURITE CULINARY MOMENT?

The first time I cooked for my mum in a restaurant setting. It was at the Radisson Blu in Cardiff and I can't remember what I cooked, it was all a bit of a haze because I was so nervous. The chef just left me to cook everything for her.

FAVOURITE LOCAL FOODIE PLACE?

I love wandering around Norwich market getting new ideas and produce. The stalls are just crammed with great local ingredients.

BIGGEST FOOD EXTRAVAGANCE?

I love high quality chocolate, particularly Valrhona. I like the Ivoire and Caramelia the best, but they are all outstanding.

DREAM DINNER?

Just to have all my family together for dinner at the pub which is just over the road from my Mum's house in Wales. I would always choose lasagne. It used to happen a lot but now I live too far away so it is special when I get back there.

IF NOT A CHEF?

I'd love to write comic books. That seems like a cool job. It's probably a bit unrealistic as I can't draw at all! If I could, I would create Batman-type adventures.

WHAT DRIVES YOU?

The idea of making someone happy by cooking great food.

A 'TAKE 5' RECIPE?

Sweet chilli salmon and cashew salad. Just mix some pan-fried salmon, noodles and salted cashews in a bowl. Add some sweet chilli sauce and toss through the salad leaves. It's a quick and tasty dinner.

SIGNATURE DISHES

Starters

Crispy soft-boiled egg, asparagus soldiers, Yare Valley rapeseed mayonnaise

Cromer crab, avocado, pickled cucumbers, pink grapefruit dressing

Pickled baby beets, pickled shallots, horseradish, basil

Mains

Gressingham duck breast, ginger breadcrumb, cauliflower purée

Lowestoft loin of cod, Cromer crab, samphire, charred baby gem lettuce, salsify purée

Confit pork belly, black pudding purée, cabbage, bacon, smoked mash

Puddings

Strawberry parfait, strawberry sorbet, pistachio crumble

Chocolate honeycomb, chocolate shards, chocolate oil, honeycomb ice cream

Roast figs, chocolate ganache, yoghurt sorbet, honeycomb

MUSIC TO COOK TO?

I love reggae and ska but I also have a guilty pleasure – pop punk like Scouting for Girls and the Ordinary Boys.

UNFULFILLED AMBITIONS?

I want to be a good father, but getting one or maybe two AA Rosettes would be nice as well!

Back to her Roots

This is Claire Yaxley's second incarnation heading up Roots. She sold her share of the business in 2013 and went into clothes design, but when the restaurant came up for sale in May 2016 she didn't hesitate to throw herself back into the trade, this time as sole owner. "Food and drink and Norfolk farmers are where my passion and knowledge lie. I love this place and I believe it has a great future."

Roots is everything a place like Norwich deserves: the city is quirky, independent and proud of its heritage, and Roots, in the heart of the historic Lanes area, is a perfect fit with its ethos of championing local producers – including wines from the nearby Winbirri Vineyard, Norfolk Gin and locally-distilled whisky – and providing freshly-made, real food.

Inside the Grade II-listed building, a stylish café offers snacks and light meals as well as a full dining menu, while upstairs a light, airy restaurant is decorated with an eclectic mix of furniture that reflects Claire's desire to make eating out a "simple and thoroughly enjoyable" experience.

Claire's is an approach based in pragmatism, honed no doubt during her years on the farm she ran with her former partner at Hickling. Known throughout the county as 'the hen lady', Claire also had 11 horses, lots of quail and a full complement of dogs and cats.

The rusticity of farm life is evident in Roots. "You won't find white tablecloths and fancy cutlery," she says. "Our plates don't match, much of the furniture comes from the farm,

we have a whole assortment of jugs and mugs. Roots is absolutely about the food that Gareth cooks."

Roots
6 Pottergate, Norwich NR2 1DS
W: www.rootsofnorwich.co.uk
T: 01603 920788
E: claire@rootsofnorfolk.co.uk
 /RootsBistroNorwich
 @RootsNorwich
 /roots_norwich

Accolades:: Waitrose *Good Food Guide* 2015

Cost: carte average £22; wine from £25

Open: B 10-11.30 (Sat-Sun), L 11.30-2.30 (Tue-Sun), D 6-9.30 (Tue-Sat). Closed Mon

Details: takeaway coffee and cakes during the day; tables outside; basement available for private hire

FOOD LOVERS' GUIDE

Read on to discover some of Norfolk's tastiest treats in our 'little black book' of all that is delicious about this tasty county. Whether you have lived here for decades, just moved in or are a welcome visitor, we hope you enjoy exploring the familiar and perhaps not-so-familiar foodie places listed on the following pages; indeed there are some spots that locals would really rather keep secret!

It's quite possible that places and things that you love may be missing; omissions made either by oversight or because we just don't know about them. Why not share the knowledge with us by emailing norfolkguide@feastpublishing.co.uk

Where an address is given it indicates that the place in question welcomes visitors.

OTB signifies somewhere further afield, just over the Norfolk border, and worth showing your passport for!

Enjoy...

ALCOHOLIC DRINKS

BREWERIES AND BEER SHOPS

Centuries of brewing tradition mean Norfolk's ales need little introduction. Big names and microbreweries giving the best of grain.

Fat Cat
T: 01603 624364
W: www.fatcatbrewery.co.uk

Grain
T: 01986 788884
W: www.grainbrewery.co.uk

Woodforde's
The Fur and Feather Inn, Salhouse Road,
Woodbastwick nr Wroxham NR13 6SW
T: 01603 720353
W: www.woodfordes.co.uk

Humpty Dumpty
Church Road, Reedham NR13 3TZ
T: 01493 701818
W: www.humptydumptybrewery.co.uk

Buffy's
T: 01379 676523
W: www.buffys.co.uk

Lacons
T: 01493 850578
W: www.lacons.co.uk

Yetman's
T: 07774 809016
W: www.yetmans.co.uk

Jo C's
T: 01328 863854
W: www.jocsnorfolkale.co.uk

Norfolk Brewhouse
T: 01328 878495
W: www.norfolkbrewhouse.co.uk

Opa Hay's and Engel Fine Ales
T: 01502 679144

Iceni
Foulden Road, Ickburgh nr Mundford IP26 5HB
T: 01842 878922
W: www.icenibrewery.co.uk

Elveden
The Courtyard, Elveden Estate
nr Thetford IP24 3TQ
T: 01842 898064
W: www.elveden.com

Panther
T: 01603 871163
W: www.pantherbrewery.co.uk

Wolf
T: 01953 457775
W: www.wolfbrewery.com

Redwell
T: 01603 624072
W: www.redwellbrewing.com

All Day
T: 0 1603 951173
W: www.alldaybrewing.co.uk

S & P
T: 07552 300768
W: www.spbrewery.co.uk

Golden Triangle
T: 01603 757763
W: www.goldentriangle.co.uk

Tipples
T: 01603 721310
W: www.tipplesbrewery.com

Winter's
T: 01603 787820
W: www.wintersbrewery.co.uk

Wagtail
T: 01953 887133
W: www.wagtailbrewery.com

Aleyard
T: 01953 681005
W: www.aleyardbrewery.co.uk

Why Not
T: 01603 300786
W: www.thewhynotbrewery.co.uk

Tombstone
6 George Street,
Great Yarmouth NR30 1HR
T: 07584 504 444
W: www.tombstonebrewery.co.uk

Two Rivers
T: 01366 380131
W: www.denverbrewery.co.uk

Waveney Brewing Co.
The Queen's Head, Station Road,
Earsham R35 2TS
T: 01986 892623

Beeston
T: 01328 700844
W: www.beestonbrewery.com

Brancaster
The Jolly Sailors, Main Road,
Brancaster Staithe PE31 8BJ
T: 01485 210314
W: info@brancasterbrewery.co.uk

Poppyland
T: 01263 513992
W: www.poppylandbeer.com

Dancing Men
The Hill House Inn, off The St.,
Happisburgh NR12 0PW
T: 01692 650004
W: www.hillhouseinn.co.uk

Chalk Hill
The Coach & Horses, 82 Thorpe Road,
Norwich NR1 1BA
T: 01603 477077
W: www.thecoachthorperoad.co.uk

Elmtree
T: 01953 887065
W: www.elmtreebeers.co.uk

Fakir
T: 07713 789 085
W: www.fakirbrewery.com

Stumptail
T: 01328 701042
W: www.stumptail.co.uk

Taylor's
The London Tavern, 2 Church Street,
Attleborough NR17 2AH
T: 01953 457415
W: www.taylorsattleborough.com

VINEYARDS & WINEMAKERS

East Anglia produces award-winning English wines, taking more trophies than any other region of the UK.

South Pickenham Estate
T: 01760 756376
W: www.southpickenham.co.uk

Tas Valley Wines
Hall Farm, Overwood Lane, Forncett St Peter,
nr Norwich NR16 1LW
T: 01953 789445

Thelnetham Vineyard
W: www.thelnethamvineyard.com

Flint Vineyard
T: 01986 893209
W: www.flintvineyard.com

Winbirri Vineyards
T: 07595 894841
W: www.winbirri.com

Broadland *Fruit Wines and Norfolk Mead*
T: 0 1603 872474
W: broadlandwineriesdirect.co.uk

Humbleyard English Wines
Paddock Farm Shop, Mulbarton NR14 8JT
T: 01508 578892
W: www.humbleyardenglishwine.co.uk

CIDERHOUSES
*Perhaps more familiar to the West Country,
our few cidermakers more than make
up for their rarity with their quality.*

Norfolk Cider Company
The Norfolk Cider Shop, Wroxham Barns,
Tunstead Road, Hoveton NR12 8QU
T: 07717 116828
W: www.norfolkcider.co.uk

Whin Hill Cider *Seasonal shop*
Stearmans Yard, off B1105,
Wells-next-the-Sea NR23 1BW
T: 01328 711821
W: www.whinhillnorfolkcider.co.uk

Jonty's Cider
The Barrel, Kenninghall Road,
Banham NR16 2HET
T: 01953 888593
W: www.thebanhambarrel.weebly.com

Crones *Organic Cider, Apple Juice and Vinegar*
T: 01379 687687
W: www.crones.co.uk

Trunch Cider Co-op
W: www.trunchcider.co.uk

East Norfolk Ciders
T: 07768 857427

Burnard's Cider
T: 07588 556889
W: www.burnardscider.co.uk

Harleston Cider Company
W: www.harlestoncider.co.uk

DISTILLERIES AND LIQUEURS
*An extension of the brewing expertise,
the art of distillation has thrown up
a real artisan flair.*

Wild Knight *English Vodka*
T: 01366 327070
W: www.wildknightvodka.co.uk

The English Whisky Co.
Whisky and Liqueurs
Harling Road, Roudham NR16 2QW
T: 01953 717939
W: www.englishwhisky.co.uk

The Norfolk Sloe Company *Liqueurs*
T: 07867 817618
W: www.thenorfolksloecompany.com

Norfolk Saffron *Liqueur*
W: www. norfolksaffron.co.uk

NON-ALCOHOLIC DRINKS

HOT DRINKS
*Discover Norfolk passion and good taste
by the cupful*

Wilkinsons of Norwich *Tea & Coffee Merchants*
5 Lobster Lane, Norwich NR2 1DQ
T: 01603 404800
W: www.wilkinsonsofnorwich.com

The T Junction *Teas and Coffees*
59, Level 2, Castle Mall, Norwich NR1 3DD
T: 01603 661066
W: www.thetjunction.co.uk

Nelson and Norfolk Tea Co.
W: www.nelsonandnorfolktea.co.uk

Gnaw Chocolate
T: 01603 501518
W: www.gnawchocolate.co.uk

Strangers Coffee
Strangers Coffee House,
21 Pottergate, Norwich NR21DS
10 Dove Street, Norwich NR21DE
W: www.strangerscoffee.com

Smokey Barn Coffee
T: 01603 322287
W: www.smokeybarn.co.uk

Grey Seal Coffee
Grey Seal Westgate, 5 Westgate Street,
Blakeney NR25 7NQ
Grey Seal Roastery Brew Bar and Art Café
Manor Farm Barns, Glandford NR25 7JP
T: 01263 740249
W: www.greysealcoffee.co.uk

CoffeeMagic
Griffin Lane, Attleborough NR17 2AD
T: 01953 454885
W: www.coffeemagic.co.uk

COLD DRINKS
*Ripe berries and orchard fruits make
for delicious juices and cordials.*

Norfolk Cordial
T: 01263 570251
W: www. norfolkcordial.com

Crones Organic *Apple Juices*
T: 01379 687687
W: www.crones.co.uk

Ashill Fruit Farm *Apple Juices*
Swaffham Road, Ashill, nr Thetford IP25 7DB
T: 01760 440050
W: www.norfolkpureapplejuice.co.uk

Greenwoods Apple Juices
T: 01953 860356

East Norfolk Apple Juices
T: 07768 857427

Sandringham Apple Juice
W: www.sandringhamapplejuice.co.uk

FOODS

BEEF
*Native cattle breeds and lush pasture
make Norfolk beef some of the best.*

Carrick Farm Butchery *White Park Cattle*
Park Farm, off Elsing Road, Swanton Morley,
nr Dereham NR20 4JU
T: 01362 637457
W: www.carrickandson.co.uk

Bagthorpe Farm *Shorthorn Cross*
T: 01485 578528
W: www.bagthorpefarm.co.uk

DJ Barnard *Hereford Cross*
Mill House Farm, Low Road, Shropham,
Attleborough NR17 1EH
T: 01953 498511
W: www.djbarnardmeats.co.uk

The Beefsmith *Red Ruby Devon*
T: 01379 853645
W: www. thebeefsmith.co.uk

The Carleton Herd *Red Poll*
W: www.thecarletonherd.co.uk

Eves Hill Farm *Hereford*
T: 07870 490159
W: www.eveshill.uk

Hall Farm *Red Poll*
T: 01508 470413
W: www. beautifulbeef.co.uk

Heckingham Hall
Red Poll and Blonde d'Aquitaine
T: 01508 548079
W: www.heckingham-hall.co.uk

Manor House Farm *Red Poll*
T: 01263 740497
W: www.salthousebeef.com

Houghton Hall *Longhorn*
T: 01485 528569
W: www.houghtonhall.com

The Calf At Foot Dairy *Jersey*
T: 07787 103508
W: www.the-calf-at-foot-dairy.co.uk

LAMB
*The sweet grasslands of Norfolk
give us some of the best spring lamb,
hogget and mutton.*

DJ Barnard, Shropham *Suffolk Cross*
Mill House Farm, Low Road, Shropham,
Attleborough NR17 1EH
T: 01953 498511
W: www.djbarnardmeats.co.uk

Heckingham Hall *Mule Cross*
T: 01508 548079
W: www.heckingham-hall.co.uk

Swannington Farm to Fork *Mule Cross*
Woodlands Farm, Church Lane,
Swannington, Norwich NR9 5NN
T: 01603 754437
W: swanningtonfarmtofork.co.uk

Friends Farm *Zwartbles*
The Street, Alburgh IP20 0DL
open Tue & Fri
T: 01986 788081
W: www.friendsfarm.co.uk

Snettisham Park *Lamb*
Bircham Road, Snettisham
nr King's Lynn PE31 7NG *seasonal*
T: 01485 542425
W: www.snettishampark.co.uk

Green Farm *Lamb and Mutton*
T: 01263 577441
W: www.www.greenfarmlamb.co.uk

PORK
*Sandy soils and good arable crops for food
make for happy herds of delicious pigs.*

DJ Barnard *Large White Cross*
Mill House Farm, Low Road, Shropham,
Attleborough NR17 1EH
T: 01953 498511
W: www.djbarnardmeats.co.uk

Swannington Farm to Fork *Landrace Cross*
Woodlands Farm, Church Lane,
Swannington, Norwich, Norfolk NR9 5NN
T: 01603 754437
W: swanningtonfarmtofork.co.uk

Scotts Field Pork *Large Black*
T: 07940 800275
W: www. scottsfieldpork.co.uk

Samphire at Sycamore Farm
Gloucester Old Spot and Saddleback
T: 01379 674413
W: www.samphireshop.co.uk

Friends Farm *Landrace and Large White Cross*
The Street, Alburgh IP20 0DL
open Tue & Fri
T: 01986 788081
W: www.friendsfarm.co.uk

The Fruit Pig Company
T: 0845 548 0046
W: www.fruitpigcompany.com

POULTRY

The old-fashioned flavour of farmyard birds comes from the right breeding, slow maturing and the best grain feeds.

Norfolk Quail
T: 01328 829249
W: www.norfolkquail.co.uk

Mortons's Traditional Taste *Free Range Turkeys*
T: 01692 538067
W: www.freerangeturkeys.co.uk

Pearts at Martin's Farm
Free Range Chicken, Duck and Guinea Fowl
T: 01263 861241

Traditional Norfolk Poultry
Free Range 'Norfolk Black' Chicken and Norfolk Black & Bronze Turkeys
T: 01953 498434
W: www.tnpltd.com

The Fruit Pig Company *Chickens for Christmas*
T: 0845 548 0046
W: www.fruitpigcompany.com

Peele's *Free-Range 'Norfolk Black' and other Turkeys*
T: 01362 850237
W: www.peeles-blackturkeys.co.uk

Godwick *Free-Range 'Norfolk Black' and Bronze Turkeys*
T: 01328 700540
W: www.godwickturkeys.com

ORGANIC FARMED MEATS

Slow-rearing, careful husbandry and additive-free production are worth seeking out.

Ash Farm Organics *Farm Shop*
Stone Lane, Bintree, nr Fakenham NR20 5NA
T: 01362 683228
W: www.ashfarmorganics.co.uk

Harveys Pure Meat *Butchers' Shop*
63 Grove Road, Norwich NR1 3RL
T: 01603 621908
W: www.puremeat.org.uk

Back To The Garden
A148, Letheringsett NR25 7JJ
T: 01263 715996
W: www.back-to-the-garden.co.uk

Longwood Farm *Farm Shop OTB*
Icklingham Road, Tuddenham IP28 6TB
T: 01638 717120
W: www.longwoodfarm.co.uk

WILD GAME

Shooting protects our farming landscape and gives us tasty great value natural meats.

Houghton Hall *Parkland Fallow Venison*
T: 01485 528569
W: www.houghtonhall.com

Snettisham Park *Farmed Venison*
Bircham Road, Snettisham
nr King's Lynn PE31 7NG
T: 01485 542425
W: www.snettishampark.co.uk

Norfolk Wild Meats *Game Meats*
T: 01379 676816
W: www.norfolkwildmeats.co.uk

Godwick Turkeys *Wild Game*
T: 01328 700540
W: www.godwickturkeys.com

Bluebell Woods *Wild Venison OTB*
T: 01502 733501
W: www.wildvenison.co.uk

SAUSAGES

In a county famed for great pork, superb bangers are a delicious offshoot.

Samphire at Sycamore Farm *Classic and Flavoured*
T: 01379 674413
W: www.samphireshop.co.uk

Friends Farm *Classic and Flavoured*
The Street, Alburgh IP20 0DL (opens Tue & Fri)
T: 01986 788081
W: www.friendsfarm.co.uk

The Sausage Shop *Wide Range*
T: 01603 555072
W: www.sausageshop.co.uk

G F White *Wide Range*
16 Red Lion Street, Aylsham NR11 6ER
T: 01263 732264
W: www.whitesbutchers.co.uk

Archers Butchers *incl. Gluten-Free*
177-179 Plumstead Road, Norwich NR1 4AB
T: 01603 434253
W: www.archersbutchers.com

The Fruit Pig Company *Wide Range*
T: 0845 548 0046
W: www.fruitpigcompany.com

Perfick Pork *incl. Gluten-Free*
Bridge Stables, Gt. Ryburgh
nr Fakenham NR21 0DZ
T: 01328 829825
W: www.perfickpork.co.uk

BACON AND HAMS

Curing and smoking are great traditions in the mixed farming heritage of Norfolk.

G F White
16 Red Lion Street, Aylsham NR11 6ER
T: 01263 732264
W: www.whitesbutchers.co.uk

Norfolk Bacon at P J Kew
The Square, East Rudham,
nr Kings Lynn PE31 8RB
T: 01485 528236
W: www.norfolkbacon.co.uk

The Fruit Pig Company
T: 0845 548 0046
W: www.fruitpigcompany.com

Perfick Pork
Bridge Stables, Gt. Ryburgh
nr Fakenham NR21 0DZ
T: 01328 829825
W: www.perfickpork.co.uk

Creake Abbey Smokehouse
T: 01328 730399
W: www.creakeabbeycafe.com

Bradwell Butchery, Bakery & Delicatessen
6 Crab Lane, Bradwell NR31 8DJ
T: 01493 661473
W: www.bradwellbutchery.co.uk

MEAT PRODUCTS

Quality farmyard meats as raw materials make for a proper ploughman's lunch.

Samphire at Sycamore Farm
Pork Pies and Sausage Rolls
T: 01379 674413
W: www.samphireshop.co.uk

Bray's Cottage *Pork Pies*
T: 01263 712958
W: www.perfectpie.co.uk

G F White
Pies, Sausage Rolls and Black Pudding
16 Red Lion Street, Aylsham NR11 6ER
T: 01263 732264
W: www.whitesbutchers.co.uk

The Fruit Pig Company *Black and White Puddings*
T: 0845 548 0046
W: www.fruitpigcompany.com

Perfick Pork *Black Pudding*
Bridge Stables, Gt. Ryburgh
nr Fakenham NR21 0DZ
T: 01328 829825
W: www.perfickpork.co.uk

EGGS

*A good full English breakfast calls
for freshly-laid eggs.*

Norfolk Quails' *Free Range Chicken and Quail Eggs*
T: 01328 829249
W: www.norfolkquail.co.uk

Norfolk Geese *Geese' Eggs*
T: 01379 676391
W: www.norfolkgeese.co.uk

Ash Farm Organics
Organic Free Range Chicken Eggs
Stone Lane, Bintree, nr Fakenham NR20 5NA
T: 01362 683228
W: www.ashfarmorganics.co.uk

Wayland Free Range Eggs *Free Range Hens' Eggs*
T: 01953 457393
W: www.waylandfreerange.com

Broadland Eggs *Free Range Hens' Eggs*
T: 01692 581965
W: www.broadlandeggs.co.uk

Top Farm Eggs
Free Range Hens', Quail, Duck and Geese' Eggs
T: 01328 820351
W: www.topfarmeggs.co.uk

Snettisham Park *Hens' Eggs*
Bircham Road, Snettisham
nr King's Lynn PE31 7NG
T: 01485 542425
W: www.snettishampark.co.uk

Havensfield Happy Eggs *OTB*
Free Range Hens' Eggs
T: 01379 669039
W: www.havensfieldeggs.co.uk

WET FISH AND SEAFOOD
(also see PLACES TO SHOP – FISHMONGERS)
*Our inshore day-boat fleet and hardworking
fishermen need our support; the fruits of
Norfolk's coast are rightly iconic and delicious.*

Cole's
Units 15-19, East Coast Business Park,
Clenchwarton Road, West Lynn PE34 3LW
T: 01553 771677
W: www.colesofkingslynn.co.uk

GR Bunning & Co.
Jubilee Hall Farm, Cranworth IP25 7SH
T: 01362 820702
W: www.bunningsfish.co.uk

Norfolk Sea Larder
New Hall Farm, Mill Road, Briston nr Melton
Constable NR24 2JF
T: 01263 862991

SMOKED PRODUCE
*The smokehouse tradition goes back centuries
and the aroma of kippers filled every village.*

G F White *Smoked Chicken, Garlic, Pheasants etc*
16 Red Lion Street, Aylsham NR11 6ER
T: 01263 732264
W: www.whitesbutchers.co.uk

GR Bunning & Co. *Smoked Fish*
Jubilee Hall Farm, Cranworth IP25 7SH
T: 01362 820702
W: www.bunningsfish.co.uk

Letzers Seafood and Smokehouse *Smoked Fish*
T: 01485 525369
W: www.letzersseafood.co.uk

Cley Smokehouse
Smoked Fish, Poultry, Pâtés etc
High Street, Cley-next-the-Sea NR25 7RF
T: 01263 740282
W: www.cleysmokehouse.com

Creake Abbey Smokehouse
Smoked Bacons and Hams
T: 01328 730399
W: www.creakeabbeycafe.com

CHARCUTERIE

With a great heritage in all things piggy, preserving pork and other meats is an artisan skill par excellence in Norfolk.

Marsh Pig Charcuterie *Salami, Chorizo, Braesola, Coppa, etc*
T: 01508 480560
W: www.marshpig.co.uk

CHEESE

Dairy farming is key, not least for our new wave of passionate cheesemakers.

Mrs Temple's *Cows' Milk Cheeses*
T: 01328 820224

Bircham Windmill *Ewes' Milk Cheeses*
Snettisham Rd, Great Bircham nr King's Lynn PE31 6SJ
T: 01485 578393
W: www.birchamwindmill.co.uk

Ferndale Farm *Cows' Milk Cheeses*
T: 01263 577640
W: www.ferndalefarmnorfolkcheeses.co.uk

Fielding Cottage *Goats' Milk Cheeses*
Fieldings, Honingham nr Norwich NR9 5DJ
T: 01603 880685
W: www.fieldingcottage.co.uk

Nortons Dairy *Cows' Milk Cheeses*
T: 01603 736569
W: www.nortonsdairy.co.uk

Norfolk White Lady *Ewes' Milk Cheeses*
via good Norfolk delis

Jacmar *Goats' Milk Cheeses*
via good Norfolk delis

DAIRY

Rich pasture and lots of sunny weather making for happy cows and great milk.

Nortons Dairy *Cows' milk, Cream and Butter*
T: 01603 736569
W: www.nortonsdairy.co.uk

Domini Dairy *Raw Cows' Milk and Butter*
T: 01359 221333
W: www.dominidairy.co.uk

Abbey Farm Dairy *Raw Cows' Milk*
T: 07776 232 440
W: www.abbeyfarmdairy.com

The Calf At Foot Dairy *Raw Cows' Milk OTB*
T: 07787 103508
W: www.the-calf-at-foot-dairy.co.uk

DESSERTS AND ICE CREAM

The perfect 'afters' for any Norfolk feast, most of us love something sweet.

Dann's Farm *Ice Creams*
T: 01362 638116
W: www.dannsfarm.co.uk

Ronaldo Ices *Ice Creams and Sorbets*
T: 01603 633127
W: www.ronaldo-ices.co.uk

Norfolk Farmhouse
incl. Sorbets, Lollies and Diabetic Ice Creams
T: 01362 638116
W: www.dannsfarm.co.uk

Alburgh Norfolk *Ice Creams*
T: 01986 788784
W: www.alburghicecream.co.uk

Hunstanton Ice Cream Company
Ice Creams and Sorbets
T: 01485 533108
W: www.hunstantonicecream.co.uk

Norfolk County Dairy and Lakenham Creamery
Ice Creams and Sorbets
T: 01603 620970
W: www.lakenhamcreamery.co.uk

Parravani's *Ice Creams OTB*
T: 01502 715970
W: www.parravanis.co.uk

VEGETABLES, SALADS AND HERBS

Farmers and market gardeners make great use of fertile soils and a perfect climate.

Ash Farm Organics *Organic Vegetables etc*
Ash Farm Shop, Stone Lane, Bintree, nr Fakenham NR20 5NA
T: 01362 683228
W: www.ashfarmorganics.co.uk

Bagthorpe Farm *Organic Vegetables*
T: 01485 578528
W: www.bagthorpefarm.co.uk

Ferndale Farm *Potatoes*
T: 01263 577640
W: www.ferndalefarmnorfolkcheeses.co.uk

Green Pastures Farm *Vegetables, Salads and Fruit*
Mill Road, Bergh Apton, nr Norwich NR15 1BQ
T: 01508 480848
W: www.greenpasturesnursery.co.uk

The Tacons Farm Shop
Asparagus, Salads and Vegetables
The Grange, Rollesby nr Great Yarmouth NR29 5AJ
T: 01493 740236
W: www.thetacons.co.uk

Hillfield Nursery & Farm Shop
Salads and Vegetables
Mill Lane, Thorpe-next-Haddiscoe nr Loddon NR14 6PA
T: 01508 548306
W: www.hillfieldnursery.co.uk

The Orchards
Asparagus, Berries and Root Vegetables
Low Road, Walpole Cross Keys, Kings Lynn PE34 4HA
T: 01553 829506
W: www.sandjcarnell.co.uk

Norfolk Chilli Farm
Fresh Chillies and Chilli Plants
T: 07980 144362
W: www.norfolkchillifarm.co.uk

FRUITS

Orchard fruits, berries and stone fruits thrive in Norfolk, perfect for nursery puds and desserts.

Plumbe and Maufe *Plum Orchards*
Leith House Orchards, Lowes Lane, Burnham Overy Town PE31 8JL
T: 01328 738311
W: www.pmfarming.co.uk

Fairgreen Farms *Blueberries*
T: 01553 840640 07742 011970
W: www.blueberrypicking.co.uk

The Tacons Farm Shop *Berries*
The Grange, Rollesby nr Great Yarmouth NR29 5AJ
T: 01493 740236
W: www.thetacons.co.uk

Hillfield Nursery & Farm Shop
Berries, Stone and Orchard Fruits
Mill Lane, Thorpe-next-Haddiscoe nr Loddon NR14 6PA
T: 01508 548306
W: www.hillfieldnursery.co.uk

The Orchards *Berries etc*
Low Road, Walpole Cross Keys,
Kings Lynn PE34 4HA
T: 01553 829506
W: www.sandjcarnell.co.uk

Drove Orchards *Apples and Pears*
A149 Thornham PE36 6LS
T: 01485 525652
W: www.droveorchards.com

BREADS
(Please see PLACES TO SHOP – BAKERS)

CAKES
Afternoon tea calls for fabulous pâtisserie and farmhouse baking; local eggs and beet sugar with great Norfolk flour.

Macarons and More
11 The Royal Arcade, Norwich NR2 1NQ
T: 01603 419506
W: www.macaronsandmore.com

Sassa's Bespoke Cakes
T: 07747 196374
W: www.sassascakes.co.uk

Little Cake Pantry
T: 07943 539197
W: www.littlecakepantry.co.uk

Mellie Makes Cakes
T: 01379 608333
W: www.melliemakescakes.co.uk

Scrumptious Buns
T: 01603 782273
W: www.scrumptiousbuns.co.uk

Sponge
T: 01263 711033
W: www.sponge.co.uk

Buns Of Fun
T: 07932 874576
W: www.bunsoffun.co.uk

Little A's Cakery
T: 01362 692705
W: www.littleascakery.co.uk

The Norfolk Cake Company
T: 01366 381250
W: www.realnorfolkcakecompany.co.uk

B's Bakes
T: 07530 853593
W: www.beesbakesnorfolk.co.uk

Cupcake & Co
T: 01603 560120
W: www.cupcakeandco.weebly.com

Pixie Hall Cakes
T: 07875 600289
W: www.pixiehallcakes.co.uk

Fudgey Fudge
T: 01842 812310
W: www.fudgeyfudge.com

LARDER STAPLES
The simple things in the kitchen are often taken for granted. But without them, our cooking just wouldn't taste the same.

Norfolk Saffron *Spices and Flour*
W: www. norfolksaffron.co.uk

Crones Organic *Cider Vinegar*
T: 01379 687687
W: www.crones.co.uk

Ashill Fruit Farm *Cyder Vinegar*
Swaffham Road, Ashill, nr Thetford IP25 7DB
T: 01760 440050
W: www.norfolkpureapplejuice.co.uk

Greenwoods Cider *Vinegar*
T: 01953 860356

Essence Foods *Infused Sugars and Cake Decorating*
T: 01362 668844
W: www.essencefoods.co.uk

Ollands Farm Foods
Christmas Puddings and Mincemeat
T: 01692 652280
W: www.ollands-farm-foods.co.uk

Bircham Windmill *Stone-Ground flours*
Snettisham Rd, Great Bircham
nr King's Lynn PE31 6SJ
T: 01485 578393
W: www.birchamwindmill.co.uk

Letheringsett Watermill *Stone-Ground flours*
Riverside Road, Letheringsett nr Holt NR25 7YD
T: 01263 713153
W: www.letheringsettwatermill.co.uk

Bonallack Great Granola
T: 07786 316610
W: www.greatgranola.co.uk

PRESERVES AND PICKLES

Sweet ripe fruit and crunchy vegetables taste great, picked in season and preserved in style.

Essence Foods *Conserves and Chutneys*
T: 01362 668844
W: www.essencefoods.co.uk

Eastgate Larder *Medlar Cheese and Jelly*
T: 07778 160063
W: www.eastgatelarder.co.uk

Season's Bounty *Jams and Jellies*
T: 07796 678490
W: www.seasons-bounty.co.uk

Jubberwacky
Jams, Mustards and Sauces
T: 01263 761525
W: www.jubberwacky.co.uk

Ollands Farm Foods
Jams, Marmalades and Chutneys
T: 01692 652280
W: www.ollands-farm-foods.co.uk

Channell's Norfolk Preserves *Low Sugar Jams*
T: 01493 330168
W: www.norfolkpreserves.co.uk

Peachey's Preserves
Marmalade, Relishes, Compôtes and Chutneys
T: 01379 676169
W: www.peacheyspreserves.co.uk

Orchard Fruits
Curds, Jams, Chutneys and Vinegars
T: 07971 990345
W: www.orchardfruits.co.uk

The Garden Pantry
Jams, Chutneys, Pickles and Sauces
T: 07814 511374
W: www.thegardenpantry.co.uk

Thistlefield *Jams and Chutneys*
T: 01366 347365
W: www.thistlefield.co.uk

Candi's Chutney *Chutneys*
T: 07867 398517
W: www.candischutney.vpweb.co.uk

Chillis Galore
Chilli Jellies, Sauces and Relishes
W: www.chillisgalore.co.uk

Norfolk Heatwave *Chilli Sauces*
T: 07733 991211
W: www.norfolkheatwave.com

Scrubby Oak Fine Foods
Vinegars, Pickles and Sauces
T: 01760 722202
W: www.scrubbyoakfinefoods.co.uk

Norfolk Chilli Farm *Chilli Sauces, Jams, etc*
T: 07980 144362
W: www.norfolkchillifarm.co.uk

Miripiri *Chilli Sauces and Jams*
T: 07828 858384
W: www.miripiri.net

CONFECTIONERY

Over coffee or any time of the day, an energy boost or simple luxury, sticky sweetmeats and chocolates hit the spot.

Samphire at Sycamore Farm
Chocolate Tiffin and Florentines
T: 01379 674413
W: www.samphireshop.co.uk

Black Shuck Sloe Gin Truffles
T: 07867 817618
W: www.thenorfolksloecompany.com

The Chocolate Deli
Guild Street, Little Walsingham,
nr Fakenham NR22 6BU
T: 01328 820100
W: www.thechocolatedeli.co.uk

The Norfolk Truffle Company
T: 01508 550325
W: www.norfolktruffles.co.uk

Just Truffles
The Pod, 3A Church Street,
Harleston IP20 9BB
T: 01379 851933
W: www.justtrufflesonline.co.uk

Carousel Chocolates
6 Red Lion Street, Aylsham NR11 6ER
T: 01263 735737
W: www.carouselchocolates.co.uk

Cherry Tree Chocolates
9 High Street, Hunstanton PE36 5AB
T: 01485 534992
W: www.cherrytreechocolates.com

Digby's Fine Chocolates
6 Garden Street, Cromer NR27 9HN
T: 01263 516802
W: www.digbyschocolates.com

The Booja Booja Company
T: 01508 558888
W: www.boojabooja.com

Docwra's Rock Shop
13 Regent Rd, Great Yarmouth NR30 2AF
T: 01493 844676

The Little Fudge Stall at Courtyard Confectionery
Wroxham Barns, Tunstead Road,
Hoveton NR12 8QU
T: 01603 783762
W: www.wroxhambarns.co.uk

Kinnerton Confectionery Company
T: 01328 862632
W: www.kinnerton.com

Gnaw Chocolate
T: 01603 501518
W: www.gnawchocolate.co.uk

Fudgey Fudge
T: 01842 812310
W: www.fudgeyfudge.com

OILS

Extra virgin rapeseed oil is as healthy as olive oil and, produced locally, is definitely a greener option.

Yare Valley Oils
Rapeseed Oils and Infused Dressings
T: 01508 538206
W: www.yarevalleyoils.co.uk

Crush *Rapeseed Oils and Infused Dressings*
T: 01263 805009
W: www.crush-foods.com

Mr Hugh's *Rapeseed Oils*
T: 01366 348025
W: www.mrhughs.co.uk

SPECIALIST AND DIETARY

Special diet choices and sensitivity should not preclude enjoyment and indulgence.

Booja Booja Company
Dairy-Free Confectionery and Ice Cream
T: 01508 558888
W: www.boojabooja.com

Bon Bakery *Gluten-Free and Vegan Biscotti etc*
T: 01603 951091
W: www.thebonbakery.com

223

Gaia's Kitchen *Vegan and Gluten-Free Dishes*
T: 07740 485638
W: www.gaiaskitchen.co.uk

Butlers of Norwich *Vegetarian Meals*
98 Vauxhall Street, Norwich NR2 2SD
T: 01603 665066
W: www.butlersofnorwich.co.uk

Just Add Grapes *Gluten-Free Savouries etc*
T: 07896 246596
W: www.justaddgrapes.co.uk

GLOBAL SPECIALITIES

Sometimes home cooking with local ingredients just needs a lift; worldly flavours and warm spices bring zing.

Bhajiman *Dry Spice Curry Kits*
T: 01603 327858
W: www.bhajiman.co.uk

Ethnic Fusion *Indian Cuisine*
T: 01362 638449
W: www.ethnicfusion.co.uk

SNACKS

Busy lives and eating something on the run or just nibbling over drinks, graze on a taste of Norfolk.

Algy's Norfolk Popcorn
T: 01362 683893
W: www.norfolkpopcorncompany.com

Cleaver and Keg *Meaty snacks*
T: 07817 501828
W: www.cleaverandkeg.co.uk

GOURMET PET TREATS

Even our canine companions can eat very well with tasty treats.

Pooch's Handmade Dog Treats
T: 01485 609091
W: www.poochs.co.uk

Ollie's Pawtisserie
W: www.ollies-pawtisserie.co.uk

PLACES TO EAT

CAFÉS AND EATERIES
Smaller or simpler eating places are often some of the most appealing to escape to.

Strangers Coffee
Strangers Coffee House, 21 Pottergate,
Norwich NR21DS
W: www.strangerscoffee.com

Grey Seal Coffee
Grey Seal Westgate, 5 Westgate Street,
Blakeney NR25 7NQ
Grey Seal Roastery Brew Bar and Art Café
Manor Farm Barns, Glandford NR25 7JP
T: 01263 740249
W: www.greysealcoffee.co.uk

The Elveden Estate Food Hall & Restaurant
Elveden IP24 3TQ *OTB*
T: 01842 898064
W: www.elveden.com

Notcutts Garden Centre
Daniels Road A140, Norwich NR4 6QP
T: 01603 453155
W: www.notcutts.co.uk

Cookie's Crab Shop
T: 01263 740352
W: www.salthouse.org.uk

No.1 Cromer Fish & Chips
1 New Street, Cromer NR27 9HP
T: 01263 512316
W: www.no1cromer.com

Deepdale Café
Main Road, Burnham Deepdale PE31 8FB
T: 01485 210305
W: www.dalegatemarket.co.uk

The Crab Hut *seasonal*
Harbour Way Brancaster Staithe PE31 8BW
T: 01485 525369
W: www.letzersseafood.co.uk

Byfords
1-3 Shirehall Plain, Holt, Norfolk NR25 6BG
T: 01263 711400
W: www.byfords.org.uk

White House Farm
Blue Boar Lane, Sprowston nr Norwich NR7 8SB
T: 01603 419357
W: www.norwich-pyo.co.uk

Creake Abbey Café
B1355, North Creake,
nr Burnham Market NR21 9LF
T: 01328 730399
W: www.creakeabbeycafe.com

Pye Baker Bakery and Café
132 Dereham Road, Norwich, Norfolk, NR2 3AF
T: 01603 625633
W: www.pyebaker.co.uk

Louis' Deli Café
81 Upper St. Giles Street, Norwich NR2 1AB
T: 01603 763377
W: www.louisdeli.co.uk

The Gluten Free Shop & Café
21 Timberhill, Norwich NR1 3JZ
T: 01603 610573
W: www.norfolkglutenfree.co.uk

Pensthorpe Natural Park
A1067 Fakenham Road,
Pensthorpe nr Fakenham NR21 0LN
T: 01328 851465
W: www.pensthorpe.com

Wells Beach Café
Beach Road, Wells-next-the-Sea NR23 1DR
T: 01328 713055
W: www.holkham.co.uk

The Apiary Cake & Coffee House
3 Thoroughfare, Harleston IP20 9AH
T: 01379 852211
W: www.apiaryharleston.com

No 33 Café Bar
T: 01603 626097
W: www.no33cafe.co.uk

Moulton Nurseries
Acle Rd, Norwich NR13 3AP
T: 01493 750458
W: www.moultonnurseries.co.uk

Norfolk Lavender
Caley Mill, Lynn Rd, Heacham PE31 7JE
T: 01485 570384
W: www.norfolk-lavender.co.uk

Moorish Falafel Bar
Lower Goat Lane, Norwich NR2 1EL
T: 01603 622250
W: www.moorishfalafelbar.com

Funky Mackerel Café
Cliff Road Car Park, Sheringham NR26 8BJ
T: 01263 826285
W: www.funkymackerel.com

224

Pretty Corner Tea Gardens
Rowan House, Pretty Corner,
Upper Sheringham NR26 8TW
T: 01263 822766
W: www.prettycornerteagardens.com

Art Café
Manor Farm Barns, Glandford NR25 7JP
T: 01263 740249
W: www.art-cafe.org

CoCoes Café-Deli
Ash Close, Swaffham PE37 7NH
T: 01760 725605
W: www.strattonshotel.com

Wiveton Hall Café
Marsh Lane, Wiveton NR25 7TE
T: 01263 740515
W: www.wivetonhall.co.uk

Dents of Hilgay
Dents Farm, Steels Drove, Hilgay PE38 0QH
T: 01366 385661
W: www. dentsfarmhilgay.co.uk

TAKE-AWAYS

Eating out for a quick treat can be distinctly culinary at some of these better places.

No.1 Cromer Fish & Chips
1 New Street, Cromer NR27 9HP
T: 01263 512316
W: www.no1cromer.com

Norfolk Riddle Fish & Chips
2 Wells Road, Little Walsingham,
nr Fakenham NR22 6DJ
T: 01328 821903
W: www.norfolkriddle.co.uk

Eric's Fish and Chips
Drove Orchards, Thornham Road,
Thornham PE36 6LS
T: 01485 525886
W: www.ericsfishandchips.com

Archers Butchers *Hot Take-Away*
177-179 Plumstead Road, Norwich NR1 4AB
T: 01603 434253
W: www.archersbutchers.com

TEAROOMS

A great British institution, whether bone china, crusts off and pinkies raised or just home-made fruitcake and a mug of builders' finest, do make time for tea.

Wisteria Tea Rooms
Newmans Yard, Norwich Street, Fakenham NR21 9AF
T: 01328 851247
W: www.wisteriatearoom.co.uk

Bircham Windmill
Snettisham Rd, Great Bircham nr King's Lynn PE31 6SJ
T: 01485 578393
W: www.birchamwindmill.co.uk

Biddy's Tea Room
15/15a Lower Goat Lane, Norwich NR2 1EL
16 Market Place, Aylsham NR11 6EH
W: www.biddystearoom.com

Rosy Lee's Tea Room
37A Bridge St, Loddon, Norwich NR14 6NA
T: 01508 520204

Heydon Village Tea Shop
The Street, Heydon NR11 6AD
T: 01263 587211
W: www.heydonvillageteashop.co.uk

The Assembly House
Theatre St, Norwich NR2 1RQ
T: 01603 626402
W: www.assemblyhousenorwich.co.uk

The Tea House
5 Wrights Court, Norwich NR3 1HQ
T: 01603 631888
W: www.theteahousenorwich.co.uk

Folly Tearoom
Hoppers Yard, Bull St, Holt NR25 6LN
T: 01263 713569
W: www.follytearoom.co.uk

UNUSUAL DINING

A new wave of quirky pop-ups and innovative destinations are shaking up how we eat.

The Albatros *Restaurant boat*
The Quay, Wells-next-the-Sea NR23 1AT
T: 07979 087228
W: www.albatroswells.co.uk

Feast On The Street *event pop-ups*
W: www.feastonthestreet.co.uk

North Norfolk Railway *dining train events*
Sheringham
T: 01263 820800
W: www.nnrailway.co.uk

The Feed pop-up stall *events and festivals*
T: 01603 627841
W: www.the-feed.co.uk

The Coffee Van, Salthouse *appears most days*
Beach carpark off Beach Road, Salthouse
no contact details

PLACES TO DRINK

PUBS
(also see PLACES TO STAY – INNS)
The great Norfolk pint is a joy; a great brewer, good cellar and passionate landlord are key.

The Cherry Tree
116 High Street, Wicklewood NR18 9QA
T: 01953 606962
W: www.wicklewoodcherrytree.co.uk

The Fat Cat Brewery Tap
98-100 Lawson Road, Norwich NR3 4LF
T: 01603 413153
W: www.fatcattap.co.uk

The Fat Cat Pub
49 West End Street, Norwich NR2 4NA
T: 01603 624364
W: www.fatcatpub.co.uk

The Fat Cat & Canary
101 Thorpe Road, Norwich NR1 1TF
T: 01603 436925
W: www.fatcatcanary.co.uk

The Plough
58 St Benedicts Street, Norwich NR2 4AR
T: 01603 661384
W: www.theploughnorwich.co.uk

The Cottage
9 Silver Rd, Norwich NR3 4TB
T: 01603 464461
W: www.thenorwichcottage.co.uk

The Fur and Feather
Salhouse Road, Woodbastwick
nr Wroxham NR13 6SW
T: 01603 720353
W: www.thefurandfeatherinn.co.uk

The Jubilee
26 St Leonards Rd, Norwich NR1 4BL
T: 01603 618734
W: www.jubileefreehouse.co.uk

The Queen's Head
Station Road, Earsham NR35 2TS
T: 01986 892623

The Lord Nelson
Burnham Thorpe, nr Burnham Market
Walsingham Road, Burnham Thorpe PE31 8HN
T: 01328 738241
W: www.nelsonslocal.co.uk

The Walpole Arms
The Common, Itteringham NR11 7AR
T: 01263 587258
W: www.thewalpolearms.co.uk

The Jolly Sailors
A149, Brancaster Staithe PE31 8BJ
T: 01485 210314
W: www.jollysailorsbrancaster.co.uk

The Angel
Old A11, Larling NR16 2QU
T: 01953 717963
W: www.angel-larling.co.uk

The Dun Cow
A149 Purdy Street, Salthouse NR25 7XA
T: 01263 740467
W: www.salthouseduncow.com

The Jolly Farmers
1 Burnham Rd, North Creake NR21 9JW
T: 01328 738185
W: www.jollyfarmersnorfolk.co.uk

The Three Horseshoes
69 The Street, Warham NR23 1NL
T: 01328 710547
W: www.warhamhorseshoes.co.uk

The Three Horseshoes
148 Lynn Road, Roydon nr Kings Lynn PE32 1AQ
T: 01485 600666
W: www.thethreehorseshoespub.co.uk

The Boars
Bunwell Rd, Spooner Row NR18 9LL
T: 01953 605851
W: www.theboars.co.uk

The Brick Kilns
Norwich Rd, Little Plumstead, Norwich NR13 5JH
T: 01603 720043
W: www.thebrickkilns.co.uk

The Carpenters Arms
Lynn Rd, East Winch, King's Lynn PE32 1NP
T: 01553 841228
W: www.the-carpenters-arms.com

Darbys Freehouse
Elsing Rd, Swanton Morley NR20 4NY
T: 01362 637647
W: www.darbysfreehouse.com

The Earle Arms
Heydon NR11 6AD
T: 01263 587376
W: www.earlearms.vpweb.co.uk

The Feathers
71 Manor Rd, Dersingham PE31 6LN
T: 01485 540768
W: www.feathersdersingham.com

The Fox
The Street, Lyng NR9 5AL
T: 01603 872316
W: www.thefoxatlyng.co.uk

The Lodge
Main Road, North Tuddenham NR20 3DJ
T: 01362 638466
W: www.thelodge-tuddenham.co.uk

The Inn On The Green
Chapel St, New Buckenham NR16 2BB
T: 01953 860172
W: www.innonthegreenfreehouse.com

The King's Head
26 Wroxham Rd, Coltishall NR12 7EA
T: 01603 737426
W: www.kingsheadcoltishall.co.uk

The Hare Arms
Lynn Rd, Stow Bardolph PE34 3HT
T: 01366 382229
W: www.theharearms.co.uk

The Hunny Bell
The Green, Hunworth NR24 2AA
T: 01263 712300
W: www.thehunnybell.co.uk

The Ship
18 The Street, South Walsham NR13 6DQ
T: 01603 270049
W: www.theshipsouthwalsham.co.uk

The King's Head
6 Norwich Rd, Brooke NR15 1AB
T: 01508 550335
W: www.kingsheadbrooke.co.uk

The Locks Inn
Lock's Lane, Geldeston, Beccles NR34 0HS
T: 01508 518414
W: www.geldestonlocks.co.uk

The Mermaid Inn
Church Street, Elsing NR20 3EA
T: 01362 637640
W: www.elsingmermaidinn.co.uk

The Nelson Head
The Street, Horsey NR29 4AD
T: 01493 393378
W: www.thenelsonhead.com

Ribs of Beef
24 Wensum St, Norwich NR3 1HY
T: 01603 619517
W: www.ribsofbeef.co.uk

The Ship Inn
The Street, Weybourne NR25 7SZ
T: 01263 588721
W: theshipinnweybourne.com

The Vernon Arms
Church Street, Southrepps NR11 8NP
T: 01263 833355
W: www.vernonarms.com

WINE BARS
Variety is the spice of life with grape and grain, try these for a vinous alternative.

Frank's Bar
19 Bedford St, Norwich NR2 1AR
T: 01603 618902
W: www.franksbar.co.uk

The Birdcage
23 Pottergate, Norwich NR2 1DS
T: 01603 633534
W: www.thebirdcagenorwich.co.uk

The Rathskeller
8 Hanse House, South Quay, King's Lynn PE30 5GN
T: 01553 773713
W: www.therathskeller.co.uk

Ceno's Wine Bar
26 High Street, Holt NR25 6BH
T: 01263 711511

Balthazar Wine Bar
Lees Yard, Holt NR25 6HS
T: 01263 710138
W: www.adnams.co.uk

PLACES TO STAY

INNS
Good food and drink are natural bedfellows in smart hostelries, along with a comfy bed for the night.

The Ostrich
Stocks Green, Castle Acre PE32 2AE
T: 01760 755398
W: www.ostrichcastleacre.com

The Berney Arms
Church Road, Barton Bendish PE33 9GF
T: 01366 347995
W: www.theberneyarms.co.uk

The King's Head
Holt Rd, Letheringsett NR25 7AR
T: 01263 712691
W: www.kingsheadnorfolk.co.uk

The Black Boys
Market Place, Aylsham NR11 6EH
T: 01263 732122
W: www.blackboyshotel.co.uk

The Recruiting Sergeant
Norwich Rd, Horstead NR12 7EE
T: 01603 737077
W: www.recruitingsergeant.co.uk

The Buckinghamshire Arms
opp. Blickling Hall entrance, Blickling NR11 6NF
T: 01263 732133
W: www.bucksarms.co.uk

The Chequers
Griston Rd, Thompson IP24 1PX
T: 01953 483360
W: www.thompsonchequers.co.uk

King William IV
Heacham Rd, Sedgeford PE36 5LU
T: 01485 571765
W: www.thekingwilliamsedgeford.co.uk

The Red Lion
Brook Street, Cromer NR27 9HD
T: 01263 514964
W: www.redlioncromer.co.uk

The Ugly Bug Inn
High House Farm Lane, Colton, nr Norwich NR9 5DG
T: 01603 880794
W: www.uglybuginn.co.uk

The Elveden Inn *OTB*
Brandon Road B1106, Elveden IP24 3TP
T: 01842 890876
W: www.elvedeninn.com

HOTELS

Linger and stay a while, savour an extra glass and stay up late feasting.

The White Horse
Main Road, Brancaster Staithe PE31 8BY
T: 01485 210262
W: www.whitehorsebrancaster.co.uk

Titchwell Manor
Main Road A149, Titchwell PE31 8BB
T: 01485 210221
W: www.titchwellmanor.com

The Duck Inn
Burnham Road, Stanhoe PE31 8QD
T: 01485 518330
W: www.duckinn.co.uk

The Globe
The Buttlands,
Wells-next-the-Sea NR23 1EU
T: 01328 710206
W: www.theglobeatwells.co.uk

The Dabbling Duck
11 Abbey Rd,
Great Massingham PE32 2HN
T: 01485 520827
W: www.thedabblingduck.co.uk

Strattons Hotel
Ash Close, Swaffham PE37 7NH
T: 01760 723845
W: www.strattonshotel.com

The Kings Head
Harts Lane, Bawburgh NR9 3LS
T: 01603 744977
W: www.kingsheadbawburgh.co.uk

The Gunton Arms
Cromer Road, Thorpe Market NR11 8TZ
T: 01263 832010
W: www.theguntonarms.co.uk

Congham Hall
Lynn Road, Grimston PE32 1AH
T: 01485 600250
W: www.conghamhallhotel.co.uk

The Wiveton Bell
Blakeney Road, Wiveton NR25 7TL

T: 01263 740101
W: www.wivetonbell.co.uk

The Victoria
Park Road, Holkham NR23 1RG
T: 01328 711008
W: www.holkham.co.uk

The Fritton Arms
Church Lane, Fritton NR31 9HA
T: 01493 484008
W: www.frittonarms.co.uk

Saracen's Head
Wall Road, Wolterton NR11 7LZ
T: 01263 768909
W: www.saracenshead-norfolk.co.uk

No 33
Boutique hotel-style B&B guest accomm.
High Street, Thornham PE36 6LX
T: 01485 512194
W: www.thornhamdeli.co.uk
33 Northgate, Hunstanton PE36 6AP
T: 01485 524352
W: www.33hunstanton.co.uk

B&Bs AND GUEST ACCOMMODATION

A cosy refuge for the night with a hearty breakfast one of life's simple pleasures.

Cley Windmill
Cley-next-the-Sea NR25 7RP
T: 01263 740209
W: www.cleywindmill.co.uk

Bunkhouse Barn at Courtyard Farm, Ringstead
T: 01485 525251
W: www.courtyardfarm.co.uk

Byfords
1-3 Shirehall Plain, Holt NR25 6BG
T: 01263 711400
W: www.byfords.org.uk

Hall Park Bed & Breakfast, Kirby Bredon
T: 01508 495567
W: www.hallparknorfolk.co.uk

Manor House Farm, Wellingham
T: 01328 838227
W: www.manor-house-farm.co.uk

Church Farm House, North Lopham
T: 01379 687270
W: www.churchfarmhouse.org

Carricks at Castle Farm, Swanton Morley
T: 01362 638302
W: www.carricksatcastlefarm.co.uk

Sloley Hall, Norwich
T: 01692 538582
W: www.sloleyhall.com

Holly Lodge Guest House, Thursford Green
T: 01328 878465
W: www.hollylodgeguesthouse.co.uk

The Control Tower, Egmere
T: 01328 821574
W: www.controltowerstays.com

Chalk & Cheese, Shouldham
T: 01366 348039
W: www.bed-and-breakfast-west-norfolk.co.uk

Westfield Farm, Foulsham
T: 01362 683333
W: www.norfolkcourtyard.co.uk

HOLIDAY LETS
Get under the skin of Norfolk as welcome guests in a local community.

Canary Cottage, Wells-next-the-Sea
T: 01328 710246
W: www.therealaleshop.co.uk/
farm-accommodation

Ollands Farm Barn, Happisburgh
T: 01692 652280
W: www.ollandsfarmbarn.co.uk

Wiveton Hall, Wiveton
T: 01263 740515
W: www.wivetonhall.co.uk

Cley Windmill, Cley-next-the-Sea
T: 01263 740209
W: www.cleywindmill.co.uk

Glebe Farm, Frettenham
T: 01603 897641
W: www.glebefarm-cottages.co.uk

Bracken Cottage, Brancaster Staithe
T: 01328 730853
W: www.brackencottage.co.uk

Stody Hall, Stody
T: 01263 862247
W: www.stodyhallholidays.co.uk

Cartshed Cottages, Sharrington
T: 01263 478278
W: www.sharringtonhall.com

Barsham Barns, North Barsham
T: 01328 821744
W: www.barshambarns.co.uk

Mendham Mill, Mendham
T: 01379 855282
W: www.mendhammill.co.uk

Great Barn Farm, Gayton Thorpe
T: 07789 031518
W: www.greatbarnfarm.co.uk

GLAMPING AND CAMPING
Nothing quite like being out in the countryside at one with nature under the stars.

Eves Hill Farm, Reepham *Camp*
T: 07870 490159
W: www.eveshill.uk

Deepdale Farm Camping and Tipis
Camp and Glamp
Burnham Deepdale
T: 01485 210256
W: www.deepdalebackpackers.co.uk

Ambers Bell Tents *glamp*
at Wiveton Hall, nr Holt and at Mannington Hall, nr Itteringham
W: www.ambersbelltents.co.uk

Westfield Farm, Foulsham *glamp*
T: 01362 683333
W: www.norfolkcourtyard.co.uk

Riddlesworth Park, Riddlesworth *glamp*
T: 01953 681254
W: www.riddlesworthpark.co.uk

Swallowtails at Holt Hall, Holt *glamp and camp*
T: 01263 825703
W: www.swallowtailholidays.co.uk

Green Heart Farm, Southburgh *glamp and camp*
T: 07899 690532
W: www.facebook.com/GHFCamping

Salhouse Broad, Salhouse *camp*
T: 01603 722775
W: www.salhousebroad.org.uk

Round The Woods, Weston Longville *glamp*
T: 01603 870394
W: www.roundthewoods.co.uk

The Fire Pit Camp, Wendling *glamp and camp*
T: 07717 315199 / 07917 406953
W: www.thefirepitcamp.co.uk

Norfolk Glamping, Yaxham Waters *glamp*
T: 01692 671771
W: www.norfolk-glamping.co.uk

High Sand Creek, Stiffkey *camp*
T: 01328 830235

Swallow Park, Belton *glamp*
T: 01493 601180
W: www.swallowpark.com

Wild Luxury *glamp, various locations*
T: 01485 750850
W: www.wildluxury.co.uk

PLACES TO SHOP

FARMERS' MARKETS
A true expression of our historic farming and artisan food and drink production.

Creake Abbey
First Saturdays 9.30am - 1pm
B1355, North Creake,
nr Burnham Market NR21 9LF
T: 01328 730399
W: www.creakeabbeycafe.com

Diss Farmers' Market
Second Saturdays 9am - 1pm
Market Place, Diss IP224AB
T: 01379 643848
W: www.disscouncil.com

Wymondham Farmers' Market
Third Saturdays 9am - 1pm
Market Cross, Wymondham NR18 0AD
T: 01953 603302
W: www.wymondhamtc.norfolkparishes.gov.uk

Aylsham Farmers Market
First and Third Saturdays 9am - 1pm
The Market Place, Aylsham NR11 6EL
T: 01263 733354
W: www.aylsham-tc.gov.uk

The Norfolk Diet *Second Saturdays 9am - 3pm*
The Forum, Millennium Plain, Norwich NR2 1DF
W: www.thenorfolkdiet.co.uk

Loddon Farmers Market
Second and Fourth Saturdays 9.30am - 1.00pm
Jubilee Hall, George Lane, Loddon NR14 6NB
T: 01502 677214
W: www.loddonfarmersmarket.co.uk

229

North Walsham Farmers Market
Last Sunday 10am - 2pm
Market Place, North Walsham NR28 9BP
T: 07450 581277
W: www.facebook.com/NWFarmersMkt/

Weybourne Meet The Producers
check website for details
The Village Square, Kelling Heath Holiday Park,
Weybourne NR25 7HW
W: www.weybourne.net

Swaffham Farmers' Market
Third Sunday 9am - 2pm
Market Place Swaffham PE37 7DQ
T: 01760 722 922
W: www.aroundswaffham.co.uk

DELIS AND FOOD HALLS
*Globe-trotting cuisines and international
flavours add interest to our local ingredients.*

Goodies Food Hall
French's Farm, Wood Lane,
Pulham Market, nr Diss IP21 4XU
T: 01379 676880
W: www.goodiesfoodhall.co.uk

The Norfolk Deli
16 Greevegate, Hunstanton PE36 6AA
T: 01485 535540
W: www.norfolk-deli.co.uk

Cook & Co. Delicatessen
25 The Thoroughfare Harleston IP20 9AS
T: 01379 853173
W: www.cookandcodeli.co.uk

Bradwell Butchery Bakery & Delicatessen
6 Crab Lane, Bradwell NR31 8DJ
T: 01493 661473
W: www.bradwellbutchery.co.uk

Alexandra Howell Delicatessen
22 Staithe St, Wells-next-the-Sea NR23 1AF
T: 01328 710214
W: www.arthurhowell.com

The Elveden Estate Food Hall & Restaurant
London Road, Elveden IP24 3TQ *OTB*
T: 01842 898064
W: www.elveden.com

Bakers and Larners
8 Market Place, Holt NR25 6BW
T: 01263 712244
W: www.bakersandlarners.co.uk

Thornham Deli
High Street, Thornham PE36 6LX
T: 01485 512194
W: www.thornhamdeli.co.uk

Wiveton Hall Shop
1 Marsh Lane, Wiveton NR25 7TE
T: 01263 740515
W: www.wivetonhall.co.uk

Creake Abbey Food Hall
B1355, North Creake,
nr Burnham Market NR21 9LF
T: 01328 730399
W: www.creakeabbeycafe.com

Byfords
1-3 Shirehall Plain, Holt NR25 6BG
T: 01263 711400
W: www.byfords.org.uk

Archers Butchers *Delicatessen*
177-179 Plumstead Road, Norwich NR1 4AB
T: 01603 434253
W: www.archersbutchers.com

Picnic Fayre
The Old Forge, Holt Road,
Cley-next-the-Sea NR25 7AP
T: 01263 740587
W: www.picnic-fayre.co.uk

Blakeney Delicatessen
30 High Street, Blakeney NR25 7AL
T: 01263 740939
W: www.blakeneydeli.co.uk

Reeve's Larder at Bawdeswell Garden Centre
Norwich Road, Bawdeswell NR20 4RZ
T: 01362 688387
W: www.bawdeswellgardencentre.co.uk

Louis' Deli Café
81 Upper St. Giles Street, Norwich NR2 1AB
T: 01603 763377
W: www.louisdeli.co.uk

Humble Pie
Market Place, Burnham Market, Norfolk PE31 8HF
T: 01328 738581
W: www.humble-pie.com

Wells Deli Company
15 The Quayside, Wells-Next-The-Sea NR23 1AH
T: 01328 711171
W: www.wellsdeli.co.uk

Stiffkey Stores
The Old Coach House, Wells Road,
Stiffkey NR23 1QH

T: 01328 830489
W: www.stiffkeystores.com

Rainbow Wholefoods
Labour in Vain Yard, Norwich NR2 1JD
T: 01603 625560
W: www.rainbowwholefoods.co.uk

The Green Grocers
Earlham House Shops, Earlham, Norwich NR2 3PD
T: 01603 250000
W: www.thegreengrocers.co.uk

The Gluten Free Shop & Café
21 Timberhill, Norwich NR1 3JZ
T: 01603 610573
W: www.norfolkglutenfree.co.uk

WINE MERCHANTS AND DRINKSTORES
*Good food needs great drink, a fine wine
and drinks retailer is essential to help find
the right bottle.*

Adnams Stores
in Norwich, Harleston, Holkham and Holt
T: 01603 613243
W: www.adnams.co.uk

The Real Ale Shop
Branthill Farm, B1105
south of Wells-next-the-Sea NR23 1SB
T: 01328 710810
W: www.therealaleshop.co.uk

Beers Of Europe
Garage Lane, Setchey nr Kings Lynn PE33 0BE
T: 01553 812000
W: www.beersofeurope.co.uk

Reno Wines
T: 01953 425995
W: www.renowine.co.uk

Fairgreen Farms *Blueberry Wines*
Hill Road, Middleton nr Kings Lynn PE32 1RN
T: 01553 840640 07742 011970
W: www.blueberrypicking.co.uk

Tastebud Wines
Strumpshaw Post Office & Shop, 30 Norwich Rd,
Strumpshaw NR13 4AG
T: 01603 713925
W: www.theromanianwinecoltd.co.uk

Harper Wells Wines
30-32 Eaton Street, Eaton NR4 7LD

T: 01603 451098
W: www.harperwells.com

Warlingham Wines
T: 01692 615384
W: www.warlinghamwines.com

FARM SHOPS

Agricultural diversification has become vital in recent years so support your local farmer.

Walsingham Farms Shop
Guild St, Little Walsingham,
nr Fakenham NR22 6BU
T: 01328 821877
W: www.walsingham.co

Walsingham Farms Shop
Norfolk Lavender, Lynn Road, Heacham PE31 7JE
T: 01485 570002
W: www. walsingham.co

Paddock Farm Shop
Mulbarton, Norfolk NR14 8JT
T: 01508 578259
W: www.thepaddocksbutchery.co.uk

DJ Barnard
Mill House Farm, Low Road, Shropham,
Attleborough NR17 1EH
T: 01953 498511
W: www.djbarnardmeats.co.uk

Swannington Farm to Fork
Woodlands Farm, Church Lane, Swannington
Norwich, Norfolk NR9 5NN
T: 01603 754437
W: swanningtonfarmtofork.co.uk

Green Pastures Farm Shop
Mill Road, Bergh Apton, nr Norwich NR151BQ
T: 01508 480848
W: www.greenpasturesnursery.co.uk

The Farm Shop
The Street, Swafield,
nr North Walsham NR28 0PG
T: 01692 405444
W: www.taverntasty.co.uk

Ash Farm Organics
Ash Farm Shop, Stone Lane, Bintree,
nr Fakenham NR20 5NA
T: 01362 683228
W: www.ashfarmorganics.co.uk

Orchard Farm Shop
Holverston, nr Norwich NR14 7PH

T: 01508480369
W: www.orchardfarmshop.com

White House Farm
Blue Boar Lane, Sprowston nr Norwich NR7 8SB
T: 01603 419357
W: www.norwich-pyo.co.uk

The Tacons Farm Shop
The Grange, Rollesby
nr Great Yarmouth NR29 5AJ
T: 01493 740236
W: www.thetacons.co.uk

Hillfield Nursery & Farm Shop
Mill Lane, Thorpe-next-Haddiscoe
nr Loddon NR14 6PA
T: 01508 548306
W: www.hillfieldnursery.co.uk

Back To The Garden
A148 Letheringsett Letheringsett NR25 7JJ
T: 01263 715996
W: www.back-to-the-garden.co.uk

Knights Hill Farm Shop
A148 Grimston Road, South Wootton PE30 3HQ
T: 01553 674212
W: www.knightshillfarmshop.net

Dents of Hilgay
Dents Farm, Steels Drove, Hilgay PE38 0QH
T: 01366 385661
W: www. dentsfarmhilgay.co.uk

Algy's Farm Shop
T: 01362 683893
W: www.algysfarmshop.co.uk

Drove Orchards
T: 01485 525652
W: www.droveorchards.com

Wiveton Hall
Marsh Lane, Wiveton NR25 7TE
T: 01263 740515
W: www.wivetonhall.co.uk

BUTCHERS

Norfolk's well-bred, well-hung, well-fed farmyard meats need little introduction.

Bradwell Butchery *Bakery & Delicatessen*
6 Crab Lane, Bradwell NR31 8DJ
T: 01493 661473
W: www.bradwellbutchery.co.uk

Arthur Howell
53 Staithe Street, Wells-next-the-Sea NR23 1AN

T: 01328 710228
Beeston House, Market Place,
Burnham Market PE31 8HE
T: 01328 738230
Hereford House, 32 Front Street, Binham NR21 0AL
T: 01328 830239
W: www.arthurhowell.com

Toombs Butchers
315 Reepham Road, Hellesdon, nr Norwich NR6 5AD
T: 01603 427478
W: www.toombsbutchers.co.uk

A & G Butchers
Church Street, Attleborough NR17 2AH
T: 01953 453163
W: www.butchersnorfolk.co.uk

M & M Rutland
13 Briston Road, Melton Contable NR24 2DG
T: 01263 860562
W: www.rutland-butchers.co.uk

Cannells Butchers
48 Mere Street, Diss IP22 4AQ
T: 01379 642020
W: www. cannells.co.uk

Farm to Fork & Fish
Norwich Road, Horstead NR12 7EE
T: 01603 266129
W: farmtoforkandfish.co.uk

Icarus Hines
69 Church Street, Cromer NR27 9HH
T: 01263 514541
3 Church St, Sheringham NR26 8QR
T: 01263 823268
W: www.icarushines.co.uk

Fleetwoods Butchers
75 High St, Gorleston, nr Great Yarmouth NR31 6RQ
T: 01493 662824
W: www. fleetwoodsbutchers.co.uk

Richard Gill
13a High Street, Downham Market PE38 9DA
T: 01366 383306

Goddards
4 Wales Court, Downham Market PE38 9JZ
T: 01366 388377
W: www.goddardsofnorfolk.co.uk

Tavern Tasty Meats
The Farm Shop, The Street, Swafield,
nr North Walsham NR28 0PG
T: 01692 405444
W: www.taverntasty.co.uk

A.E. Howard Butchers
69 High Street, Heacham,
nr Huntstanton PE31 7DW
T: 01485 570439
West Newton, nr Sandringham PE31 6AY
T: 01485 542219
Lynn Road, Gayton, nr Kings Lynn PE32 1QJ
T: 01553 636234
W: www.jehoward.moonfruit.com

The Elveden Estate Food Hall & Restaurant
London Road, Elveden IP24 3TQ *OTB*
T: 01842 898064
W: www.elveden.com

Perfick Pork
Bridge Stables, Gt. Ryburgh,
nr Fakenham NR21 0DZ
T: 01328 829825
W: www.perfickpork.co.uk

Friends Farm *opens Tue & Fri*
The Street, Alburgh IP20 0DL
T: 01986 788081
W: www.friendsfarm.co.uk

P J Kew
The Square, East Rudham,
nr Kings Lynn PE31 8RB
T: 01485 528236
W: www.norfolkbacon.co.uk

F L Edge & Son
Market Street, East Harling NR16 2AD
T: 01953 717203
W: www.fledgeandson.co.uk

J & D Papworth Farms
16 Millers Walk, Fakenham NR21 9AP
T: 01328 855039
34a Market Place, Swaffham PE37 7QH
T: 01760 724753
46 Station Road, Sheringham NR26 8RG
T: 01263 823189
33 Market Place, North Walsham NR28 9BT
T: 01692 403059

G F White
16 Red Lion Street, Aylsham NR11 6ER
T: 01263 732264
W: www.whitesbutchers.co.uk

H V Graves
24 Gladstone Place, Briston,
nr Melton Constable NR24 2LE
T: 01263 860333
W: www.hvgraves.co.uk

Archers Butchers
177-179 Plumstead Road, Norwich NR1 4AB
T: 01603 434253
W: www.archersbutchers.com

White House Farm
Blue Boar Lane, Sprowston nr Norwich NR7 8SB
T: 01603 419357
W: www.norwich-pyo.co.uk

Coxfords Butchers
11 Market Place, Aylsham
T: 01263 732280
W: www.simonpayne.wix.com/coxfordsbutchers

BAKERS
Unsurprisingly in such a great arable county, baking expertise is as strong as our farming skill.

Bradwell Butchery Bakery & Delicatessen
6 Crab Lane, Bradwell NR31 8DJ
T: 01493 661473
W: www.bradwellbutchery.co.uk

H V Graves
24 Gladstone Place, Briston,
nr Melton Constable NR24 2LE
T: 01263 860333
W: www.hvgraves.co.uk

Bircham Windmill
Snettisham Rd, Great Bircham
nr King's Lynn PE31 6SJ
T: 01485 578393
W: www.birchamwindmill.co.uk

Pye Baker Bakery and Café
132 Dereham Road, Norwich, Norfolk, NR2 3AF
T: 01603 625633
W: www.pyebaker.co.uk

Bread Source
13 Red Lion Street, Aylsham NR11 6ER
T: 01603 898503
W: www.bread-source.com

Linzers Bakeries
357a Aylsham Road Norwich NR3 2RX
31 West Earlham Centre, Norwich NR5 8AD
T: 01603 483742
W: www.linzers.co.uk

Dozen Artisan Bakery
107 Gloucester Street, Norwich NR2 2DY
T: 01603 764798
W: www.dozenbakery.co.uk

Murrell's Artisan Bakery
71 Gordon Avenue, Norwich NR7 0DP
T: 07946 367582
W: www.murrellsbakery.co.uk

Butlers of Norwich
98 Vauxhall Street, Norwich NR2 2SD
T: 01603 665066
W: www.butlersofnorwich.co.uk

HUSK *Limited opening*
Blacksmiths Shop, The Street,
Heydon NR11 6AD
T: 01263 587557
W: www.huskwoodfiredbakery.wordpress.com

FISHMONGERS AND SEAFOOD
With a long famous coastline, Norfolk's fresh fish and seafood are a delicious treat.

Arthur Howell Fishmonger
60 Staithe Street, Wells-next-the-Sea NR23 1AQ
T: 01328 712127
W: www.arthurhowell.com

Farm to Fork & Fish
Norwich Road, Horstead NR12 7EE
T: 01603 266129
W: farmtoforkandfish.co.uk

Letzers Seafood at The Crab Hut
Brancaster Staithe Harbour PE31 8BW
T: 01485 525369
W: www.letzersseafood.co.uk

The Fish Shed
A149 Main Road, Brancaster Staithe
T: 01485 210532
W: www.fishshed.co.uk

Cookie's Crab Shop
A149 Coast Road, The Green, Salthouse NR25 7AJ
T: 01263 740352
W: www.salthouse.org.uk

Gurneys Fish Shop
Market Place, Burnham Market PE31 8HF
T: 01328 738967
W: www.gurneysfishshop.co.uk

Westons
5 Westgate St, Blakeney NR25 7NQ
T: 01263 741112
W: www.westonsofblakeney.co.uk

Davies Fish Shop
7 Garden Street NR27 9HN
T: 01263 512727

AM Frary Seafood
On Wells Quay *March to November*
T: 07901 656608

The North Norfolk Fish Company
8 Old Stable Yard, Holt NR25 6BN
T: 01263 711913
W: www.northnorfolkfish.co.uk

Northgate Fish
17 Northgate St, Great Yarmouth NR30 1BA
T: 01493 858041

Dabs'n'Crabs
Hemsby Road, Scratby nr Gt. Yarmouth NR29 3AJ
T: 01493 731305 07855 417046

Howard & Son
17 Fye Bridge St, Norwich, NR3 1LJ
T: 01603 624928
W: www.fishmongersnorwich.com

Lincoln's Family Fishmongers
27 St. Augustine's Street, Norwich NR3 3BY
T: 01603 662050

Brill Fish
4 Tan Lane, Caister-on-Sea nr Gt. Yarmouth NR30 5DN
T: 07840 269653

Donaldsons Fishmongers
Austin Fields, King's Lynn PE30 1PH
T: 01553 772241

World Of Fish *OTB*
6 Cooke Road, Lowestoft NR33 7NA
T: 01502 517171
W: www.world-of-fish.co.uk

PICK-YOUR-OWN
Buying direct is a fun way to get the ripest seasonal crops fresh from the fields. Always check opening and availability before setting off.

White House Farm
PYO Berries, Stone and Orchard Fruits, Veggies
Blue Boar Lane, Sprowston nr Norwich NR7 8SB
T: 01603 419357
W: www.norwich-pyo.co.uk

Hillfield Nursery & Farm Shop
PYO Berries, Stone and Orchard Fruits
Mill Lane, Thorpe-next-Haddiscoe
nr Loddon NR14 6PA
T: 01508 548306
W: www.hillfieldnursery.co.uk

Fairgreen Farms *PYO Blueberries*
Hill Road, Middleton nr Kings Lynn PE32 1RN
T: 01553 840640 07742 011970
W: www.blueberrypicking.co.uk

The Tacons Farm Shop *PYO Berries*
The Grange, Rollesby
nr Great Yarmouth NR29 5AJ
T: 01493 740236
W: www.thetacons.co.uk

The Orchards
PYO Berries, Root Vegetables and Stone Fruit
Low Road, Walpole Cross Keys,
Kings Lynn PE34 4HA
T: 01553 829506
W: www.sandjcarnell.co.uk

Wiveton Hall *PYO Soft Fruit*
1 Marsh Lane, Wiveton NR25 7TE
T: 01263 740515
W: www.wivetonhall.co.uk

Swafield Fruit Centre *PYO Soft Fruit*
Hill Fruit Farm, Swafield
nr North Walsham NR28 0PG
T: 01692 403332

Drove Orchards *PYO Orchard Fruits and Berries*
Thornham Road, Thornham PE36 6LS
T: 01485 525652
W: www.droveorchards.com

COOKWARE
Good chefs, amateur or pro', need the best cooks' toys.

Bakers and Larners
8 Market Place, Holt NR25 6BW
T: 01263 712244
W: www.bakersandlarners.co.uk

Loose's
Orford Yard, Red Lion Street, Norwich NR1 3TB
T: 01603 230505
W: www.loosescookshop.co.uk

Jarrold Department Store
1-11 London Street, Norwich NR2 1JF
T: 01603 660661
W: www.jarrold.co.uk

The Kitchenary Cookshop
Taverham Garden & Crafts Centre,
Fir Covert Road, Taverham, Norwich NR8 6HT
T: 01603 261932
W: www.kitchenary.co.uk

Roys Department Stores, across Norfolk
T: 01603 782131
W: www.roys.co.uk

Larter and Ford
15 Market Hill, Diss IP22 4JZ
T: 01379 642720
W: www.larterandford.co.uk

Denny & Sons
1 The Thoroughfare, Harleston IP20 9AH
T: 01379 852248
W: www.dennyandsons.co.uk

GARDEN CENTRES
*There is nothing like growing your own,
plucking the first crop as it shoots.*

Green Pastures Garden Centre
Mill Road, Bergh Apton,
nr Norwich NR151BQ
T: 01508 480734
W: www.greenpasturesnursery.co.uk

Bawdeswell Garden Centre
Norwich Road, Bawdeswell NR20 4RZ
T: 01362 688387
W: www.bawdeswellgardencentre.co.uk

Chris Bowers and Sons *Fruit Trees*
T: 01366 388752
W: www.chrisbowers.co.uk

Norfolk Herbs
Blackberry Farm, Dillington, Dereham NR19 2QD
T: 01362 860812
W: www.norfolkherbs.co.uk

AG Meale & Sons Ltd
Wayford Nurseries, Stalham NR12 9LJ
T: 01692 580226
W: www.agmeale.co.uk

FUN STUFF

FOODIE EVENTS AND FESTIVALS
*No better advert for all that is great about
tasty Norfolk, go explore the artisan vibe.*

Norwich Food and Drink Festival *late June*
T: 01603 881939
W: www.norfolkfoodanddrink.com

Crab and Lobster Festival, Sheringham and Cromer
late May
W: www.crabandlobsterfestival.co.uk

Aylsham Food Festival *early October*
T: 07833 096931
W: www.slowfoodaylsham.org.uk

City of Ale, Norwich *late May - early June*
W: www.cityofale.org.uk

Acle Food and Drink Festival *early October*
T: 01493 701081
W: www.visitacle.com

North Norfolk Food and Drink Festival, Holkham
early September
Holkham Hall Estate
W: www.northnorfolkfoodfestival.co.uk

Norwich Beer Festival *late October*
W: www.norwichcamra.org.uk

Porkstock, Sprowston *mid September*
White House Farm, Sprowston, Norwich
T: 01603 419357
W: www.porkstock.co.uk

Sandringham Food Festival *early August*
Sandringham Park PE35 6EN
W: www.sandringhamfoodfestival.co.uk

Brecks Food & Drink Festival *mid-September*
in and around Swaffham
T: 01760 722255
W: www.brecks.org/food-and-drink

Big Onion Festival *early September OTB*
Elveden Estate
T: 01842 898068
W: www.bigonionfestival.com

EXPERIENCES AND EDUCATION
*Getting close to ingredients, produce and
harvest is all part of being a true foodie.*

Marsh Pig, Claxton nr Norwich
Charcuterie Courses
T: 01508 480560
W: www.marshpig.co.uk

Sue Hudson, Bressingham, nr Diss
Breadmaking Workshops
T: 01379 688374
W: www.breadworkshops.co.uk

Scrumptious Buns *Cake Decorating Classes*
T: 01603 782273
W: www.scrumptiousbuns.co.uk

FOOD LOVERS' GUIDE
Your deliciously indispensable companion to enjoying Norfolk, edible and otherwise

Denver Mill *Breadmaking Workshops*
T: 01366 384009
W: www.denvermill.co.uk

Hall Park Bed & Breakfast, Kirby Bredon
Breadmaking Workshops
T: 01508 495567
W: www.hallparknorfolk.co.uk

COOKERY SCHOOLS
Inspired to do more than pick up a good recipe book, learn hands-on from a masterchef.

Macarons and More
Pâtisserie, Baking and Confectionery
T: 01603 419506
W: www.macaronsandmore.com

Richard Hughes Cookery School
Wide Range of Courses
T: 01603 712215
W: www.richardhughescookeryschool.co.uk

Kim's Norfolk Kitchen *Baking etc*
T: 01263 768421
W: www.kimsnorfolkkitchen.co.uk

Ethnic Fusion *Indian Cuisine*
Etling Green, nr Dereham
T: 01362 638449
W: www.ethnicfusion.co.uk

EVENT CATERING
Sometimes we just want to relax and host, leaving it in the hands of the professionals.

Somerleyton Estate *Outside Catering*
T: 01502 734907
W: www.somerleyton.co.uk

Archers Butchers *Hog Roast*
T: 01603 434253
W: www.archersbutchers.com

Hushwing Café *Betsy pop-up 'tea and cake' van*
T: 07887 295094
W: www.hushwingcafe.co.uk

The Duck Truck *Duck wrap pop-up*
T: 07919 160271
W: www.theducktruck.co.uk

Ethnic Fusion *Indian Cuisine*
T: 01362 638449
W: www.ethnicfusion.co.uk

WEDDINGS AND PARTIES
Getting married is one of the most special days, try these for a truly individual Norfolk wedding.

Garden Pavilion at Thursford *Wedding Venue*
T: 01328 878477
W: www.thursford.com

Macarons and More *Wedding Cakes*
11 The Royal Arcade, Norwich NR2 1NQ
T: 01603 419506
W: www.macaronsandmore.com

Sassa's Bespoke Cakes *Wedding Cakes and Favours*
T: 07747 196374
W: www.sassascakes.co.uk

Cley Windmill *Wedding Venue*
T: 01263 740209
W: www.cleywindmill.co.uk

Voewood *Wedding Venue*
T: 01263 713029
W: www.voewood.com

Kimberley Hall *Wedding Venue*
T: 01603 759447
W: www.kimberleyhall.co.uk

Somerleyton Hall and Estate *Wedding Venue OTB*
T: 01502 734907
W: www.somerleyton.co.uk

HEALTH SPAS
A proper detox can work wonders for over-indulgence and good living, or just a little 'me time'.

The Secret Garden Spa
Congham Hall, Lynn Road, Grimston PE32 1AH
T: 01485 600250
W: www.conghamhallhotel.co.uk

Imagine Spa
Blofield Heath - Norwich; Knights Hill - King's Lynn; Old Hall Caister - Great Yarmouth; Park Farm - Hethersett
T: 01603 813424
W: www.imaginespa.co.uk

FESTIVAL CULTURE AND FAMILY FUN
Feeding the soul is just as important as feasting. Get a fill enjoying eclectic, rustic, local entertainment.

Royal Norfolk Show, Norwich *late June*
The Showground, Dereham Road, Costessey, Norwich NR5 0TT
T: 01603 748931
W: www.royalnorfolkshow.rnaa.org.uk

Rural Pastimes Show, Euston nr Thetford *mid June*
Euston Park, Euston Estate, Thetford IP24 2QH
T: 07931 544408
W: www.eustonruralpastimes.org.uk

Worstead Festival *late July*
T: 07551 259777
W: www.worsteadfestival.org

Norfolk & Norwich Festival *late May*
T: 01603 877750
W: www.nnfestival.org.uk

Holt Festival *late July*
W: www.holtfestival.org

Red Rooster Festival *early June*
Euston Hall nr Thetford *OTB*
W: www.redrooster.org.uk

Snettisham Park *Deer Safari and Farm Park*
Bircham Road, Snettisham nr King's Lynn PE31 7NG
T: 01485 542425
W: www.snettishampark.co.uk

Deepdale Christmas Market *December*
Burnham Deepdale
Main Road, Burnham Deepdale PE31 8FB
T: 01485 210305
W: www.dalegatemarket.co.uk

Thursford Collection incl. Christmas Show
off The Street, Thursford nr Fakenham NR21 0AS
T: 01328 878477
W: www.thursford.com

Bewilderwood Treehouse Adventure
Horning Road, Hoveton NR12 8JW
T: 01692 633033
W: www.bewilderwood.co.uk

235

Recipe index

Starters, sides and light bites

Mains

Cyril's mussel chowder, smoked cod, rapeseed mash, pancetta and Norfolk Dapple — 18

Argentinian-style of rosé veal Jacob's ladder — 30

Norfolk quail, schnitzel leg, hay custard, oriental mushrooms, coddled egg, hedge garlic and rainbow chard — 38

Rare-roasted rump of Shorthorn beef, slow-cooked cheek, Smoked Dapple gratin, cavolo nero, sorrel and wild garlic — 48

Pan-roasted fillet of local rainbow trout, sweet potato and pickled vegetables — 50

Roasted pumpkin, wild mushroom and Jerusalem artichoke risotto — 51

Thai-buttered Brancaster lobster, Asian noodle stir-fry, sweet chilli dipping sauce — 58

Pork tenderloin ballotine with sage and shallots — 60

Pumpkin and cheese gnocchi — 70

Slow-roast rare breed pork belly — 80

Seared Belted Galloway beef fillet, honey and ale-braised short rib, wild mushroom risotto — 88

Asparagus spears, rack of Holkham lamb, fondant potato, carrot purée and pea shoots — 108

Roasted rump of Norfolk lamb, tagine sauce and spiced couscous — 130

Gunton fallow deer dumplings with wild rowanberry jelly — 138

Wild sea bass, saffron potatoes, brown shrimps, samphire and chive beurre blanc — 158

Cromer crab, green herb & pea risotto — 161

Plaice cooked on the bone with King's Lynn brown shrimp butter — 181

Roast cannon of Wolterton lamb, wild garlic dauphinoise potatoes, crushed peas and mint, madeira jus — 188

Grilled sea trout, broad bean, baby tomato, basil compôte, fennel oil — 190

Norfolk coast wild sea bass, peas and broad beans, wild garlic and dill — 200

Roast hogget rump, lamb shoulder, haricot beans and basil — 200

Pan-fried chicken thighs, Marsh Pig chorizo, wild mushrooms, spinach, confit egg yolk — 208

Norfolk oxtail bonbons — 210

Puddings

Torta di nocciole — 31

Thornham apple — 40

Maple and pecan brownie — 50

Sharrington strawberry trifle — 61

Miniature dacquoise sponges — 70

Dark chocolate bavarois — 81

Pear tarte tatin — 91

Apple & vanilla bavarois — 111

Strawberry bavarois — 131

Sea buckthorn berry posset — 140

Gingered rhubarb mess with basil sugar — 150

Norfolk 'strawberries & cream' — 160

Cherries and raspberries jubilee — 170

Peach melba, vanilla ice cream, raspberries, crisp meringue — 181

Lemon tart — 191

Orange sponge cake and rhubarb purée — 201

Vanilla pannacotta — 210

NORFOLK TABLE: OUR FAVOURITE PLACES

Where shall we go for lunch? You won't go wrong with one of these twenty places, where the warmest of welcomes and the tastiest of Norfolk food awaits. Kick back over a relaxed pub meal deep in the timeless Norfolk countryside, drop in at the well-known spots dotted along the coast, or choose a characterful town or city centre restaurant. In the mood for finer dining? We've got that covered too. The twenty chefs in this book aren't the only ones in Norfolk of course, but we are particularly fond of them and their restaurants. We know that they will be delighted to welcome you.

The White Horse
Brancaster Staithe PE31 8BY
www.whitehorsebrancaster.co.uk
01485 210262

Tipi in the Paddock & Owsley-Brown Catering
Conkers, Common Road, West Bilney,
King's Lynn PE32 1JX
www.owsley-brown.com
01553 840190

Titchwell Manor Hotel and Restaurants
Titchwell, Brancaster PE31 8BB
www.titchwellmanor.com
01485 210221

Congham Hall
Grimston, King's Lynn PE32 1AH
www.conghamhallhotel.co.uk
01485 600250

Thornham Deli
High Street, Thornham PE36 6LX
www.thornhamdeli.co.uk
01485 512194

Strattons Hotel
Ash Close, Swaffham PE37 7NH
www.strattonshotel.com
01760 723845

Market Bistro
Saturday Market Place,
King's Lynn PE30 5DQ
www.marketbistro.co.uk
01553 771483

The Duck Inn
Burnham Road, Stanhoe,
King's Lynn PE31 8QD
www.duckinn.co.uk
01485 518330

The Dabbling Duck
11 Abbey Road,
Great Massingham PE32 2HN
www.thedabblingduck.co.uk
01485 520827

The Victoria Inn
Park Road, Holkham,
Wells-next-the-Sea NR23 1RG
www.holkham.co.uk/victoria
01328 711008

The Fritton Arms
Church Lane, Fritton NR31 9HA
www.frittonarms.co.uk
01493 484008

The King's Head
Harts Lane, Bawburgh, Norwich NR9 3LS
www.kingsheadbawburgh.co.uk
01603 744977

The Gunton Arms
Cromer Road, Thorpe Market,
Norwich NR11 8TZ
www.theguntonarms.co.uk
01263 832010

The Globe Inn
The Buttlands,
Wells-next-the-Sea NR23 1EU
www.theglobeatwells.co.uk
01328 710206

Kindreds Restaurant
2 Bridewell Street,
Wymondham NR18 0AR
www.kindredsrestaurant.com
01953 601872

The Norfolk Riddle
2 Wells Road, Walsingham NR22 6DJ
www.norfolkriddle.co.uk
01328 821903

The Wiveton Bell
Blakeney Road, Wiveton, Holt NR25 7TL
www.wivetonbell.co.uk
01263 740101

The Saracen's Head
Wall Road, Wolterton,
Near Erpingham NR11 7LZ
www.saracenshead-norfolk.co.uk
01263 768909

Shuck's at the Yurt
Drove Orchards, Thornham PE36 6LS
www.shucksattheyurt.co.uk
01485 525889

Roots
6 Pottergate, Norwich NR2 1DS
www.rootsofnorwich.co.uk
01603 920788